THE SAYERS

THE SAYERS
TRIED AND TESTED
AT THE HIGHEST LEVEL

Stephen Sayers

Stuart Wheatman
Steve Wraith

Mojo Risin'
Publishing Ltd

First published in 2015 by Mojo Risin' Publishing

British Library Cataloguing in Publication Data:
A catalogue record for this book is available from
the British Library

Several people got shot, punched, knocked out, stabbed, bitten and robbed over the course of this book

ISBN-13:
9781911482017

Cover photograph
Nigel Smith, NRS Photography

Cover design
Andrew Brewster, PrintNV

Printed & bound by Books Factory

Proudly published Up North

This book is dedicated to
Sylvia Riley and Tony 'Legs' Lennie

To my Auntie Sylvia, the original Sayersie; the woman who was my second mother and was always there when I needed her. Fond memories will be with me 'til the day I die.

Without the assistance of Wor Legs, this book could never have been completed. For that, I am eternally grateful. Rest in peace, cuz. Love ya!

CONTENTS

FOREWORDS

I first met Stephen when I was moved from HMP Full Sutton to HMP Frankland. He invited me to his table and what a banquet it turned out to be.

I knew of Stephen and his family and they had a very strong control within the prison in Durham and indeed, Newcastle.

The hospitality I was shown was first class, as was the food. I never realised at the time that new prisoners of any prominence were welcomed to this feast; several tables were used to form an unusually long table to host these special guests of honour, of which I was one.

The second person to arrive after me was Charlie Kray, he was also a new arrival and subsequent guest of honour at this prison banquet. On both occasions I noticed that the prison staff, while viewing from the CCTV, were slightly gobsmacked with these happenings. Our food consisted of a wide range of dishes that were specifically cooked for these occasions by fellow inmates.

I will never forget the hospitality nor the kind friendship that Stephen showed me during my time as a Category A Prisoner in HMP Frankland. He was and still is a genuine man who made me feel welcome. Even though we were prisoners, we were treated with respect.

A lot has been said and published about Stephen and his family; I too have been on the receiving end of the media. Perhaps it takes one to know one when it comes to villains. My utmost respect and admiration goes out to Stephen and his family who made me feel most welcome in a hostile environment, such as prison life is.

I would like to wish Stephen all the very best with his new book and hope one day to repay the respect and friendship that I was shown during my time in HMP Frankland.

Canny bag o'Tudor Stephen! Very best wishes and thank you once again.

PD1510 FERRIS.
Paul 'The Wee Man' Ferris

❁

Tried and tested is a very strong title to any book. There are not that many firms, families or men who can wear such an accolade, especially nowadays. It's a very strong statement to make; one which only a handful of families can back up. The Sayers are a family where such a compliment fits and fits well.

The first time I had any dealings with them was many years ago: I had to give my assurances to someone. Kenny 'Panda' Anderson was the go-between and, after a few phone calls, we managed to negotiate a peace between the Sayers family and someone else who turned out to be a snidey bastard. The Sayers came out of it the winners, but what really stuck with me was that they kept their word.

There are a lot of firms out there who will promise you blind to get what they want, and then once the chips have fallen, they turn on their word and break the rules. In our world people like that are not worth a light. It is your word and the ability to see the larger picture that makes men stand out from the rest. I can place my hand on my heart and say they are men of their word – good people as we say down south – staunch, and people you can rely on, men who me and my family regard as friends. We may not go to each other's parties, but I feel that with them I have a family in the North East.

John Sayers spent a lot of time with my father back in the 90s when they were both double Category A prisoners in Whitemoor. Between my father, John and Vic Dark they ran the prison. No one had more respect than them. The screws are not our pals and they will never be our pals but they respected my father, John and Vic.

I met John a few times on visits and I can honestly say that my father held him in very high regard, calling him and Stephen personal friends – not pals or associates. That goes a long way in our world.

Joe Pyle Jnr

RESPECT FOR THE SAYERS

'Stephen Sayers is a man who has earned his reputation the old-fashioned way; on the pavement. His family's reputation is a good one and they are well-respected in London and the rest of the UK. The Sayers are my kind of people.'
Fred Foreman

'The Sayers are most definitely doers and they are the only family people talk about in London from the North East. Stephen is a gentleman, but don't mistake his politeness as a weakness. A lot of people talk the talk but can't walk the walk. This family does both.'
Dave Courtney

'I count the Sayers from Newcastle as close friends. They are a staunch, loyal family and well-respected throughout the criminal fraternity. Have they been tried and tested at the highest level? Most certainly.'
Eddie Richardson

'There have been many criminal families over the years who have made their mark, but as history shows, many have lived in London. The Krays, the Richardsons, the Addams and of course ourselves, the Frasers. The Sayers brothers have changed all of that; old-fashioned criminals with old-fashioned values. They have earned their place at the top table.'
The Fraser family

CHAPTER 1
WELCOME TO MY WORLD

'You little bastards! Where are you?'

We lay deadly silent. Never moving an inch. I could hear Mam pleading with him to leave us alone, which would always end up with her getting a good hard slap. He was a six foot tall, 17 stone and as strong as a bull from lifting beer kegs all day. None of us stood a chance against that. No one in their right mind would cross him.

We tried to ignore him but we could hear his voice getting more and more aggressive. We were all looking at each other and shaking with fear. Mam was still pleading again – doing anything she could to protect us – telling him we were just kids. He didn't like any backchat. There was silence… then an almighty slap followed by a long scream. Instinctively, the three of us jumped out of bed and ran downstairs and started screaming at him to stop it. He just saw this as sport and lashed out at us, catching us on our backs with his heavy hands. We cried… tears on top of tears. We then climbed onto Mam, who was also in tears, and tried to protect her. He stopped and looked at us all cowering and called us all 'soft shites'. He walked to the kitchen and cracked open a bottle of Newcastle Brown Ale. It had gained the nicknames Mad Dog and Wife Beater around the doors – very appropriate in this case. We all knew what was coming next. He called the three of us in and then started the interrogation.

It was always the same: he would start off by saying that he would batter us if we went thieving.

'What do you say if the police arrest you?' he'd ask.

We stood silently with our backs still red raw with the heavy-handed slaps with tears still streaming down our faces, sniffling like kids do. If one of us piped up and said, 'We say nothing, Dad,' that would be the trigger for the slaps to come raining down on us again.

Mam would always try to help but Dad was just too strong. What made it a million times worse was that he was picking on his own family and it didn't seem to bother him one bit. He would then grab us by the hair and drag us into the back yard while we'd scream and plead for him to stop. Then… nothing. Nothing at all. He'd be done. He'd leave us in the backyard. It didn't matter if it was freezing cold, he'd just leave us there, shivering.

We would climb into the dog's kennel one by one and then huddle together for the night ahead. John and I kept Michael in the middle to protect him and we covered ourselves in stinking old coats that our dog Judy lay on. Judy seemed to sense our distress and snuggled into us to try to keep us warm. She was good like that. We'd watch through the window as my dad beat our poor mam. In his mind, maybe he thought leaving us to sleep in the dog's kennel would make us better people. That memory will be with me 'til the day I die. From that day on we all swore that we would never let anybody lift their hands to us again. We were kids, we were small, but things like that bond you closer than anything.

❂

During the six weeks summer holidays I would work on my Uncle Albert's barrow in town. Each day I'd wake up with the noise of my granny shouting 'Do you want a cup of tea, son?'

I'd get myself washed and ready and would head downstairs where Uncle Albert would be waiting. He'd always get his stock before coming to ask me if I wanted to go to work with him and then we'd walk from Gran's on Westgate Road to the Grainger Market in town where we we'd be greeted by my uncles Thomas and Georgie Kelly, who were in the same game. As a youngster doing this, it was a great buzz. Just to be part of something, something grown up, something that was useful and part of life… like I was learning something but didn't really know what at the time. They'd compare stock and then we would make our way to the van that would be parked on Nunn Street and start unloading the barrows.

Uncle Albert would put his barrow outside The Clock bar and we would get to work. We'd flash the barrow up so it looked presentable to the customers, getting all the signs written out, all the stock piled and priced and then we'd be ready for action. There was always something going on around the Grainger Market; you could guarantee come half past ten in the morning my cousins Michael and Terry Pattinson would drive past us. You could actually set your watch by them! They were always that late to the market in the morning people used to say they were actually arriving early for the following day, but they just used to laugh and crack on. They had their own pace and nobody was going to speed them up.

Next up were the price labels up and scales out. The good thing about working for my uncle was that he would always buy me a sandwich and a cup of tea whereas the other barrow boys would tell me to help myself to fruit off the barrow. I prefered a sarnie – still would – but especially when you're surrounded by fruit; it wasn't a treat if it was in front of you and free, was it? Those holidays were great times; not a care in the world, working outside with the sun on my face, a full belly and a bit of money in my pocket. The only bad thing with holidays is that they have to come to an end and I'd have to go back to school and start a whole new year. That feeling inside when you knew the holidays were ending... six weeks that just weren't long enough, endless days, light nights... and you'd feel it all coming to an end and there wasn't a thing you could do about it.

I wasn't a massive fan of going to school. Everybody from our area went to Saint Mary's and I reckon I must have had about 20 cousins there too. I wasn't a great scholar but I did actually go there from time to time and show my face. It seemed my home life was in turmoil more often than not, so sometimes school seemed like the better option.

This brings us back to my dad. At the time, he was living a double life. Seriously. He wasn't a spy or anything glamorous like that, but it was just as bizarre: he lived with two families and he was quite open about it. My mam could do nothing about it because Dad would have just lifted his hand to her. He stayed at our house three days a week: Tuesdays, Thursdays and Sundays. Sundays were not *that* bad; Dad started to drink in the house rather than down the pub and my mam would try and keep him sober for as long as possible. It was the Tuesdays and Thursdays that I hated the most because on these nights he would be blind drunk and would get really violent.

I remember sitting at school one day and it was just after we'd had our lunch. The teacher mentioned what day it was it was: Tuesday.

'Shit,' I thought to myself, my dad would be mortal and we could all be in for a hard night ahead, depending on his mood. Without a drink he was a loving, caring dad but the 'evil' drink changed him and he'd think nothing of laying into me and my brothers and then my mam for trying to stop him. It would be the same procedure week in week out. But it started getting worse – and that's when he started dragging us outside to the back yard and leaving us out there to fend for ourselves for the night.

We were in the house having our tea, listening for him to arrive. There was an eerie silence; always the dark threat, like a storm brewing above the house, the black clouds gathering and building by the minute. We'd steal nervous glances at each other, eyes would dart around the room at any sound we heard, hoping it would pass and calm would prevail.

Dad had a haulage business at the time and all his wagons worked for Scottish and Newcastle breweries. He had five or six wagons and his yard was on Skinnerburn Road on the Quayside and, in those days, the draymen who delivered the beer would have a drink in all the bars they delivered to – so you could just imagine the state they got themselves into on a daily basis. Nice work if you can get it, eh?

This night we heard his wagon up the street and he was shouting out of the window. He could probably be credited with inventing road rage; you've seen nothing like it. He was mortal drunk. *Again*. So Mam sent us to bed to get away from him. He came in and he was full of himself, shouting for his tea. It was a typical scene for our family. It's only when you see something like *Our Friends in the North* where Geordie's dad used to goad him and beat him that you realise it may have been like that for other kids and abused mothers… as though it was the right of the bread-winner to get hammered after a hard day's work and make them pay for his life not being what he wanted it to be. He couldn't have been happy because he was living his double life… trying to escape something and have a different version of himself with other people.

Anyway, I'm no psychiatrist. We were very young; we didn't deserve to be treated like that. No one does. Michael was four, I was six and John was eight. We all got into the same bed and waited. Our breathing slowed as we struggled to hear what was going on. But, of course, it turned out we didn't need to struggle. You'd be able to hear him from outside or a few houses down the street.

And that was when it all kicked off: him slapping her, us running downstairs to help and getting thrown out into the yard. But me and my brothers are quick learners. After our first night in the kennel we decided to give it a facelift. It was about six foot long and four foot wide, and three and half foot tall. Bizarrely, we only had one dog – I know it sounds like enough room for a pack of them! It was a pretty decent size for just one and a cosy size for three extra kids... she probably *did* mind, but she didn't show it. As a kid or grown-up, there's no better feeling than your pet snuggling up to you on a night and to do it in those circumstances made it all the more special for us. So, for all of us really, we gave it a makeover that would have George Clark wetting his pants: carpets and blankets in to keep us warm and snug and kept Judy in the lap of luxury in-between our visits. The kennel became a regular 'punishment' in our early days and, looking back on that time of my life now; I can see that it changed us.

He drummed it into us all that under no circumstances should we say *anything* to the police. It's one thing that's stayed with us and served us well.

I remember another one of my dad's drunken interrogations quite clearly: he made our John go out of the room, placed a bottle on the chair and then shouted for him to come back in. Me and our Michael were just watching, but the both of us were very suspicious. You have to understand the script never changed. It was always about how to conduct yourself when arrested or in a police station and some of the tricks the police would do to fit you up. Our John walked into the room and he just stood there looking at this bottle on the chair and also looking at me and our Michael for some kind of hint. We couldn't help him because we were none the wiser. John decided not to touch the bottle. Dad gave him a slap with the back of his hand

and that was that. Test over. Getting the back of the hand was seen as a result.

Dad's training wasn't wasted. Ten years later, three men robbed a newsagents in North Shields and the owner got squirted with a toxic substance; probably ammonia. They got away with £10k and John and a friend of ours called Peter Morrison (aka Cabs) were nicked for it. After getting woken up in the middle of the night by two detectives our John was taken to the interview room. When he walked in there was a bottle on the chair for one purpose and one purpose only – for our John to pick it up and leave his finger prints on it. John had a flashback as the memory of our dad and his interrogations came flooding back. He knew instantly what was happening so he ignored the bottle, much to the annoyance of the police. He got a not guilty in the end.

My dad was a villain; there is no getting away from it. He was a bloody good one at that, but he did dabble in legitimate business now and then and he ran a very successful scrap yard at one time in Newcastle as well as his haulage business. I started hanging around there and making a few quid from the age of eight or so but I was aware that my dad had his fingers in a few pies – and it seemed that more than often he would be up to no good. He would always say to us that if he ever got nicked we'd need to get rid of anything he left in the house. He would never leave anything in the house though, so I guess it was just a precaution... but it was one which would serve us well.

So, we got word that my dad's cousin had been arrested. Even at this age, we knew the procedure: we checked the house over from top to bottom, there was nothing incriminating lying round or hidden away. It was one of those old-style houses where downstairs, two rooms had been knocked into one and had glass doors separating them.

I was just about to sit down when I saw an old suitcase on the floor that we must have missed earlier. I don't see how you could miss something like that; I'm surprised we hadn't tripped over the thing when we were searching. I picked it up as our John came into the room and wasn't sure whether to open it or not, but curiosity got the better of us and we put it on the table and unclipped the locks before slowly opening it. The suitcase was neatly packed full with money on both sides. I'll never forget the look on our John's face; no doubt the expression on my face was just the same. As we were looking at each other my mam walked in and her face was a picture too. We all just stood and stared for what seemed like two or three minutes before the realisation hit my mother and she slammed the suitcase shut.

'Ah, me babies... me babies. You can't see this. We'll all be arrested.'

She threw herself over the case to protect us from it. Even at eight years old I'd learned not to panic and, with the help of our John, we managed to calm her down. We told her that we knew what we had to do. We assumed that the police would come bursting through the door at any minute, so there was no time to lose. We emptied the suitcase into an old army duffle bag and we were off with it before the police turned up.

We headed up Elswick Road to the cemetery. To most people it was just a rundown, vandalised and over-grown cemetery. It was anything but that to us; it was everything. It was our playground, head quarters and our stamping ground and we knew it like the back of our hand. Even at that age, we'd earned a bit of a reputation with local constabulary (hard to believe, I know) and to them we were the Elswick Mafia Boys. Not a bad name to have, eh? The grass in the cemetery was over four foot long in places, which made a great hiding place. This was just as well because within minutes of us getting there with the bag, we saw the police arriving at our house. They were there for a while searching high and low but found nothing. As they were leaving I saw one of them stare straight over to where we were hiding, like he could sense us watching him... or worse, he could actually *see* us. It was getting dark though. Unless he was Robocop, we should be safe. We stayed hunched down, one hand each on the bag, poised ready to leg it, our hearts racing.

There was one tomb in the cemetery that we could both move. We'd used it as a place to hide in when we were playing games, so we instinctively knew to make our way over there. Sure enough, there was a gap and it just took a bit of pushing and pulling to move the concrete slab to give us just enough room to drop down into. We'd chucked an old length of rope into the duffle bag so we got it out, tied it to the handle and lowered the bag down into the darkness. It all seemed a bit too easy... like it was *old rope for money...* and that's when we heard shouting and screaming. Not from inside the tomb though! It was someone being chased by the police, with their torch lights swinging from side-to-side as they ran. Without thinking we both slid our way down into the tomb, pulling at the grass and stones to cover our tracks, but leaving a little gap to spy from. We held our breath as we watched the copper's boots pace up and down past our hiding place, looking at each other, our eyes widening at how mad the situation was. I was sure we were going to get caught. It was like the police knew we were in there but were just toying with us, letting us suffer in an old grave before deciding enough was enough. After another pass, they called it a night. That's when me and John breathed out for the first time in what seemed like hours. It was only when we could see their backs far away that we knew we were in the clear. You might think that hiding in an old tomb would scare the shit out of an eight-year-old boy, but not me. Not saying I was like Robert the Bruce hiding in his cave or anything, I mean… it was dark and dingy but the thing for me was that the tomb was secure just like the dog kennel in our back yard. To be there in the tomb with our John, protecting my dad's money (or whoever's it *had* been) felt natural to me and I never doubted myself for a second. I knew in my heart what I was doing was right.

Once the coast was clear and we climbed out with the bag, we couldn't help ourselves. We took another look into it.

'How much do you think is in?' asked our John.

'I reckon a million dollars,' I replied.

I put my hand in my pocket, pulled out a penny and I chucked it on top of the notes.

'There's over a million now,' I said and we both started laughing. Eight years old and millionaires! We were never going to be nine to five'ers after that, were we?

As the days went by, we stayed in the cemetery and kept watch over the tomb. It was crazy what you could witness on Elswick Road late at night. There was prostitution on the streets during the 70s and all the pubs were full. There was a lot of drunken violence and domestic violence kicking off all the time. If it wasn't something on the street, we could hear the dramas going on inside people's houses from our hiding place. We'd armed ourselves with a little stick and we'd nabbed a kitchen knife each on the way out and, with our loyal dog who would attack on our command, we felt like little soldiers guarding the Crown Jewels.

We were there for three days and nights. It turned out that they'd already nicked my dad and had him and his cousin in for questioning on an unrelated offence. The mandatory holding time when you were nicked back then was three days and, once they were released without charge, we handed the money back over. We expected a bit of praise but it didn't come. We did what we were supposed to do, so why should we be thanked? That was my dad's take on it. He said our true reward was in the experience of it all. Looking back I agree; he was right.

About a year later some bloke got nicked in a foreign country trying to pass some of the notes over. It turns out that they were forgeries! In fact they were the best the FBI had ever seen at the time. It felt even more like we'd been part of something bigger.

As I turned 11, my dad abandoned our family altogether and decided to bring his other family up instead. Even though this put an end to the drunken interrogations and beatings, all I ever wanted was my dad back home. It's what every kid wants deep down.

A few weeks after he moved out I saw him in the street and I begged him to come home but he just ignored me. On another occasion he passed me in his car with his new family and I waved at him but he blanked me again and drove straight past. I was devastated and I couldn't stop crying. I felt so unwanted and lonely. No one should have to go through that. I'm not putting all of this together to say whether he was right or wrong or good or bad. He was all of them, just like everyone else is. We do things, we act and we react and, a lot of the time, we don't really understand why; we just do it and live and breathe and carry on because that's what life is... getting through it by whichever way you decide to.

Those memories have never left me and, on many occasions, I have revisited the incidents in my mind and they have given me the strength to move forward and overcome any obstacles that have been put in my way.

So, what did my dad's unique method of fatherhood produce? I'll tell you. Three hardened criminals who feared nobody and who could tackle any situation. Do I hold a grudge against my dad for the way that he treated us? Do I fuck... I love him. Rightly or wrongly, it was his way of preparing the three of us for a life of crime and his teaching gave us the advantage over all our rivals. Many would say we were born into it. All we did was go into the family business, just like loads of you lot did who are reading this. Would I say we were born into it? Probably, but I'll let you decide.

We all become who we want to be in the end though, don't we? You can be born into anything, shaped and moulded by your environment, your parents, family, your peers – we all take our influences from all over the place. To some extent, we – the Sayers – are a product of our environment. Which isn't a bad thing! We love the West End and our name became synonymous with the place and I love that. And to be able to have lived a life that you the reader is interested in is a great feeling for me. You've read all the stuff in the newspapers, you've heard all the rumours, all the whispers in bars and you may know a few things about us, our reputations and what we've done. Now it's time to hear the real story – the story of the Sayers family and my side of it all.

So... sit yourself down, get comfy, and let the bad lads into your life...

CHAPTER 2
GROWING UP

I was born on the 12th of August 1965, 7.30pm, at 13 York Street in Elswick, Newcastle, to John Brian Sayers and Yvonne Bulman. I was a house birth and I weighed in at a healthy 10lb... and I screamed the fucking place down. My dad timed it perfectly; he was released from a nine-month sentence on the day I was born and was there to welcome me into the world.

As a kid, I would hang around the barrows with my Granny Liza and cousins Philip, Joe, Tony, Peter and my brothers John and Michael as well as Frankie Kelly most of the time. It was brilliant. I'd stop at my Granny's overnight and then we'd be up sharp for breakfast. More often than not, there'd be around 20 people downstairs having a cuppa before the day ahead, even at stupid o'clock in the morning. Uncle Albert might be there before doing a day's graft on the suitcases selling gold or watches and the like and there'd be another cousin selling scarves or something – always *someone* selling *something*.

Barrows back then were illegal, so I used to keep toot for the police coming to make sure everyone had a decent chance of making it through the day without getting nicked. Even back then they didn't have anything better to do than hassle people trying to make a living. It didn't look too suspicious if a bairn was up a lamppost just minding his own business, rather than a grown-up spotter... and I got paid for it. I'm sure this conditioned me to always having one eye looking over my shoulder. I know how hard it is to believe, but I've just never really got on with them. I could spot one a mile away – and that was using my sight, not sense of smell.

From the earliest days I can remember, the barrows were always a big part of my life and the activity around them was fantastic. The buzz and the excitement of being in amongst it all was brilliant to experience as a kid. It must have been around the early 70s when I was five or six years-old; wide-eyed and taking in anything and everything, people-watching, learning how the barrows worked, even down to how much things cost and working out mental arithmetic... all good training for later life.

Summer holidays doing this was amazing and all the summer fruits were on display on the barrow; vivid colours and the smells were so inviting you just wanted to eat everything. Well, you'd have a bellyful once and then learn your lesson from it. Uncle Thomas Kelly and Uncle Albert Sayers worked on that corner. They had a barrow each and it was a busy junction by The Clock. The barrows looked amazing; there was a good flash up (display) and they were taking money. Back then there were no big supermarkets, so everyone was heading to the city centre for fruit and veg and they were the freshest you could get.

The lamppost between the barrows had a big wooden box leaning against it. I'd climb onto the box and stand looking up and down the street when I was on watch-duty. There was a particular tall, skinny bizzy (police officer) who'd taken a personal dislike to all the barrow boys and he was a right sly fucker; you had to be on your toes when this one was about. One of the family would give us the word when he was on the beat and news spread quickly amongst us. He was so well-known amongst our family because of his arrests that we disregarded whatever his name was and what he represented. For all of us, he had one name and went by one name only… *the long streak of piss*.

Over the previous few weeks he had arrested quite a few of the barrow boys for causing an obstruction while street trading. An obstruction, while street trading? It's like arresting the policeman for being a long streak of piss or a complete idiot… it just goes without saying. We were very busy at the time – it was great to have so much demand for what we were all selling. The only good thing I could say about this is that work for me and my young cousins was in demand. My family were not granted street licenses until the 1980s, so it was illegal to sell fruit and veg from barrows in Newcastle until then. It seemed we were destined to be lawbreakers! But they, we, were only out to make an honest living doing what we knew. My family had been doing it all their lives. My Great Grandmother and her 11 children… most of them went to jail for the barrows. How mental is that? For selling fruit and veg. In those days conditions were harsh in prison, but sending an old woman there was seen as normal.

I suppose this is another reason why I've never really liked the police. Every day *something* would happen; most weeks someone would be arrested. We couldn't just have a day at work and go home. It was constant fear and you could never let your guard down. You know when you hear about victimisation? This was it. The old cliché of go out and arrest some real criminals was very true in this situation. You had to have eyes in the back of your head and never completely relax because the long streak of piss would be onto you, and this fucker had a reputation for being cunning. But you learn to fight cunning with cunning. One day I turned my head and saw something shine out the corner of my eye. It was the sun bouncing off huge sheets of glass from a glazier's van – obviously fixing another shop window that had been put through. I followed the van as it crawled alongside the shops and the driver stopped to unload and do his job… and that's when I saw the bastard, creeping behind the van. He'd been using it as a cover and was biding his time before pouncing. I looked at my Uncle Thomas and Uncle Albert, 'Hedge up!'I shouted. But they couldn't see him and just carried on serving. I needed to act quickly.

'Nitto!'I shouted – slang for stop. 'He's there behind the van! It's the long streak of piss!' I was pointing and shouting as if I had seen the devil himself. I was blowing my own cover, but it was necessary. 'There he is! The long streak off piss!'

I jumped down from my watchtower, and took the price signs down and removed any weights as fast as I could. I did as much as I could before walking away. My uncles saw me doing this and jumped into action: they picked the barrow and started taking it away down the street, so by the time the long streak of piss caught up and stopped them there were no prices up on the barrow and no other evidence to suggest they'd been selling. My aunty Sylvia was also working there at the time and even grabbed their money pouches and hid them in a shopping bag. Of course, he must have known that what little fruit and veg that was left belonged to my uncles and it also suggested that they'd sold a lot to not have much stock left... but could he prove it? Could he bollocks! He was a bit pissed off to say the least; out foxed by a child.

It didn't end there though. Three of my traveller cousins, Frankie, Philip and Tony arrived and Peter and Joe Riley along with my brothers Michael and John with our other cousin Frankie Kelly. We all stood looking at the long streak off piss with hatred in our eyes because we knew this man had brought so much misery to hardworking people with his relentless persecution – essentially he'd taken food off our tables. As we all stared him out, his radio bleeped and a message came through before he said he'd be back to see us later and ran off. We were on edge for the next few hours and determined to prevent this man on getting one over us, so me and my young cousins spread out all over the place and in the little side streets so we had plenty of time to give notice when he returned. He never did come back, but we knew that wouldn't be the end of him. We headed back over to my Granny Liza's in Westgate Hill Terrace. I felt like the little hero of the day. Uncle Thomas and Uncle Albert praised me and gave me ten bob apiece for my actions.

I asked if I could stay the night, as my travelling cousins had come to visit. They came up from their camp every weekend and I loved spending time with everyone. There was my Uncle Joe Reilly and his wife, my Aunt Sylvia (my dad's sister), my cousins Joe, Frankie, Phillip and Lisa. I was never refused a bed for the night at Granny Liza's; I just always thought it was polite and respectful to ask first because it's in my nature. She loved having us around and being surrounded by family.

Everyone that came to my granny's would always be welcome and would be offered something to eat; a big bowl of vegetable broth and freshly roasted hot beef sandwiches were her specialties. It's making me as hungry writing about it as it is for you reading it. Freshly baked warm crusty bread with homemade broth...

Anyway. If that isn't the best food to have after working outside all day, I don't know what is. She knew how to look after us all. Her house was always full of family and close friends with a very comfortable atmosphere and a loving feeling of togetherness. Add to that the smell of the food, the conversation and laughter and it's the perfect mix for a strong family.

I'd always be there watching and listening and absorbing everything I heard like a sponge. The stories amongst the elders in my family would fascinate me. Looking back now, the stories were all crime-related – excluding my mother's side of the family who were law-abiding people. My mother was highly intelligent and educated and worked as a civil servant and ran Swan House dole office in Newcastle for a number of years until her retirement. She was multilingual speaking in Latin, French and German fluently. One of her favourite hobbies was to time herself and see how fast she could complete the latest *Times* crossword. To have that kind of influence on a youngster as well as the more villainous side was like going to crime college.

My mam was from a wealthy background. Her dad, my grandfather, was Harry Bulman nicknamed 'Jonna' Bulman prior to his death he had owned a large and very successful demolition company and had invested in quite a bit of property throughout Newcastle. When my mam and dad got married he gifted them the big house in York Street that we grew up in – the house I was born in.

During the early to mid-70s, the price of potatoes rocketed. They went from being around £1-£1.50 a bag up to £10 a bag in a very short space of time. Whatever the reason behind this was, my dad and his associates looked to get a piece of the action. That was the thing with such a mind – see something, hear something, sniff it out, see what can be made off the back of it and jump on it quickly before anyone else gets in first. It was just like any other business, really… without the honesty.

I remember being with him one time, sitting outside a warehouse on Newcastle's Quayside on a pallet of potatoes. My dad had a funny sense of humour; he told me to give him a shout if I noticed a boat or ship coming round that bend of the Tyne behind us. Then he proceeded to jump on a forklift and move pallets of potatoes back and forth. As time passed, I was lying there sunbathing with my eyes shut and almost doing off when I nearly jumped out of my skin at the sound of a ship's horn blasting out. I opened my eyes and saw possibly the biggest and loudest ship I had ever seen so close up. There was no need to shout to Dad – he'd seen the ship coming long before me. It wasn't like anyone could miss the thing. He drove straight over towards me on the forklift, parked it up and got off. As he stood next to me he rubbed his hands together with anticipation.

'Son, I hope we can fit all this in the warehouse.'

The potatoes were getting loaded out of the cargo part of the ship by the tonne. I was just looking on in amazement. I couldn't believe the size of the warehouse, it was huge. Just like the ship. I couldn't take it all in. I was up and on my feet, but before I could go any further Dad shouted at me to go home.

'Can I not stay here, Da?' I asked.

The last thing I wanted to do was go home. Not now! It was all starting to happen – the buzz, the excitement, but he promised I could return the following day. To me this was a massive adventure. I knew fine well that those potatoes were not going to be paid for which made it all the more exciting. I couldn't wait to get back down there and didn't want to tell our John and Michael, as I knew they'd want to come along too.

At 5.30am there was a loud bang outside the house. I looked out the window and there was our John getting in the wagon with Dad. I was devastated. Our John was the oldest brother and I suppose that's why he got taken instead of me. There was very little I could do about it. I jumped back in to bed but I couldn't get to sleep. My mind was racing – the excitement was back, but I was also a bit put out that I was missing out on the adventure I'd started. It was *my* adventure. It didn't even cross my mind for a split second that it was a school day until I heard Mam shout to wake us up for school. There was no way I was going in with everything that was happening down on the quay. To avoid suspicion, I got my uniform on, had my breakfast and then walked with Mam to see her onto the bus to work. She gave me a cuddle and a kiss and told me she loved me and to have a good day at school. I smiled and told her I would and then waved as the bus drove off... I turned straight around and headed back home, up the lamp post above the front door, along the guttering at the side of the house and climbed though the bedroom window above the front door. I was on a mission: got our John's Chopper bike and went peddling down to the warehouse. I knew exactly how to get there. It took me half an hour or so and, when I arrived, I was taken aback with the sheer quantity of potatoes in the warehouse. It was full to the brim and they were still unloading them. I could see Dad from a distance, making arrangements with the man who was in charge of renting the premises. There must have been ten tonnes of potatoes in the main part of the warehouse and in the adjacent room it was full of chocolates – pallet after pallet of chocolates. And cigarettes – there was a cigarette wagon getting unloaded as I looked on, amazed. This was a long firm in full flow and, even at a young age, I knew the mechanics of it. Fucking hell... what a buzz! Just seeing it all happening and unfolding was brilliant.

Just in case you didn't know, a long firm fraud involves setting up a front company and making modest orders with suppliers, paid for on time so that the company can build up credit. Once your credit is good, you can place a much bigger order and then sell on the goods at knock-down prices before the supplier knows what's up. By the time they come looking for their money, the company's been stripped of its assets and dissolved. It's a very profitable crime and it's been going for donkey's years. It fascinated me watching this take place and it all just felt so natural, like it was preparing me for the criminal life that lay ahead of me.

The place was hub of activity and there were vans and wagons getting loaded with potatoes all morning. Like, where had all the people and vans come from, how was it all set up and what and when and who? Dad accepted that I'd used my initiative and told me and our John to count the bags of potatoes that were getting taken out and to make sure we got it right as these people would skim from you straight away. It was typical of my dad, and he drummed it in to us to never trust anybody. He would always say, 'trust is a good thing, but trust not is even better.' So, using this new-found wisdom we had a queue of around 25 vehicles waiting to be filled up with potatoes and closely scrutinised. Dad found this rather amusing and told me to lighten up because at that rate we'd not sell anything. He then got me and John together and walked us into the warehouse through the side door where a wagon was reversing in. One of my dad's cousins got out and rubbed me on the head and asked how I was and if I was being good. I found this a very strange question to ask. I don't know about being good... but I was certainly being careful and nobody was stealing from us; quite the opposite. Dad told us to count wagons in and out and we were on top of the world, totally in our element: controlling blokes in wagons, telling them 50 cases of cigarettes to one, 50 cases of whiskey to another, chocolates here, cigarettes and cigars there... counting, double-checking... triple-checking... until the place was empty apart from a load of Cadbury's chocolates. Everything had to be out of the warehouse that night, so I ended up taking them home. And, when I say a load of chocolates, I actually mean a palette full. We couldn't get moved for weeks, but I did my best to eat us out of the predicament.

Friday and Saturday nights when the local bars were closing and people started spilling out onto the street, it was common for them to make their way to the chip shop or the Chinese takeaway. I mean, it was the same on any estate and I'm sure it still is to this day. In Elswick, the bars and takeaways were only a kick up the arse away from each other – well within convenient staggering distance for the inebriated and rather peckish chap to round off an evening. In the 70s there were a lot of Irish workers living in the area and working for a firm called Murphy's. The Irish lot mixed well with the westenders and some of them married the local lasses – overall they were good people that enjoyed a good drink – and there wasn't any of the 'they're taking our jobs' mentality that there is today. Another thing there was a lot of in the 70s was street prostitutes that used to work along Elswick Road (I hope I haven't done a typo and said they were *in* their 70s rather than saying it *happened* in the 70s). Nine times out of ten they'd be related to people in the area that we knew, so there was no hostility towards these women. It was quite the opposite in fact; if they ever got any trouble from men kerb-crawling, we used to throw bricks at their cars and they'd soon make a sharp exit. There was a lot of solidarity in the West End and, if any strangers came into the area and brought trouble for a local, then we'd all stick together. It was a real community; looking out for each other. That bond has gone these days as the area has been demolished. Any community that was left was totally obliterated along with the houses. Whatever bond remains is certainly not as strong as it used to be because the families have been scattered to different parts of the city. It's just what happens: people move away, new people move in, they keep themselves to themselves and community spirit dies because no one who lives there is actually *from* there and so there's no history or memory left to keep it all together.

One night my dad sent me and our John out to the chippy to get a fish supper. We were standing in the chip shop queue and we had our Alsatian, Prince, with us when we heard a disturbance coming from outside. I recognized the voice as coming from a working girl by the name of 'big' Jean, who was a friend of the family. She always had time for us and she would always send her love to members of our family when she saw us – nice lady, whether she happened to work nightshift or had a more respectable occupation. The noise from outside the door was getting louder and louder so I had to have a look. Outside I could clearly see this Irish man was drunk and being aggressive towards Jean, who was having none of it. Then, in a typical woman-with-a-handbag manner... she banged him on the head a few times with it. It was like something out of an old sitcom. Unfortunately for the Irish bloke, when she hit him, blood squirted out of his head and he fell straight to the ground. His head was split open and he was out cold. That part of it didn't usually happen in sitcoms though. Jean just stepped over him and took her business elsewhere. I couldn't believe what I'd seen! We collected Dad's supper, got the dog and went down the house all excited about it. To us, going to that chip shop late at night was an adventure. A few weeks passed but the memory of Jean hitting him was still vivid in my mind. I couldn't get over the fact that a woman could knock a man out... not only that but *with a handbag? A somewhat large black leather handbag.*

So there we were: a few weeks later about to go to the chippy and as were we about to walk up, I could hear loads of shouting and balling from the bar across the road and sure enough, it was big Jean and another drunken Irish man (not that I'm assuming a stereotype here, my Irish friends). She was shouting at him, he was shouting at her and neither seemed like they'd back down. Taking a closer look – as you do – I noticed she had the very same bag on her arm and I had a feeling I knew what was coming next! This was the real reason we wanted to go to the chippy on Elswick Road, not for Dad's supper. I bet he thought we were brilliant for being so obedient and keen to do something for him as well. Just as I suspected, I watched as Jean's arm wind up like a fast bowler then – CRACK – she struck the man with her bag right across the head just like the last one. He fell to the ground unconscious just as quick as the other one as well. She saw me looking over and came over and asked what we were doing out so late. I said we were going to the fishy for my dad.

'Ha'way. I'll take you along home,' she said.

Well, one thing's for certain; you'd be pretty safe at night being walked home by big Jean. Whoever you were! As we were walking off, another Irish man came out of the pub and found his mate sparked out on the ground. 'What happened to you, man?' he was asking as he tried to revive him.

As we got near our house, big Jean stopped off at a back alley and told us to wait. Curious to see what she was doing, I followed her and watched as she unzipped that infamous bag, pulled out a big red house brick and threw it on the ground. Mystery over! What a woman! It was no ordinary handbag.

We all loved sport in our house and we were very competitive. I was like all the other young lads my age, bang into football and I supported Newcastle United. As a player I was a left-footed striker. I'd been the top goal scorer in my school and then the year after I was in the upper class and I was still the top scorer for the season and four of us got asked to go for trials at Newcastle. There was me and my best school pal Bryce Moses and two other good friends Anthony Cross and an Irish lad called John Gibson. John came over from Northern Ireland in the 70s with his family, but was one of us straight away; an adopted Geordie. The early trials went quite well and me and the lads were called back on more than one occasion. Jimmy Moses and another lad called Robert Cross could also play a bit too and were also called.

One of the trials got cancelled and the next one was arranged for a few weeks later, so I had a bit of time to kill. Now, remember the palette of chocolates? Well, there was so much chocolate in the house that I think my mother was considering doing away with the furniture and just using chocolate instead; even a replacement for the fireguard. But to save the family from such an embarrassment, I was still on my mission to rid us all of confect. Chocolate consumption was reaching new levels… in fact, so had I on the scales. When I turned up for my next trial a few weeks later I had put on two stone and I was a proper little fatty stood at five foot seven. In total, I put on three stone since my first trial a few months earlier. So, there I was, in the rescheduled trial and I couldn't run or move fast enough to catch a cold, never mind challenge another player. It was like I was just chasing after the ball. It was frustrating because I'd been fast and hadn't even realised I'd let myself go. And, of course, I was just letting myself down. I got substituted after fifteen minutes, which I was glad about because my shorts were cutting right in to me. Part of me was devastated, but that was the end of my dream of pulling on the Number 9 shirt and scoring at the Gallowgate End. I had eaten my way out of a goal-den opportunity and fucked it up with my fat face.

The extra weight made me look older. I was only ten at the time but I looked about 13 or 14 years old. We were playing football in the Gem Park just off Westgate Hill and when we finished our game I picked the ball up. It was a present from Mam for my birthday and was my pride and joy. It was a good kickabout and I was starving. Why did kickabouts always end at teatime? But this one did and I set off walking home along Elswick Road, bouncing the ball like a basketball player. All of a sudden a big blue transit van pulled up on the road alongside me. The back doors and side doors open and the police came jumping out and pinned me against the wall face first. They were the police, not your common-or-garden police... these fuckers were Special Patrol Group and it was their job to fight violence with violence wherever violence may be. They were known for their heavy-handedness. To me, they were just a group of bullies thinking that a uniform legitimised picking on a child. So they had my face pushed into the wall and asked me where I'd been, why I was sweating and who had been chasing me. I couldn't really reply, even though the urge to tell them that the football was a rather blatant clue they'd failed to spot. One of them asked me again why I was sweating and asked if I had been chased by the police for burgling a house. I knew not to speak to these people. I gave my name and that was it. As soon as I said my name, one of them punched me in the kidneys before they pinned me down on the floor and kicked and punched me. They were kneeling with all their weight on my body and the pain was unbearable. They kept bending my arm up my back and asking me to tell them where I'd been. It was excruciating pain; for anyone to endure, not just a ten-year-old. I cried, as ten year olds do in that situation. I was determined not to speak a word; I didn't care how much the copper was hurting me with his knee in my back. Then... they just stopped. They released my arms and let me go. Once I got to my feet (none of them helped me up) one of them asked how old I was. I told him I was ten and I remember the look on his face; how his expression changed in a split-second to one of total shock. The rest of them were the same. They realised they'd just assaulted a ten-year-old boy. They sped off and I sat on the curb on Elswick Road, doubled over with pain from the kicking. I looked up and saw my ball rolling down the hill. I sat there for a few moments, pulled myself together, then went down to the house and got changed. I thought it was pointless telling my mam. She would have screamed to high heaven and my dad would have probably got himself nicked. I feel it was just another part of my education. If I didn't like them before, I fucking *hated* the bastards now!

As I got older it seemed I lived a double life of my own. I was working the barrows by day and thieving by night. The life of crime was pulling me in like a magnet. I knew I was in its grip and I was happy to go with it; it felt natural to me... so natural that I didn't even realise it was happening. It was just life – families who live more by the law than we did have their own set of values and their idiosyncrasies by which they live: school, a family holiday once a year, dinner, homework, university, job, career, mortgage, marriage, 2.4 kids, sensible car or maybe a 4x4 for negotiating those tricky roads to and from Sainsbury's. Our family and our environment was different.

As I saw it, it was us against *them*: the system, the establishment, the law... the man... whatever name you want to give it. We all shared the same strong philosophy.

Over the years I'd received one hell of an initiation and education and, as a child, I was certainly influenced by those around me. With that kind of start, it's no wonder I went down the path that I did. For starters, there was that copper who used to persecute us for being street traders. To me, that scumbag represented authority and taught me not only to be wary of them, but to have an instant dislike towards them all. He was out to get us and it made us resent the law but it also made us have to live our lives around the law. And when our Auntie Sylvia died in 2015, over 400 people attended the funeral and it was even front-page news of *The Evening Chronicle*:

"The 78-year-old, who was part of the well-known Sayers trading family and was instrumental in a campaign for the industry to be recognised as a legitimate business. Members of Sylvia's family, including her grandmother Maria Kelly, known as the Queen of the Barrows, were jailed for trading before the laws finally changed in 1981 when Newcastle City Council allowed licensed street trading."

You don't get tributes like that if you haven't made your mark in life, do you? And the thing is, we changed the law! It was wrong and we were pioneers in having the right to work as street traders. I bet that if or when that copper pegs it, there won't be that kind of grief or respect shown so publically.

Some people may try to justify why and how they fell into crime. In me and my brothers' case it just felt so right to us. As far as we were concerned, we were prepared and bred for it. Let's not forget we had quite a few fighters and boxers in the family who not only taught us their trade, but they taught us how to fight with bad intentions. The difference between bad intentions and no bad intentions is winning and losing. It's just sheer determination in succeeding against all the odds and putting everything you have got into achieving your goal. Even more so if you're in a fight, it becomes the biggest advantage.

Working in my dad's scrap yard was a fantastic experience for me in many ways. As a kid, something like that is the best playground you could ever imagine; an adventure every day and the best environment to learn the ropes. It was on Skinnerburn Road, which runs along Newcastle's Quayside, parallel with the Tyne. At the time there was about six or seven people working there, Davey Mares, Derek Bennett and a man called Bimbo are just a few to name. They all worked on the yard and Davey was in charge of them all. We also had a resident in the yard – my dad's friend called big Trevor Harrison. Trevor had nothing to do with the yard; he just lived there in his trailer. Most scrap yards would have a fierce dog – we had Big Trevor and when he would arrive back 'home' after a full day of drinking, he really was someone to stay well clear of.

On one particular occasion me and Big Trevor's son Jimmy were sitting on a car bonnet with our shirts off, sunbathing with the music turned up so we didn't hear a wagon pull up outside. I was lying there in a blissful world enjoying the rays and doing anything but work. I guess it was perks of being the boss's son. Well, it was! Who wouldn't sunbathe on the job if they could get away with it? I was awoken by a sudden snap and a yelp that came from my right-hand side. Jimmy was clearly in pain and a split second later so was I. Then I saw him from out the corner of my eye – Big Trevor full of drink with a horse whip in his hand. *A fucking horse whip*? Jimmy and I instinctively knew what to do. We scarpered! But unfortunately for Jimmy, he got whipped again all the way down his back. The old cliché to many would be 'a cuff round the ear' or 'a slap on the wrist' – you don't generally hear 'I'll come after you with a horse whip' that much, do you? Ahhh, those were the days: being able to whip a child and get away with it! Anyway, I used to get my own back (pardon the pun) and torment Trevor as much as possible. He'd still find a way of getting one over on me though... clever as an old fox he was. Because he'd be so drunk, most of the time he wouldn't even remember chasing after us or whipping us until we reminded him the following day. He'd never apologise once he'd sobered up though. He'd just shout, 'Go on, fuck off before I kick you up the bollocks. You Sayersie bastard.'

Charming. Lovely social skills, eh?

Thinking back, maybe I was too keen to grow up. I felt I was mature enough to hit the world when I was a kid because I felt I knew things others my age didn't and I wanted to learn more about 'our world'. Staying at school and learning all their ways just wasn't for me. I couldn't learn the things I needed to know at school; I could only learn them on the streets... by doing it and living it. The idea of going to school was to create an opportunity to make a living the conventional way. Outside of school, I could learn firsthand how to make money and learn from an active and successful business. I would never learn that at school.

Davey Mares used to drive the wagon to the scrap yard half a dozen times a day and he would always take me with him. He was an absolute diamond! One day as we were driving, he just pulled up, jumped out and walked round to the passenger side and said, 'Jump over. You're driving.' I looked at him with a big smile on my face, 'Are you sure?' I was as nervous as hell. 'Move over,' he said. He put a hat on my head and give me a coat to sit on to boost me up and make me look bigger. I've never been one to cower away from situations or avoid a good challenge and, as soon as I knew he was on the level, I was well up for taking this one on. I jumped over and adjusted the mirrors as if I knew what I was doing... mirror, signal, manoeuvre and all that... then I pulled away. And stalled it. Davey was sound about it though. He didn't embarrass me or discourage – he gave advice and helped me to concentrate on what I was doing. I mean, I was 11 years old and driving a wagon carrying two cars on the back. He was my passenger, so it was in his interest to be nice to me! I started it back up, took my time, looked in the mirror and I was away. I couldn't believe it! I drove over the Tyne Bridge and over to some scrap yard in Gateshead to weigh these two vehicles in. I felt like a big man – on top of the world. It became a regular job for me and my confidence soared. So, in no time at all, my real education had started to pay off.

I slowly lost interest in other scrap yard activities such as gear boxes, dismantling radiators and all that (although I always enjoyed winding old Trevor up). I still loved the yard and being part of it because it was ours, but I swapped my fascination for anything crime-related, especially in how to break into and steal cars and vans. What the people down at the yard didn't know about stealing cars wasn't worth knowing. They knew it all. Not only did I acquire this knowledge, but I practiced it on every opportunity I could (out of sight of my dad, of course!). He caught me jiggling the locks of cars on numerous occasions and would ask me what I was doing. I'd always come out with some silly excuse, but I think he knew. Of course he knew. He was my dad and nothing got past him.

Over time Davey Bimbo and Derek left the yard and I was there on a day to day basis just by myself. My good friend Fish Tams would come and see me all the time with bottles of pop and sandwiches. There is a close bond between the Sayers and the Tams family because the older generation we good friends and we all grew up in the same area together. I would regularly lock the yard up and walk up Forth Banks to the Kings Head pub which, at the time, was owned by an uncle of mine. It was always full of a collection of right old characters from town and this was where you'd find a lot of members of the Tams family. Old Giddy Tams was my favourite; I always had a lot of time and respect for him and he did for me. There wasn't a man in the country that could beat him at dominoes. Not because he was the best player, but because he was the best cheat (I always liked old Giddy. I had a lot of respect for him as I do the rest of the Tams family – they are my friends).

It was a visit to this bar where I saw my dad and he asked how things were going in the yard and I told him it wasn't too good. Bottom line was that we needed some stock. To me it seemed like he'd lost interest in the whole thing, probably due to the strain of the double life he was living. It saddened me for a lot of reasons and it made me more determined to keep it open. I know my interest had waned but there was no way I wanted to just let it go either. I felt it was part of us; something to bond us together and with no stock to sell there was no money and things were not going to change. The scrap yard had been my life for the previous two and a half years and I'd loved every minute of it, so I was not prepared to let it close down without a fight. Secretly, I was hoping and praying that if I got the business back on its feet it would get my mam and dad back together. I used to pray for it every night.

It was a Wednesday in Newcastle and there was a football match on; Newcastle were playing at home which was ideal as far as I was concerned. Newcastle's football ground is near enough to my mother's house to hear the roar of the crowd especially when Newcastle scored. Certainly back then. You don't hear it so much these days. I had a set of keys for the scrap yard that I'd kept in my pocket. I had my tea that night then made my way along Buckingham Street. I knew where I was going and I knew what I was looking for. I had my mother's shopping bag with my boiler suit in, a woolly hat and gloves, and a pillow to sit on and I went looking for Ford cars to break into. As I said earlier I was short of stock so my plan was to find the dirtiest scruffiest car that looked like it belonged in a scrap yard, as many cars did back then. I found what I was looking for and there was a dozen or so in the same street. I walked up and down the street checking everything out and eyed the cars up properly.

Now, I know I said I'd been interested in stealing cars and this would have been an ideal opportunity for me. The street was empty; the cars were there for the taking. I'd probably have opened the boot of each car, removed the spare tyres and put them all in the boot of the scruffy old one that I'd first sussed out. With around ten spare tyres and some hydraulic jacks, I'd easily have been able to start the car up and drive it down to the yard. There'd be plenty of time because the match had only kicked off 15 minutes ago. If I'd wanted more, I could have been back there in minutes and gone through the same procedure four times in different streets, bringing four new cars and car wheels to the yard to get us started again. Easily. I could then have walked home with a sense of self-achievement. If I was that way inclined.

As my dad was spending less time at the scrap yard it didn't bother me business-wise as I knew that side of it inside out. When the next home game came around, I could have probably stolen five more cars because I'd probably have learnt a bit more and taken my bike, so I could get round the streets quicker in my recce mission, and just put it in the back of each car I was TWOCing. I could have taken around 20 cars a month at that rate, if you think about it.

Through keeping the place afloat, I'd accumulated a decent handful of cash and put it to one side for a rainy day. It was hard graft but it felt good hat I was able to do it all on my own. Dad was rarely there to see what I was doing, if at all. It would have been nice because I think he'd have been proud of me. One day he told me he needed to see me, so he came down to have a word. I knew what it was about – he was going to close the yard. But there was something inside me that felt we could still keep going: I'd brought two of the lads back in on four quid a day and I'd got a wagon repaired on a fiddle job for £100 when the work had been quoted at £250. In my eyes, this was what being in business was all about.

My dad pulled up and it was quite busy with four or five customers in at once and some new stock; twenty cars with various parts missing from of them. I will never forget the look on my dad's face as he came in and saw all the vehicles. He pulled me and asked me what was going on. I said I'd been busy. 'Busy doing *what*?' I told him that I'd earned him some money and gave him what I'd saved and told him I'd paid for the wagon as well. This was the first he had ventured down to the yard in three or four weeks and I was hoping it would revive his interest but it didn't. It did not get mam and dad back together either. It got closed down and I was absolutely devastated. Sometimes when I was 12 and feeling bored and a bit lonely I take a car and drive it down there. By then, dad was with his other family. We still saw him though, it just carried on differently.

I was hanging around outside the famous Dolce Vita nightclub in Newcastle one night with a couple of pals including Tom Brayson and Joseph Ramsey. The club was closing and I could see a lot of the older westenders having trouble with some people – some things never change! A few fights broke out there were men and women fighting at the same time. It wasn't the most pleasant sight in the world, but nothing out of the ordinary for me. It was a bit of a free-for-all with around 20 people braying the shite out of each other. I just stood back and watched – it's always good entertainment, isn't it? I saw a certain westender knock half a dozen people out with a hammer that he'd happened to find in the back lane that seemed to have sealed his victory. I mean, once you introduce a hammer, it's game over. With that, we left. Nothing more to see.

As we were driving though town we saw a group of five or six of the people who'd been fighting and they'd armed themselves with sticks – no idea where they'd find sticks in the middle of town in the early hours, but they'd managed it. We pulled over and a few words were exchanged… and then an incident occurred where one of the men was hit in the face with a steel wheel brace. The police were soon on the scene and we took off in a high speed chase before skidding off the road at 70 or so mph and straight in to a big street lamp. Two girls were on the other side of it walking home and the lamp post undoubtedly saved their lives as we'd just have flattened them otherwise. They stood screaming in shock, unable to move. And neither could I. My ankles were fucked and I couldn't put pressure on my feet. I tried to get out, but as I did so, a big bizzie ran over and slammed the door on me… right against my ankles. The pain was immense. At that point, the bizzies weren't really sure what we'd done. They probably thought we'd stolen the car as the driver ran off after the crash and was never caught.

They got us to hospital in an ambulance to the RVI instead of the hospital in the nearer General Hospital in the West End. When we were ushered into A&E there was a man sat with a huge bandage on his eye, obviously in a lot of pain, waiting to be seen to. The two girls from earlier were there and still looked like they were in shock. We waited for ages and then we heard loads of noise and shouting from a group of people heading in our direction. Talk about bad luck! It was the people who we'd had the run-in with earlier. It then clicked! The bloke with the bandage on his head was the guy who'd fallen out with the wheel brace. It was unreal, like a scene from a daft comedy. At the time, it wasn't that funny though. They wanted to set about us but we were in no fit state to walk, never mind fight back. The nurses saw what was going on and screamed for the police to assist us helpless young lads being picked on by the angry mob. Fair play – they came running in and were very heavy-handed with these people, which was very amusing when you consider we were certainly not the victims and they were only trying to get revenge.

I was lying on a stretcher along with my future two co-accused. I didn't know what Joe's injuries were but I could see a lot of blood coming from Tom's feet and, as far as I was concerned, my ankles were broken as the pain was unbearable. If this wasn't a FFS moment, I don't know what was. There's one thing worse than time dragging on in A&E, and that's time dragging on when you're in such agony.

41

The police assessed the situation placed us all under arrest, so it managed to get even worse for us. To top it off, we spent a few more hours in there before Tom went in for an operation. I came out of X-ray and they give me some crutches; badly sprained ankles but nothing broken.

We were taken to Pilgrim Street police station. I remember going up the stairs and falling over a few times with a mug bizzie laughing behind me as I struggled to get up the steps while he was barking orders at me. I managed to reach the top of the stairs though. At the charge desk in reception I couldn't put any weight on my feet and this mug made it quite clear he was not a fan of the Sayers family.

There I was having to empty my pockets out with great difficulty and I had this shithouse bully cunt tormenting me. He thought it would be a good idea to kick my crutches away from me and I slipped and banged my head really hard off the counter. I went dizzy then fell to the ground in agony, thinking I was going to fall unconscious. I heard them laughing at me and I refused to stand up. I wouldn't give my name or date of birth to sign in to say that I'd been arrested.

The desk sergeant told him to help me up and put me on my crutches and, as I still wouldn't give my name, he told him to take me down stairs and let me sleep it off. I refused further medical assistance after the fall, so off I went hobbling downstairs when the cowardly cunt behind me put his hands on my back and ran me down them. I immediately fell and started tumbling down the stairs. The copper shouted for assistance, saying I'd attacked him. I fucking wish I had, but he'd not have been able to shout for anyone. He used a lie to justify his bullying tactics. To digress, I saw this cowardly cunt five years later in Walkers nightclub. He ran to the toilet and locked himself in a cubicle and started screaming he was sorry and that he wasn't a policeman anymore. I didn't touch him. I just watched him scream like a woman in labour as I give him a piece of my mind. He showed his true colours again: a cowardly cunt without his uniform. When it was man to man he was nothing. I would have fucked him easily but it would have lowered me to his level – it actually felt better to not raise my fists to him.

Back at the station and loads of police came running down and I heard one of them say, 'Enough is enough. You've had ya fun.'

They charged me, Tom and Joe with GBH with intent and we were going to be up in court on the Monday. We were remanded for a week. After around six weeks I got Judge in Chambers and then six months later the trial started at Kenton Bar Crown Court. There was no doubt that I'd end up in the detention centre, Joe got Borstal and Tom 'Brass Neck' Brayson received two years imprisonment. I was 15 years old.

On the bus on the way back to prison after sentencing, all the lads knew me. My reputation was growing even back then. While I was getting off the bus all the older lads found it funny as they'd been in detention centres in their youth and shouted and laughed. Was I scared? I'm not sure. I don't think I was. I think I was anxious but it seemed more like a feeling of butterflies in my stomach than anything… like I was raring to go. Of all the advice I've heard over the years, one piece has stuck with me: walk into the room like you fucking own the place. And that was true here. As a youngster in that situation, you can't show any fear because it's survival of the fittest and the Alphas will be looking for easy prey in all the new lads.

I walked into the centre like a little tough guy and hadn't been in the building ten seconds and a screw spoke to me in a very disrespectful way. I replied in the same tone of voice. A screw who was hiding behind a mesh curtain came out and hit me with the back of his hand right across the face. It hurt me.

'Do that again and I will do you in front of your friend,' I said. The two of them approached me and he drew his arm back to slap me again. As it came down, I blocked his arm and grabbed it and bent it up his back turning him round and pushed him over the desk. There was nothing he could do. The other screw pressed the bell and a load of them ran in and dragged me off. The governor walked past and asked what was going on then saw my face and asked why it was red raw. I told him I fell over. Even though it was me against them I would still never grass the man. Screw or not, it's not in my nature under any circumstance. The governor moved on to his next meeting. With the situation resolved, I didn't get put on report. The bully screw seemed to respect me after that, or maybe he was just a coward who feared me.

Detention Centres were tough places. They were set up to be a short, sharp shock based on the first eight weeks of basic training in the army... but with plenty of brutality added in by the sadistic screws. Being brought up fighting on Elswick Road, I fancied my chances with pretty much every single screw in there. I am not saying that I would have beaten them all at the time, but I would have definitely died trying. It's not like I just swaggered around all the time – I knew how to carry myself and how to hold my head up high. I was a Sayers and that counted for everything. In there, I was flying the flag and representing a name and a family, no matter how young I was. To me, it was the start of being a Sayers and I wasn't going to crumble. It wasn't about being rehabilitated back then – yeah, it would show you the toughest time possible to try to beat the badness out of you and it worked for a lot of lads. My experience of it was to absorb it all and take it as training; free training for those who were bad enough to get there and to graduate from. There was no way in the world I was going to let any screws intimidate me there was not one of them or all of them together that could have been half as bad as my father when he was drunk. When you've been through something like that you can rise above anything. I did my time and took it like a (young) man. To me, that was when I started to really grow up and realise where my life was taking me. In hindsight, it was probably taking me down the wrong path, but then my book would have been called *The Sayers: I worked in an office for 30 years and lived by the Law* and no one would have been interested. What I mean is, I could tell that I was no Ordinary Joe and it felt like my life had already been mapped out for me by having the name Sayers. It was pointless resisting. I knew what I was and I knew what I was going to be.

CHAPTER 3
THE WILD WEST

The Greyhound bar on Pitt Street in Newcastle is full of history for our family. My dad ended up buying it around 1990 and it was also the same bar that my cousin Frankie Donnelly tried to shoot my other cousin Frankie Slater.

In the mid-80s I used to go there a fair bit. It became a good base for me and a very good friend I was working with called Michael 'Pie' Kirtly. He was a diamond of a geezer and as game as a pebble – we were definitely a good match for each other. Around that time, thieving out of motor vehicles was a very common practice – it was easy pickings and easy pickings meant easy money. People were far from security conscious and let's not forget that technology in those days was nothing like today; CCTV cameras and Big Brother watching you were just an idea in a book. Thieving was rife in the West End and there were a lot of people who would specialise in breaking into vehicles whether it be wagons, vans or cars. It didn't matter what kind it was, as long as it had wheels and doors and something to hoist inside it. Most people used a piece of tungsten with a hole drilled out of the centre, with a leather lace knotted through the hole – kind of like a conker on a string – but it would shatter a car window on impact. This device was called a 'popper' and I'm proud to say it originated on Tyneside… well done, lads! It was simple and very effective.

The Greyhound was one of those bars that attracted people of the same mindset, so you'd always hear conversations of either someone having a good tickle (a good financial result) or comments along the lines of, 'I've got myself a good bookie or a florist.' This meant a villain somewhere had stumbled across a bookie's (betting shop) which would be privately owned, probably in a discreet district somewhere. The bookie would unknowingly be getting some attention from a firm of bad lads who'd have one objective: to steal money. Unknown to said bookie, he'd be educating the firm on his every move so they could plan their own. A quiet eye would be kept on this creature of habit until Grand National day when the tokens could quadruple, if not more. It was just a waiting game, a master plan and a big win.

The day of the National would come and everybody would be in place. The lads would be watching him leave work and follow him to his destination which, more often than not, would be the pub. Once the bookie entered the pub, it was game on. They'd always leave their briefcase (with the prize in it) inside their car, whether it be in the boot or under a seat. To them, leaving it in their car was safer than taking it anywhere with them – but that was where they were wrong. The reality was that they were creating the easiest blag. The lock would be forced or the window would be smashed or, worst case, the car would get taken. The firm would normally consist of two or three people, depending on the graft. One would drive, one would burgle the car and one would put a bicycle lock on the pub doors just in case he or anyone else came out. The prize would be discreetly removed from the vehicle and that was it – job done and they'd be away to divvy up and share their takings.

The same technique worked with florists on occasions like Valentine's Day or Mother's Day as the takings would be considerably higher. Their vans were all full with cash in them days as credit cards were not the norm like they are now. With florists, a very big order of flowers would be placed for a delivery where there they'd have to park up and walk a couple of minutes to the house door. If there were two people delivering, an order of up to £100 would be placed as you could get armfuls of flowers for that in the 80s, and it meant that the driver would have to take half of the flowers to the house. In doing so, they were leaving the van unattended and, in that split second, that was when the blaggers would pounce. They'd be in and out within seconds – easy. There was also the invention of ram raiding, which I'm sure was another North East thing. Cigarettes were always a favourite – light and easy to sell on. Anything else didn't come near. Videos were also a big thing back then, but apparently they were a pain because most of them would get broken when the van was rammed through the shop window.

There was a good community spirit in the Greyhound and everybody was anti-police. We'd constantly get up to mischief and humour has always had a big bearing on our lives. We were young, probably in our late teens to early 20s but always young at heart. Probably daft at heart would be more fitting, like when me and Fish Tams, Pie Kirtly and Charlie Huggins were at a loose end one day; it was nice and sunny and far too hot to go thieving, but it was never too hot for frisk (fun). The four of us were parked up at a petrol station, and before you start thinking it, no – we weren't going to turn it over. We had just spent our last £15 on a packet of cigarettes, some tab papers and matches, fuel, pop and sweets and we got out and walked behind the shop to where an automatic car washing machine was. One of the lads brought the spare box of poppers. We opened them up and shared them out and started tying them to the threads on the wheel of the giant buffers of the car wash. We even melted the tied bristles with a lighter so they'd stay on properly... then we sat back with our fizzy drinks, sweeties and cigarettes and waited to see what mischief would evolve. Inside, I was hoping it wouldn't be someone we knew! We started laughing too much out in the open and it would have been obvious it was us, so we got back into the car and positioned it by the side of the petrol station next to other cars. We still had a good view of the shop and desk but couldn't see the carwash.

A couple of hours went past and we were still sat with the windows closed with the car full of clouds of marijuana smoke. A big man in a suit, driving a new but dirty Jaguar pulled up. Our toes started to curl as we realised he was not there for fuel... anticipation of some silliness mixed with the countless spliffs was too much... we could hardly contain the laughter building up. He got out and bought a token before getting back in his car and straightening his sunglasses. We were stoned off our nuts, bouncing up and down like a bunch of kids. Fuck only knows what it must have looked like to the outside world – bearing in mind that the weed smoke completely filled the air to the point that we could hardly see in or out. We had to open the windows to let it all out and the fits of giggles had us by the time we heard the sound of the window poppers hitting the Jag. It was loud! And crackling and banging. I mean, these were nuggets of tungsten spinning round at however fast they go, whacking straight into bodywork, glass and chrome. We were laughing uncontrollably. As the buffers hit his windows they shattered instantly, sending the glass and soap suds into the car. Every window – front, back and sides – were shattered. It was like it was under machine gun fire. We could hear the car horn blasting away and he was revving the car trying to get out. But there was nowhere to go with those huge buffers either side of him. Even if he got out of the car, he'd probably not make it out alive (maybe we should have thought that one through a bit first). It must have been hell in there. The noise of popping and grinding steel was relentless and, as the last buffer raised up above the windscreen, or where the windscreen used to be, he drove out screeching his back wheels and spinning to the front of the garage. It looked like he'd gone stockcar racing via a foam party. There were no windows left; it was scratched to bits and the inside of the car was flooded and full of foam. You couldn't even see the man until he got out… and he did get out *very* quickly and started screaming to the high heavens. In fact, I'd go as far as saying he was *fucking foaming*. There was an awful lot of steam coming from him as he ripped his jacket off and slammed it to the ground and with the amount of steam rising from his back and he looked like he was in pain and beetroot red. I could only presume that this man had paid for the deluxe hot wash.

He steamed (no pun intended) to the shop and marched straight up to the cashier. We knew the cashier geezer from Benwell and he was a proper cheeky laddie as well. We couldn't hear what was said but the cashier got grabbed by the throat and dragged straight over the counter and onto the floor. We were doubled up in laughter, trying to start the car but it wouldn't turn over as we had been there for hours playing the radio and the battery had died. Fucking brilliant... we couldn't make a quick getaway. What made matters worse was when we were pushing the car to bump start it, it rolled and stopped on Charlie's foot. And of course, that only made us laugh even more and couldn't even move it off his foot because we were weak with laughter. He was screaming in pain, we were screaming with laughter, the man in the suit was screaming at the geezer on the floor who, I'm guessing, would have been screaming with pain as well.

In all the commotion with Charlie's foot we totally forgot about the angry man with the smashed up Jag. He got back into his car and drove past us at speed. Then we saw the cashier as he staggered out of the shop shouting, 'You lot fucking caused this!' You could see by his face he had been punched and must have been crying. In shouting that, he just increased the laughter amongst us. There was no malice in what we had done. Honest!

Not long after the carwash incident we were driving though Newcastle when we saw a wagon with its back shutter halfway up and a couple of blokes were loading boxes of cigarettes into a newsagents. They were making quite a few trips in and out of the shop. We were intrigued...

and waited to see if they were bringing any cash out with them. Hmmm… we then followed them to their next drop on Grainger Street and unloaded more into another shop and left the shutters halfway up again as they went about their business. They unloaded around a dozen or so at a time. I got out of the car and walked past the wagon and had a good look inside. It was packed full of cigarettes. I saw the padlock lying there, so I quickly nabbed it knowing that they'd be unable to lock the shutter. On their return, the delivery men seemed very puzzled that they'd managed to lose the lock. It was a waiting game with us wondering where the next drop would be. We didn't have to wonder any longer as one of the drivers shouted over that they would have to get off to their next drop in Leeds. Fuck that. We didn't even have enough fuel in the tank to get past Durham. We drove past and I chucked the lock in the back of their wagon so they could lock up safely when they got to Leeds.

A blag could be on or off that quickly and we always kept our eyes open for the next opportunity. As time went on, people were broadening their horizons and looking at the bigger picture. That's how westenders made money. You have entrepreneurs who set up businesses and whatnot but that's all we were doing as well. We were entrepreneurs in our own way – acquiring, selling, making money. It was how we made a living back then. westenders were like pirates but with more scruples. And we took every and anything we wanted. Fun Loving criminals, man.

There was another time I was with Pie Kirtly – on our way to the Greyhound again. It's not that we had a drinking problem or anything, far from it. The Greyhound was an excellent base for us.

We were taking the scenic route with no real direction. Our stomachs were rumbling and our petrol tank was as empty as our bellies. In fact, so were our pockets. It wasn't an ideal situation, but from what I have learnt over the years, it shouldn't matter if you have money or not... you should never go hungry. The petrol light was flashing and we needed to get some juice into it immediately, so we found ourselves driving around Percy Street in Newcastle and dropping anchor in the multi-storey car park. We heard that you could eat well and refuel from parked cars and we saw a nice new Datsun and wondered what would happen if we put a tube into their petrol tank and siphoned the petrol from theirs to ours. It was certainly a possibility.

I clocked someone carrying some shopping bags from Marks and Spencer's food hall. I didn't know anyone at the time that shopped at these types of shops as they were so expensive. It was looked upon as a luxury – still is – but it didn't mean it was out of bounds for us. The way we looked at it was if they could afford to shop at Marksies then they weren't as skint as us and they certainly weren't as hungry as us. Conscience clear.

The couple just loaded the bags into their car and walked away to carry on with their shopping I could've easily had the lock open in seconds and removed the food that needed to be oven cooked. I'd have been left with two bags full of goodies and a packet of serviettes, along with two bottles of

Lambrusco.

We could have driven to Leazes Park, just five minutes away, if that. It was a lovely summer's day – perfect for a lavish picnic. But we also needed to rectify the empty pockets situation.

As the day went on we didn't seem to get any further forward, so we called it off and decided to meet up later for a few pints and a couple of joints.

That night a few of us ended up in a flat in the West End and a little bit worse for wear after smoking and drinking for a few hours. I remember someone had a police radio scanner, so we had a listen just to pass the time and kill our boredom. We were listening to different radio transmissions and I'll never forget the names of these people, but I'll change them for the sake of this story to protect the innocent and the guilty: Mr and Mrs Jackson from Gateshead were reporting a burglary that was taking place across the road in a cash and carry from where they lived. Nice law abiding citizens they were as well. From what we could make out it was about to come on top for these lads as the police were en route. With us being good criminal Samaritans we decided to give these lads a heads-up so they stood a chance of getting away.

Bearing in mind that the coppers were naïve and would give anything up over the radio, not only did they give this couple's name out but they also gave out their address. It was mental. They'd probably give their PIN numbers away if you listened long enough! One of the lads called up 192, gave the operator the Jackson's name and address and asked for the phone number. Easy! It was time for a little bit of fun.

On Tyneside we have a slang word used for leaving or leaving at high speed: nashing. You can nash on, do a nash or just nash. It's all up to the nashee, really. Usually, when a criminal was active and wanted their partner in crime to leave immediately he would give the signal to, 'fucking naaaaashhhh!' You get the idea.

Someone phoned Mrs Jackson who'd been back on the phone to the police three more times since giving a detailed account of what was occurring at the cash and carry. She obviously thought it was the police responding to her emergency call, and the first thing she said when she answered our call was, 'And about time too,' in a well-to-do voice. Bloody hoity-toity do-gooder! She'd obviously been drinking. 'Can you see these people?' my mate asked. 'Yes, we can see them. There are three of them and they are trying to force the door open with something that resembles a crowbar.' That'll be an actual crowbar then.

We knew the clock was ticking and these three individuals who were only trying to get a few quid as we saw it, were about to be arrested. He asked Mrs Jackson where she and her husband were situated in the house. She said they were both looking through the upstairs bedroom window and the thieves were no more than 30 yards away. He explained to her that, 'Officer Nash was on the scene, but was having difficulties with his radio. She took the bait and asked what she could do to help. She shared the handset with her husband and they were both speaking down the phone like they were Dempsy and fucking Makepeace. He told them to open their bedroom window and switch on their bedroom light – done – and told them it was their job to scare the burglars in the direction of Officer Nash. They were keen to do their bit and my mate struggled to keep his laugh in as we heard them open their window and shout, 'Naaashhh!' at the top of their voices.

He managed to pull himself together and ask Mrs Jackson what was happening. 'Well, they are just staring at us, officer,' she said. I reminded them that Officer Nash was in place and he was waiting for the burglars to be chased in his direction; they had to show willing to help apprehend these no-good crooks. He told the Jacksons to repeat his next line word-for-word. Firstly, hold the telephone in one hand and go to the window. 'We haven't moved and neither have the burglars,' she said. Good, good. He fed them the line and after she drew breath, we heard: 'We have phoned the police and they are on their way. Nash! Nash! *Nash*! This did the trick and the lads were off on their toes. Villains 1, Police 0.

We carried on smoking that night and couldn't stop giggling. What a laugh, man. We still had the scanner on and we'd been aware of a certain individual who'd been repeatedly contacting Northumbria Police and reporting anything and anybody. Another vigilante, but this one would just take things too far. He'd report people who he thought were drink drivers or innocent people just walking home minding their own business. Some people dream of winning the lottery, some dream about being a star, but this arsehole dreamed of been a Crown Prosecution witness, no doubt about it. He was ripe for the picking and we'd heard his name come over the radio reporting things for quite a few weeks. He seemed to have a bit of an attitude as well... and even the police were sick of his constant phone calls. Hmm... should we do Mr Plod a favour and have some fun with Mr Bell? Well, we wouldn't usually. But, we were in good spirits and it was going to be an all-nighter, so why not, eh? That night Mr Bell's name came up at least three times in the space of half an hour, reporting different incidents that he believed were going to happen. We didn't like it. He needed a different hobby, so a good lesson was called for. We got hold of his number the same way as we did with the Jacksons and the criminal Samaritans sprung into action again.

The call was made to Mr Bell, who answered very abruptly and aggressively. He demanded to know why we had not been responding to his tip offs and why no arrests had been made. How dare he talk to 'the police' like that! The response was simple: 'Because we are fucking sick of you!'

This certainly fuelled the fire and Mr Bell screamed down the phone, 'How dare you speak to me like that. I have assisted you for over 28 years now and I have not had so much as a thank you. It's disgusting!'

'You're right. It *is* disgusting. Have you not heard of insurance companies, Sir? We have CID to investigate these crimes. This is what keeps us in a job, so we have to turn a blind eye now and then.'

Mr Bell was foaming. 'I am reporting you. What's your number?'

'Well if you do, bonny lad, we have your address and there is a few of the lads going out on the drink for the derby on Sunday and we will make it our business to issue a search warrant for your home and you will gain firsthand experience of the finest police brutality.' One of the other lads chipped in. 'And I'll personally get you three years in jail for the drugs I'll plant in your house, you nosey old bastard.'

Mr Bell couldn't believe what he was hearing and replied with a completely different tone of voice. 'Is this a joke?'

My mate continued, 'I'm going to tell you this once and once only: there is a cracking young tanned blonde and rather large-chested Woman Police Officer on duty tonight and not only do I fancy my chances but I think our lass has cottoned on to it. When I get home, can I say to my wife that I have been round yours investigating one of your countless accusations?'

Mr Bell wasn't happy with that suggestion. 'I cannot believe this! I am going to call the police!'

'But we *are* the police, you silly cunt. Now get ya head down and go to sleep and mind ya own businesses.'

'I want your name and badge number now!' Mr Bell screamed. It just so happened that the lad on the phone had been pulled over a few days earlier and still had the producer leaflet on him with the copper's details on, so he read them down the line.

Mr Bell continued, 'I am going to see my local MP about you!' The criminal Samaritans wished Mr Bell the best of luck and hung up.

We never heard him on the scanner again. It looked like our tactics had put paid to the local busybody and probably saved a lot of people from getting nicked. That was just a bit of banter, really. We never meant anyone any harm by doing that and certainly never took it seriously or any further than that.

I was in my mam's house in York Street having a cup of tea with my good friend Tom Brayson one day when our John turned up to see what we were up to.

We left soon after and went to the Blue Man pub that used to be at the top of her street. We were in there for about 15 minutes before I went to the toilet. I couldn't get in as someone had their back to the door, so I put a bit of pressure on it. I could hear voices and a few heated words, and then, all of a sudden the door opened and I heard a voice, 'Stephen, I'm sorry. I didn't know it was you.' There was no one else in there with him, so he must have been having a bit of a word with himself. He had something in a bag which looked very suspect and, in his agitated state, he dropped it on the floor: a white, engraved ivory cross about a foot long.

I asked him what it was and he told me it was a religious artefact that had been stolen from St Nicholas Cathedral in Newcastle. To be honest, I was disgusted that this pathetic excuse for a human being could stoop so low. I was and still am a God-fearing person. I may not go to church or pray as much as I should, but nevertheless, I am a believer. I had heated words with the lowlife and let's just say there was a decision made and I left the toilet with the cross, he left unhappy.

I showed our John and told him what had been said and we left. We went to see our solicitor who at the time was Rowe and Scot and they contacted the church, which was across the road from their office. We went across there to meet the priest, who was a perfect gentleman, and we passed the bag over to him. He checked the contents and he could not thank us enough for returning it. Reporters from the local newspapers were there to and took our photo to capture the occasion and gave a happy ending to the story of the missing cross.

Spoiler alert! Just so you know, there's a bit of a heads up here for a future crime we got nicked for...

Years later, when I got done for a blackmail charge (cough), my solicitor Richard Haswell contacted Saint Nicholas Cathedral and spoke to the same priest who we handed the cross to. He remembered me and said he would be more than willing to help with a character reference and a letter of thanks for returning the item. He was a man of his word; he was very grateful for what me and our John had done and the letter I received explained that the artefact we had returned was over 200 years old and therefore priceless, and that *the people of Newcastle should remember Stephen and John Sayers for their actions. This artefact could not be replaced at any cost and the people of Newcastle should always be in their debt.*

Not a bad endorsement, eh?

Another spoiler alert, I did ten years for the blackmail...

When I finished the sentence I received a phone call from my cousin Frankie Slater saying his mam had died. She was a lovely lady and the funeral was held at the West Road crematorium and I attended with my cousin Tony 'Hymie' Sayers. While we were there, me and wor John had the chance to have a five-minute talk with the pastor who held the sermon; a good man called Tom Leighton who I'd known all of my life. We knew the man because he used to do a lot of good for the community at the church hall. In the daytime pensioners would go there to socialise and have their dinner in a good clean and safe environment. Then at night Tom and his good wife Miriam would run a youth club, which was full of Elswick people. It was a well-run club and it certainly helped to get us all off the streets and kept us out of trouble.

While we were having our chat with Tom, he told us that at Christmas time he and some others would go to the houses in the West End and give toys to families that were less fortunate and needed a bit of help. He said the things he gave them were sometimes quite old and wondered if we would be able to help him in any way. There was no hesitation on our behalf; we told him we'd be only too happy to help. With Christmas just around the corner, me and my good friends had a couple of whip rounds and we raised £500. Tommy Dillon and Billy Dixon went to see a few market traders and they donated some large boxes of toys full of action men, Barbie dolls and countless dresses, cars, games – you name it – there was something for every boy and girl. I thanked the lads for their kindness. Not only did we have boxes of toys, but we still had the £500 too. We dropped all the toys of at Prudhoe Street mission where Tom and Miriam sorted them all out for delivery.

What we did that day for the needy made me feel really good inside, so much so that me, our John, Billy and Tommy kept the tradition going until Tom and Miriam retired five years later. I might be a tough guy, but when it comes to things like that, I become a big softie.

I can remember my first Christmas out of jail when I had finished my ten-year sentence. I can remember walking downstairs and seeing the smile on my kids' faces. Then I realised that there'd be kids waking up that morning and, because of us, they'd have some toys to wake up to.

CHAPTER 4
MEET VIV GRAHAM

In the 80s, Newcastle's city centre nightlife was opening up like never before. Gone were the old men sitting with their cloth caps on and bottles of stout and whippets (although they're still around in the CIU clubs), playing dominoes and talking about the hard time they get from their wives.

Nah, the 80s meant big hair, tight denim... and that was just the blokes! Seriously though, times were definitely changing. We had that Loadsamoney North-South divide, but we still saw our economy booming. The dolly birds had arrived and the bars were bouncing. Money was flowing in and in them days you never had drinking areas such as Jesmond, the Quayside, Ouseburn or The Gate – the Bigg Market was the heart of the party and anyone who was anyone was there. It was not unusual to see 50 or 60 people queuing up to get into pubs and there were more licensed premises than any other city centre in the country. We even had a floating nightclub on the Tyne! Early on in the decade, we had *The Tube* being shot at Tyne Tees on City Road with Jools Holland and Paula Yates bringing massive household names from the music industry, flying the flag for the Geordies. The downside? There wasn't one, really. Unless you call groups of blokes battering the living daylights out of each other on a night out a downside. You see, cities will always be evolving, but men will always have that side to them that's never going to evolve: that side of us where we fight. Whether you're hard or not, a man just has an innate capacity for a scrap. It's in all of us no matter how much you

63

try to bury it in your psyche. The clubs were full to the rafters and tough guys were making a reputation for themselves. This was the time when anything went. You could get away with so much naughtiness because technology hadn't evolved either and was nothing like it is now – no CCTV, no smartphones, social media and, in many respects, nights out and the control of bars and clubs was a lawless area. It was the time when you could invent the rules and there were a few people who were starting to emerge on the scene as the rule-makers; people could muscle in, take over bars and security and power struggles were inevitable.

There was one man that stood out amongst them all – not just by his physical size but also his ability to instantly knock anything he hit spark out unconscious, which he did on a regular basis. He was a good amateur boxer: very strong, 13 and a half stone was his fighting weight until he came across a man called Andy Webb. What Andy doesn't know about bodybuilding is not worth knowing. If anyone can take credit for giving Viv his strength and size it was Andy. Andy roided Viv up with around four stone of muscle in all of the right places, which changed Viv from being extremely dangerous into a lethal weapon. Viv earned a reputation for battering anyone who stood up against him.

I first met him at Wheelers nightclub in Gateshead, where he started working the doors under the watchful eye of Paddy Leonard and a bloke who went on to become a mentor to him, big Billy Robinson. It was easy to see how different Viv was. Even back then. It was inevitable that he'd end up in a position of power. And, as his reputation and power grew, it was sadly inevitable that he'd end up in an early grave as well. Newcastle has had plenty of tough fighting men over the years but Viv seemed to tick all the boxes. I would go as far to say the only person who resembled shape, size and was as equally effective with their hands was Mike Tyson. I'm not saying that Viv would do Tyson... what I'm saying is if Viv hit Tyson or anyone else on the jaw they were going to sleep, such was the power of that man. Viv's name kept getting mentioned to me all the time saying he had beat this one up or he had knocked this one out. He seemed to have done everybody.

The westenders were certainly not afraid to stand up to him, but who'd even want to? There was a massive divide between the West End of the city and any doormen. We didn't like any person in a position of authority – especially when they weren't from the West. That was it for us: we didn't like getting told what we could and couldn't do by anyone in a uniform. Whatever you were wearing – a blue one with a silly hat or a penguin suit when standing on a door – to us lot that signalled conflict and we always reacted to it. No fucker told us what to do. In Elswick, we ran the place. It was ours – always had been and always will be. We rule it all and we take that mentality with us wherever we go. Don't give us a dodgy look as we walk in past you or we'll take your face off. Don't dare attempt to stop us going in because you'll get hurt and don't ever try to get heavy-handed with any of us because we stand firm and we stand together. So, for a number of years, there was plenty of stories of westenders clashing with doormen and when violence was used, both sides suffered casualties. And if the West End were involved you could always guarantee there would be weapons used. The doormen couldn't stop them, so work flooded in for the likes of Viv and his associates. The only way to deal with it was fight fire with fire and that's what Viv would do. He was a bloke who stood for no shit in any of his pubs or clubs. The westenders didn't like that approach at all. And in return, he didn't like the westenders. It was conflict all the way: beatings and retaliation would go on all the time. We brought the Wild West wherever we went. There was no doubt about it; Viv had a firm grip over a lot of Newcastle city centre. The way we saw it was that we ran Newcastle and he ran the doors in Newcastle. Technically we were on the same side, but we were on different sides in many other ways. We all had fierce reputations and there'd always be talk of rivalry because of it.

When you've got a few people with big reputations, that kind of talk goes without saying. There's always been families with reputations where each generation is born into it and that's what you stand for. Each and every time you saw off a challenge, you moved up a rung on the ladder. As we saw it, we were three brothers who stood our ground from being kids and having the back-up of a big family and friends. In that sense, we built our reputation early and quickly. You don't just become a 'name' by accident.

I'd visit my mam in York Street all the time. Not just to be fed and watered. Honest! I was there one brilliant sunny Sunday morning and had a cup of tea and a cheeky sarnie – I was going out for a drink that day and thought I'd put a lining on my stomach. The lads dropped in before we headed into town: John Mac, Tom Brayson and my cousin Frankie Kelly and we left my mam's with the immortal words echoing up the street after us:

'Promise to stay out of trouble, my boys.'

'Don't worry, Ma,' I replied and the lads shouted, 'Don't worry, he's with us.'

As you can imagine, my mam worried a *lot*. We strolled long to the Balmoral on Westgate Road for about 12.30pm, where we were greeted with open arms from about 50 West End lads: Tony Charmers, Charlie and Davey Huggens, Snake Mains, Jimmy Hardy and Fish Tams, to name a few. We had a good day's drinking, and we left at 8.30pm and went to Raffles on Pink Lane. Not a bad little session.

Pink Lane was infamous for prostitution at one time, but the area had been cleaned up. It always had that air of notoriety about it for a long time after. I suppose with all the football lads drinking there and fighting away supporters, the reputation of Pink Lane was never going to recover quickly.

There were about 30 of us Elswick lot and, after a few more drinks, we were all a bit worse for wear – but in a good way. We never went out to cause trouble – no one wants that on a night out. Maybe because we generally went out in big groups people would think that but to us, it just meant the more people, the more fun there was to be had. We were in the lounge bar when a friend of mine called Malcolm Barmer asked me to speak to somebody on the telephone. As I walked through the bar to get to the phone, I saw a stocky little man talking and looking in my direction out of the corner of my eye. I didn't not take much notice of him, but sensed *something*. People tend to look at you when you have a bit of a reputation, but most of the time they'll look away in an instant. This kind of look was a different one. Anyway, I took the call and started talking to Malcolm again.

We were engrossed in a *shouting into each other's ears over the music* conversation when I heard a voice say, 'Hello, Malcolm. What are you doing with him?' It was the little stocky fella; Jimmy Somerville (no, not him from The Communards) who was also known as Psycho. Now, you don't get called Psycho for nothing, do you? This man was extremely violent and dangerous. He was 37, around 17 stone and loved to fight. This was also the same man who three years previous had tried to bully my brother and co-accused while they were banged up in Durham prison. By asking Malcolm that, he was obviously laying down a challenge... basically, he was saying it to me and was looking to see my reaction. But I was in my 20s, and my criminal CV was growing quicker than the average bad lad, and I also loved to fight. In fact, it was probably my hobby at the time. I had no fear of anyone – I don't think I ever have. And I'm still the same. I've always taken anyone on because that's how I am. To me fear is only a figment of your imagination. I was no bully, but I took on all comers and wouldn't shy away from a confrontation. If you do so, it just eats away at you inside and causes you to fear the next one – and that's a difficult rut to get into. I've always tackled anyone head-on and dealt with a problem or a situation there and then; no dwelling, no afterthought or 'what if' – just straight in and sort it out.

He made his move and advanced towards me so I got in first and hit him with a right-hander, full of bad intentions, busting his nose. With blood all over his face, he staggered back but didn't go down. This wasn't going to be a one-punch-fight and he was as tough as they come. He caught me with a couple of good clean blows, but I got in just below his ribs and winded him. It turned into a real battle. Pain can weaken some people, but it seems to make me stronger. He was roughly five stone heavier than me and, although he was weakening, his weight was his one advantage.

He tried to grab me in a bear hug but I pulled away, 'Come on, then. *Come on*!' No one in the bar wanted to get involved, but they all cleared space for us as much as they could. It was pretty crowded in there and it's not the biggest bar in the world anyway. The atmosphere was dark and I could here people shouting, 'Do him!' I doubt either of us knew whose side the shouting was on at that point.

I gave him no recovery time and steamed in again with four or so big punches. It was a decent flurry, striking with power and accuracy. I could see his left eye was closing and we were both spitting blood as we stood toe-to-toe. He came at me again and our momentum carried us toward the door and the barmaid shouted for us to take it outside.

Hearing this I dropped my guard, 'Come on then... outside.' But he took advantage of my error and grabbed me and got me in a headlock. Jimmy's trademark was biting his victim's noses or ears and he got my nose in his mouth and started biting hard. I had to act quickly because he could turn the tables and finish it in this position. I managed to get my finger in his eye and I tried pull it out. It wasn't a time for finesse – if he was going to play dirty, then I would as well. He released my nose... and this was *his* big error. I jumped up and caught him flush with a head butt. It rocked him and I knew the end was in sight. I grabbed him and butted him again and again. He staggered and fell against the bar so I jumped on him and continued head butting him. My nose was throbbing and the pain was driving me on.

It felt good. It felt better than good. Sheer strength and determination was keeping him on his feet but he was fucked. I head butted him again and then followed that up with a good body combination. The fight was mine for the taking and I took it. I could only imagine what the crowd of onlookers must have been thinking: our shirts were ripped off and we were covered in blood, breathing heavily, both our fists still clenched. I caught him with another couple of punches and he finally dropped to his knees.

I moved in to end it and felt a load of arms around me, keeping me back.

The red mist had hold of me as well and we all know there's no going back when that happens. It was too late to stop. Bearing in mind I'd taken some big hits myself, it was like it could only end when one of us couldn't move. My friends were dragging me off him but I was breaking free and going back to lay into him again. My friends finally got me outside and this gave Jimmy a breather and time to lick his wounds. When I was out there I could see him looking at me through the big glass windows. *Was he for real*? It was like pouring petrol onto a fire. I broke free from my friends and ran back into the bar.

'Come on, Psycho! Come on!'

He had nothing more to give. He looked at me, 'No more, Stephen. No more.'

It fucking killed him saying that. I could hear the pain in his voice, but it had to be one of us. His nose looked really bad. Well, so did the rest of his face. He offered me his hand to shake. I accepted and there was a feeling of mutual respect. It wasn't like we were going to embrace and be best buddies – it was just inevitable that we'd end up fighting. It was just the when and where that was unknown. One of the barmaids handed him a towel and he wrapped it round his face to stop the bleeding.

For me, other than settling a score, it changed my game. It cemented my reputation. It put me on a higher level at a young age, moving me up the ladder a lot quicker. When you've got two big families going at it like that, it's only really afterwards that you realise the importance of it: it was family honour and everything that goes with it and it was a very good win for the Sayers. And fair play – that's how bad blood is sorted out. You have a fight, a straightener, whether you want to do it with fists only or anything else; and that's it. Last man standing is the winner or someone throws the towel in. You shake hands and you walk away with respect for each other. That's how it works. It was fair. All this unfairness, shooting people and whatever the fuck else anyone wants to do only leads to shit. A fight is never sorted

71

out with a bullet – it just starts a feud that will last through generations of family, all looking over their shoulders, waiting to be avenged. That's not what you want, is it? You don't want a legacy of shit, so you nip it in the bud as quickly as possible and, bizarrely, you even end up as friends some of the time.

In hindsight, we both should have been prepared for the fight. We were in that we were both game, but probably we should not have been drinking and not did it in a bar... but maybe it was better that it was just a thing that had to boil over naturally. It could have happened anywhere, really.

We sorted out our differences there and then like two old-fashioned Geordies... stripped to the waist, all blood and snot, in the thick of it. Let's not take anything away from Jimmy, he was what he was and he backed down to no man. He was one hard bloke, that's for sure. We fought like animals and shook hands like men. And that that was it – our beef was over.

CHAPTER 5
A NEW BREED OF CRIMINAL

There was a certain group of professional blaggers from the West End of Newcastle who were very active throughout their criminal careers and specialised in major robberies. They were well trained, disciplined and *very* experienced. They had a good combination of brains, braun and extreme bravery. They knew how to work as one; as a unit. I've mentioned before that my family are always there for me and stand together and show strength and resilience and no fear – that's what this lot were like.

One day the word came through amongst the boys that they had a good 'card marker'. A card marker is an individual on the inside who knows about the timings of large cash movements. The graft is only as good as your card marker's knowledge and, if he or she has first hand information from working there, it does not get any better. I mean, the card marker is your inside eyes and ears, the provider of all the information you'd ever need!

Back in the 80s nearly everyone got paid in cash. We didn't have the systems in place that we have today, so if a villain found a business where a few hundred people were working, there was a high probability that a large amount of money would be moved there to be distributed amongst the workforce.

In this instance, the card marker gave the lads a heads up about money that was being transferred to pay the nurses and cleaning staff at the eight hospitals in the area. The money would be picked up from a security cash depot in

Washington and taken to Pritchard Security depot in Gateshead. The lads were on it and plans were set in place. They did their research properly by watching the vehicle's movements over a prolonged period of time and the only problem they would have to overcome as far as they could see was when the vehicle left the cash depot it would drive approximately 500 meters until it got to a roundabout. At that point, there was a choice of three exits but the security van never took the same route. That would mean anyone wanting to hit it would either have to do so during that 500 metre stretch, or take the chance of having to cover three possible scenarios, and that would have an impact on the plan. They decided to strike at the roundabout.

At 8am on a Wednesday in late March, 1987, the lads headed to Washington and were ready and waiting. They sat in the vehicle with the windows steamed up, trying not to draw any unwanted attention to themselves. They sat there for five or ten minutes in silence, readying themselves, all of them psyched with adrenaline, before the radio crackled into action. One of them picked the radio up and said, 'Repeat, Repeat,' and a message came back.

'It's on its way.'

Everybody knew what to do. These boys had been doing this for some time. The balaclavas were rolled down over their faces and the pump-action shotguns were cocked with the safeties removed. These boys meant business and nobody would stop them.

As the security van approached the roundabout they noticed a car very close to it, but nothing would hinder the job. Within seconds there was a car in front of the van and one at the back, boxing it in and forced it to a standstill. There were three security guards in the front of the van and two of the armed masked gunmen positioned themselves at the driver's and passenger's doors, pointed their shotguns at them and told them all to get out. There was a man in the back of the van who refused to open the door.

The three front seat occupants were now laid face down on the ground with their hands on their heads. There was no messing: the lads had a job to do and so did the security guards. They were there to protect the money, but does a security guard's wage pay enough to risk getting your head blown apart by a shotgun? It doesn't. The stakes were too high for the robbers and they wouldn't back down at such a hurdle. Besides, when you've locked yourself into a security van and you can see that going on, it probably feels like your safest option to stay put.

One of the security guards was brought to his knees at the back of the van and had a gun placed to his head. The demand was simple – if the back door didn't open in three seconds a man would die. The security guard in the back of the van had a change of heart and opened up. He was dragged out, placed on the ground and, with a gun to his head, was told not to move. He didn't.

At that point, some traffic had built up behind them – around six cars – with all the occupants watching events unfold. One of the lads ran over and pointed the gun at them and demanded they threw their car keys out. All the occupants did as he said with no hesitation. At the same time another lad had got into the back of the security van. He emptied it in moments taking five boxes. Job done, they were back in their vehicles and they were off within a few minutes. There was no stopping them and the security guards didn't know what had hit them. Everyone complied and no one got hurt – textbook-style bit of graft. Once out of the way, the lads switched cars twice; both times setting the previous car ablaze to prevent the police planting evidence. They then headed to the slaughter to share out the wages.

The boxes felt a bit light as they headed into the house and there was a feeling that the half a million haul that they were expecting was not what they'd got away with. When the boxes were opened the contents didn't even look close to £50k. The radio was on at the time in the background and a newsflash said that, 'a firm of armed robbers had stopped and successfully robbed a security van on a daring daylight raid.' It carried on to say that they had successfully escaped with £300k. It was nice of them to mention that the money had been compressed by a machine and it had steel bands around it. When one of the lads cut the bands off the money instantly expanded. Not a bad morning's work for a four-man team; each clearing £75k minus the expenses of the card marker, cars, safe house, boiler suites etc. Once the money was shared out the gang went their separate ways. That night the robbery hit the local news on a programme called *Northern Life*. Northumbria Police released a statement which was short and simple: 'We are now dealing with a new breed of criminal.'

With the blags that were going on at the time for these criminals, they must have netted around £4.5m easily. If you bear in mind when that was and equate it to today's money, you're talking around £45m. Now that's a lot of money!

On the 12th of August, 1987 – my 22nd birthday as it happens – at approximately 10.30am, a group of carefully selected armed robbers met up. These lads had been put together specifically because of the qualities they possessed. They knew it was going to be big, but what they didn't know at the time was *how* big. It was going to be Britain's biggest post office robbery.

A Royal Mail train was delivering a large amount of cash to Newcastle, which would then be moved to a main sorting office in Orchard Street. The money would then be sent to other districts in the region, one of them being Sunderland. This happened every Wednesday. There was one big problem though... the security van was followed by armed police from Orchard Street to Sunderland. The plan was for the robbery to take place at the post office depot when the money was being unloaded. Because of the police escort, there had been a couple of abandoned attempts to pull off the job but the lads were nothing if not determined.

On the day in question, the spotters were out and everybody was in position once again. They were getting notifications that the police car whose job it was to protect this vehicle was still behind, until it came to the junction next to the bridge leading into Sunderland. This was the stage where everything was in the balance. For whatever reason on this occasion, the police didn't follow the van through the city centre. Nobody will ever know why; only the police themselves. The armed robbers were hiding in the back of a vehicle with other men from the firm plotted up in their positions waiting for notification that it was on. Everyone sat in silence until the message came over the radio: 'The dog has made its own way home; I repeat – the owner has lost his dog.'

It was on!

Everyone knew their job. Nobody spoke a word. The only noise that could be heard was the noise from the pump-action shotguns being loaded with heavy shot. With heartbeats going twenty to the dozen, balaclavas were pulled down and the robbers got ready to strike. Now for the part that made this work so special... the split-second timing of it. It was vital to them.

The van parked up in the depot and the big double gates were shut behind it. Five security guards came out into the compound for extra security. Meanwhile, there were two vehicles parking a little bit further up the street. The boys were ready, knowing that it was all systems go. Seconds turned into minutes and the minutes turned into tens of minutes... the tension built and built... and then, 'Go! Go! Go!'

Hearts raced faster, adrenaline pumped through their veins.

Suddenly a big Range Rover came from behind the transit van at high speed and rammed though the heavy reinforced gates. It pulled up alongside the cash van and the lads got out and into the yard. There was a wheelbarrow with sacks of money in. Two of the lads dragged the barrow towards the van and started throwing money inside.

The security guards were placed face down on the ground with shotguns placed to the back of their heads, 'If you want to be a hero you die a fucking hero. Now get your noses on the fucking ground.' They did as they were told.

A group of post office workers walked past and made an attempt to get involved, but the robbers were not having it. The one at the front was stopped in his tracks; 'Lie down on the ground or I'll blow ya fucking head off!' would have been enough to stop any wannabe hero.

Meanwhile, the other lads stacked the cash up ahead of schedule. With that, they were off. The van was full of huge sacks of money and every radio station on the scanner blasting into their ears: 'Major armed robbery committed. All vehicles attend Sunniside Post Office.'

The bad lads had a good head start though. They changed vehicles, burned the other ones out, and were on their way to the safe house to share out the loot. How many were on the graft, you will never know and exactly how much was taken will never be known either, but the boys made history that day.

Northumbria Police were in no mood to celebrate, but that night I was. In my taxi on the way to Walkers in Newcastle and the driver couldn't stop talking about a robbery in Sunderland, bigging it up as though people were proud of it. There was a sense of a pat on the back from the general public for the underdog – not in a Robin Hood sense, but like there was some praise for *the people* taking something back. Of course, the taxi driver had no idea who I was and it was a bit of a buzz to hear someone talking about me and my family with such regard. We were named as those behind it because we were thought of as the only ones with the audacity to do such a thing: we had the brains, the knowhow and the good looks... the coppers generally had no idea, no intelligence and no evidence to go on. But that never stops them, as we know.

The reputation of the Sayers brothers was spreading like wildfire and nobody really knew our faces outside the West End. We always kept a low profile because we were brought up not to seek attention... when you're a dastardly bunch of career criminals the last thing you want is to be recognised.

He continued to talk about these Sayers brothers and told me that they now ran Newcastle and had an army of armed men at their disposal. 'They sound mint,' I said. I afforded myself a smile as I paid him and thanked him... and yes he got a canny tip! It definitely helped to hear him talking about me – about *us*. It totally set me up for a good night – but not only that, it started setting me up personally and professionally. If you're only 22 and the taxi driver is talking to you about you and he doesn't even realise it *is* you, then you're doing something right. You're creating a buzz. It was a bit surreal: 'Here, you'll never guess who I had in the back of my cab the other night...'

As I arrived at the club there was a queue as long as the building. I walked straight to the front door and saw the doorman who gave me a nod to let me and Tammy, my girlfriend at the time, passed all security hand in hand. I was centre of attention and not just because it was my 22nd birthday – and you know what? It felt good. I was young and in a good position in life – certainly getting to where I wanted to be. Not many can say that. In no time at all, the champagne was flowing and there was a hyped-up party atmosphere. The club was bouncing, full of people dancing, the DJ was doing his thing and the lighting was adding to it all. It was obvious from way back that Newcastle would end up as one of *the* places to be for a good night out. Before you jump to any conclusions, I wasn't the one buying. I hadn't swaggered in like Johnny Big-bananas ordering bottles of Cristal or anything like that. People could not have been more generous and respectful. We partied the night away and it was brilliant.

A few days later my phone rang and a good friend told me that my mam's house was being raided. Armed police were ransacking the place and the street was closed off with a dozen vehicles all with blue lights flashing and creating a scene. They were there to arrest me. They raided our John's at the same time, but unfortunately for him he was home. They went after Tony 'Legs' Lennie and Ken Sanvid as well. Tony wasn't there at the time of the raid. I received legal advice to leave Newcastle as I was also going to be fitted up for the robbery. Over the course of the next two days, John and friend Ken Sanvid were charged with armed robbery.

At a hastily arranged ID parade, one witness pointed at our John on the line-up and said that it wasn't him... but it looked very much like him. Another witness picked John out saying he had attended the robbery just moments after it happened and saw our John wearing a boiler suit and holding a pump-action shotgun and a balaclava on his head but rolled up so you could see his face... and that he was smoking a big old pipe that looked like it belonged to Sherlock Holmes. That was the calibre of witness that Northumbria Police were providing. Elementary, I hear you say. There wasn't a shred of evidence linking him to the robbery but that didn't matter. Evidence never matters when they've got something in mind and they're desperate to prove it. John got remanded in custody and found himself behind bars for 13 months.

Fuck all that: I was not prepared to be fitted-up and spend 20 years in jail for a crime that I didn't commit, thanks to fabricated evidence from those Northumbria Police clowns. I left the region and got to a safe house down south with some trusted friends.

The publicity that the robbery received was crazy and a reward of £75k (ten per cent of the robbery takings) was on offer to help convince Joe Public he was doing the right thing by shopping these dastardly robbers. It would be a nice earner for anyone – especially a straight-goer.

CHAPTER 6
ON THE RUN

Tony 'Legs' Lennie was a one-off where frisk was concerned; he was a one-off and was one of us. Word came through that the police had raided his mother's house (my Aunt Mary Lou's) and that he was now on the run as well. I had to find him. That would be easy these days, but back then you couldn't just tag someone on Facebook and ask the world where they were. There were no mobile phones – we just made do back then, didn't we? It took approximately four days, 20 separate phone boxes and call after call filled with codes. It was all cloak and dagger stuff, but needs must. We didn't want to bring it on top for each other.

Finally we met on Weymouth beach on England's sunny south coast in the middle of August. I could think of worse places to meet. I was there early and watched him walk past in front of my vantage point. I had a good view of everything, just in case something wasn't right. I watched as he was looking for me, looking for a sign... my eyes were all over looking for the police. I followed him, keeping a short distance behind to check that nobody was around. When it became clear he was not being followed, I approached him at a nearby café. As I made myself known we looked at each other and burst out laughing and hugged. It was typical of us: we were both in the same predicament but could still smile and see some humour in the whole thing. It was great to see my cousin.

'Where should we go, cuz?' he asked.

'I don't know,' I replied, but I suggested we book a hotel.

So we did. We found one close to the beach and it was beautiful with big glass windows and sea views. It felt safe and it felt a million miles from reality and the amount of shit we were in. As we were sat having a meal a *Crimewatch* preview came on the television. I heard the BBC announcer could be heard say, 'After the news we have a list of Britain's most wanted men.' Legs and I looked at each other. It sent a shiver down both of our spines.

We paid and returned to our room sharpish and put the TV on for *Crimewatch*. We didn't take any risks and didn't want to waste any time – we started packing our bags while it was starting and were prepared to leave in case our faces were on TV. But we were safe – nothing happened, no mention of us, and no dodgy photofit pictures were flashed up. There was still the feeling that we were on borrowed time and that we'd be featured on it next month. But that was in a months' time and we were 'on holiday' until then.

We unpacked and spent a bit of that time at the hotel and on the coast during the peak holiday season. It was easy to blend in because it was so busy down there. It didn't last forever though. As the holiday season came to an end we had to think of a new hiding place – it would have looked a bit dodgy either out in the open or hiding ourselves away in the room day and night. The only winter resorts in Britain at the time that we were aware of were Aviemore in the Highlands of Scotland or Blackpool over in the north west of England. We weighed it up: snowy Scotland or rainy Blackpool... fish 'n' chips and bingo or deep-friend Mars bars and Irn Bru... Blackpool got the nod because we enjoyed the sea air too much! Legs had wanted to go to Scotland but there was no way in the world I was going anywhere that cold. There were plenty of fun pubs in Blackpool... what could go wrong? Seriously though, it wasn't really a jolly and we weren't just out for a good time. If you've ever been on the run, you'll know this. It's a nerve-wracking thing to have to do. Of course, you've got to let your hair down from time to time otherwise you'd crack up. It's never that glamorous sharing a pokey hotel room with another bloke and spend most of your time there watching daytime TV. There was no *Jeremy Kyle Show* back then either.

We headed back up north. It took us a full day to get from the south coast to Blackpool and it gave us a sense of comfort to be heading back closer to home, I think. Although Legs spent the whole journey trying to convince me to keep going, I'd made my mind up – I'd made *our* minds up – and I was certain it was the right move for us.

When we arrived we found a hotel and got ourselves booked in. We went straight to our room where I switched the TV on just in time for the news at 5.45pm. The newsreader announced that the Conservative Party were holding their conference in Blackpool. At the time, the IRA was bombing the mainland and threats had been made towards Maggie Thatcher. Security was to be top priority and the news report showed dozens of police walking along the sands and promenades and even a mini battleship in the sea! *What the fucking fuck*? Scotland suddenly felt really appealing. Whose ridiculous idea was it to come to Blackpool, anyway? We didn't even unpack; we just went downstairs and checked out. I knew a travelling family who lived close by, so we headed there for the night. They made us welcome, fed us and gave us a bed for the night. Brilliant hospitality, just as you'd expect from the travelling community. It was brilliant to have contacts like that – very useful in that situation, but it was reassuring knowing we could trust them and that we'd be safe that night. Trust counts for everything in this world.

When we woke up the next morning we talked about our plans with the family and they offered us food and shelter for as long as we needed and we took them up on their kind offer. The camp became our home for the next three months and it was a godsend. And we still managed to socialise in some of the mad pubs Blackpool had to offer, so it worked out really well for us. Maggie left Blackpool and good riddance to her and the heat was off. I won't name that family in these pages, but they know who they are and I'd like to thank them.

One night I was standing in a nightclub in the middle of Blackpool, packed full of Scottish people which isn't so bad when you come from Newcastle as they're practically neighbours. I was talking to a beautiful dark-haired lass whose family originated from Newcastle. I'd gone to the bar to get her and Legs a drink and, as I was heading back with them, I heard a loud roar like being at a football match. There were people shouting for Celtic and others for Rangers on opposite sides of the dance floor. The chants got louder and louder until the two groups of about 50 or so on each side started fighting each other, with chairs being used, tables overturned and bottles flying left, right and centre. It was mental!

We were stood there watching it unfold. Normally, we'd have been in amongst a bit frisk like that, but we were wanted men and couldn't afford to get nicked. And then, just as I'd handed Legs and co their drinks, the brawling crowd edged its way towards where we were standing. Fuck me; the Jocks certainly know how to fight. They were just braying the shit out of each other for all they were worth. It was like a tornado of violence, picking up debris as it came for us and spewing out casualties as it gathered momentum. It wasn't a good place for us to be. People had been seriously hurt and there was blood everywhere. Worse still, the police would arrive in no time.

We tried to leave through the fire exit but the doorman stopped us in our tracks and said that nobody was getting out until the police arrived. Now this was a fucking serious situation to be in. There wasn't time to get into a scuffle with the doorman. I turned round and couldn't see Legs anywhere but there was no time to lose; he was a big lad and knew what he was doing. I told the doorman my girlfriend was pregnant and we had to get out of there. I gave him a £20 note and he smiled and opened the door and we legged it over to a waiting taxi just in the nick of time.

A police van pulled up outside the club with the blues on and six coppers steamed into the club. They'd need a *lot* more than that to stop that fight! But that was their problem – ours was still ongoing until we got away from the place. As we got in, the taxi driver turned and asked if I was Scottish. I told him I was a Geordie and, to put his mind at rest, told him that the madness had nothing to do with me. He went on to explain that the fight was an annual event. He said the Scots were good spenders but once they'd all had a good drink they tended to fall out over football and the police would wade in. It sounded just like Geordies and Mackems... but without actually being on speaking terms first.

He dropped us off at Rumours (there was always a Rumours in a place like Blackpool. Or Whispers) next to Yates's wine lodge and I saw Legs stood waiting for us. The girl had to head off – she thanked me and we said our goodbyes and me and Legs decided to have one for the road before heading back to the camp. It was last orders anyway and we needed a drink after that! He went to the toilet while I got the round in. I waited. And waited. *Come on, Legs.* He didn't come back. I asked the doorman at the front door if he'd been thrown out but they couldn't even remember us going in.

The place closed and there was no sign of him, so I headed back to my hotel. I was hoping he was there but there was no sign of him there either. The following day came and went and I began to fear the worst. In fact, I don't even know what the worst was. What could I do though, file a missing persons report? *The fucking irony...* he goes missing while we're on the lam. If he'd been nicked, I know he wouldn't have said anything, but it would have meant that the heat would be on in Blackpool and it wouldn't be long until the police came to the hotel. I packed our bags and waited for the daft bastard, thinking that he'd probably met a bewer and gone back to hers. Time was getting on though. I got restless and more than a little bit paranoid. I decided to stay one more day and see what happened.

I was lying having a cat nap when I heard a fumbling at the door. I jumped up immediately and ran over and opened it. False alarm. There was some bloke standing there with his key in his hand drunk looking for his room, that turned out to be the next door along. My heart sank when it wasn't Legs. I felt helpless. And it was fucking boring without him as well. I made up my mind: I'd leave the next morning.

I had an uneasy sleep that night tossing and turning, thinking through the various scenarios. Had he been arrested then? Had he lost his key and forgotten where we were staying? I was worried sick at that point. I knew he had the spare key because took it the night we'd gone out. If the police did have him they didn't have the key with the hotel name on, so I knew there was no chance of them turning up and walking in uninvited. I got a few hours' kip though. I woke up the next day and went down for breakfast. I was just on autopilot, planning my next move and keeping my head down all the time. I went back up to the room and had a shower and prepared to leave the hotel when all of a sudden there was a knock at the door. I'd given up any hope that he'd return and anyway and I'd just walked past the cleaner on the way to the room.

I opened the door and there he was; larger than life and twice as daft. I was so happy and relieved to see him and to my surprise he was standing with my good friend John Brooks – Brooksey.

'Where the fuck have you been?!'

'Cuz, you won't believe what happened to me. I went outside to smoke a spliff and I heard someone shout my name and, when I turned round; there was Brooksey in a car. I went over to him and he told me to get in, so I did.'

Brooksey had apparently found the love of his life and Legs decided to head off with him... without telling me. I started feeling angry with him for leaving me for days but then Brooksey chipped in explaining that it was his fault. They had been on a two-day bender. Typical. Oh, and Brooksey had been in bed with the love of his life: a girl who he said was as brown as a berry with hair down to her ankles; a waist like a wasp with legs up to her armpits. I thought to myself, 'What sort of human being have you been having sex with?' She sounded really bizarre. A fucking hairy wasp with long legs? It made me want to try whatever it was they'd been smoking. He said she was called Montinique. He said she had a friend who also gives cracking massages... and curiosity got the better of me. I had never had a proper massage, so off we all went in a taxi.

Brooksey told the taxi driver to take us into the middle of the town centre. When we arrived it was really busy. We paid the driver and headed to a shop doorway where Brooksey pressed an intercom. The door clicked open and we walked in and up the stairs before coming to another door with an intercom. This time a man came out and invited us in. Hmmm... I was starting to think it could be a massage parlour until we got through that second door and I realised we were *in a massage parlour* surrounded by bedrooms and curtains and whatever else. It suddenly

90

seemed to hit Brooksey too, because he started running from room to room screaming for Montinique. He opened three doors in quick succession, disrupting the 'business' that was taking place. The workers were far from happy with his antics and I dare say their minders wouldn't be too happy if we chased more of their punters away. So much for low profile, eh?

But then Montinique appeared and saved the day. She was with five of her friends who were dressed for work in stockings and all the gear. Brooksey stopped and looked at her and said, 'It's me... Brooksey. *Your* Brooksey. I've come back for you, my love.'

Oh, man. It was such a romantic moment... cut short by Montinique who replied, '*You*?! You're a fucking pervert!'

Brooksey wasn't having any of it and tried to convince her that it was merely a case of mistaken identity. Sadly though, it wasn't. She repeated her insult to which he replied, 'I've spent all my money on you, ya dirty bitch!'

And then love's young dream was over.

'Phone the police!' she shouted to the bloke who'd let us in. It was time to leave. The last thing we needed was the police arriving and nicking us in a brothel; what a fall from grace that would have been. Imagine *The Evening Chronicle* headlines: "Pervert armed robbers on the run caught in a backstreet Blackpool brothel with wasp-looking long-haired prozzie." Read all about it, indeed.

I didn't want to be a ridiculous headline, so I tried to pull Brooksey out by the arm, but he kept breaking free and shouting and screaming at his former lover. By the time we got him outside there was quite a large queue at the bus stop near the door. The working girls were all hanging out of the window screaming and shouting at Brooksey and he gave them a mouthful back. What a palaver, man. People stared and pointed at us. They laughed at us as well, which would have usually wound me up until me and Legs started laughing along with them. What a ridiculous situation to get into. All the time *low profile* was echoing in my head and the hysterics just got worse.

We finally got him away from the establishment and we had a few peeves in a bar to calm him down. I also met a girl down there called Maxine and we spent a bit of time together. She was a Vegas showgirl, no less. Not sure if she actually was one, because I'm not sure why a Vegas showgirl would leave those bright lights for the not-so-bright lights of sunny Blackpool. Still, with the summer season coming to an end and no more Z-list washed-up comedians to heckle, we decided to leave Blackpool. When I popped round to Maxine's to say goodbye to her she wasn't home. I always wondered what happened to her.

We decided it was time to go back home to Newcastle. My cousin Frankie Slater came and picked us up and took us to a safe house. He drove us into Newcastle in the back of a van. We couldn't see a thing, but more importantly, nobody could see us. It was nice to be back. I love that feeling when you're on a train returning back to the Central Station and you see the Tyne Bridge. Everyone always looks out for it; it makes you feel warm inside and you get itchy feet, wishing it would just pull into the station rather than chugging along at a snail's pace.

Anyway, none of that happened. Our aim: recharge our batteries, catch up with friends and family and get our affairs in order before fucking off to our next destination. Another mate was going to sort us some moody passports out. Luckily, and due to it being the 80s, you could rock up to any post office and get a 12 month passport over the counter in ten minutes or so. All you needed was fake paperwork with any name on it. It was that easy. The Post Office, man. They were fucking useless. No wonder they were a target for armed robbers. Frankie brought back some lamb and cooked us a nice dinner on our first night back home. It was a welcomed feed.

We spent a few days in Newcastle before taking a trip abroad. Tenerife was the chosen destination and, 24 hours later Legs, Slats and I were looking out of an aeroplane window waving goodbye to old Blighty. Another chapter of my life was about to begin.

On the plane, I did my best to relax. I'm probably not the only one. Looking across at the other two while we were drinking warm Stella and munching on dry roasted peanuts, I couldn't help but think of the scrapes I'd been in over the years. For a relatively young bloke, I'd done quite a lot, seen quite a lot and been in some 'interesting' situations. There were things I was proud of and things I was not so proud of, just like everyone else. Most of what I'd done was probably different to what most others my age had done though. What I was proud of was that I had genuine people I could rely on. My family has always been there and have always been strong.

I looked across at Legs and Slats. We'd booked seats away from each other to be safe, but me and Legs exchanged a glance and I gave him a wink. Legs gave me a look that transported me back to a time I was out with him in Newcastle with a few others. There was a bar in town called 42nd Street that was always packed full from 4pm 'til 8pm most nights before slowing down a bit after that. They used to run a great happy hour on trebles, which was probably the main reason why anyone went there. We were there one night celebrating Richy Hall's birthday; a close friend of ours. As you can probably imagine, the alcohol flowed and we were mortal drunk after enjoying as many trebles as we could while happy hour was on. There was about eight of us in total with me (obviously), Legs Lennie, my other cousin Tony 'The Corey' Sayers. Our Tony was not a violent or dishonest person – he was quite the opposite, but don't hold that against him! That said, he was a Sayers and was loyal and more like a brother than cousin.

By 9pm, as usual, the place was very quiet so we left. There's never any point in staying in bars when there's more of you than the sum total of customers as well as staff. Once we climbed the stairs and got out into the street, the fresh air hit us and took us to another level. We staggered around for ages before arriving at Walkers nightclub. The walk must have started to pull us round and we started feeling a bit better once we were inside. I spotted an aunty and uncle and started talking to them. They were with a group of friends at the bar, so we had a drink and carried on with the banter. That's one of the things about being part of a huge family;

they say anywhere in the world you are, you can always guarantee you'll bump into a Geordie and it's the same for us: anywhere you go in Newcastle, you're guaranteed to bump into a Sayers. As I was talking to them, I noticed some trouble kicking off – two big six-foot-plus roid-heads pointing their fingers and being very aggressive towards my cousin Tony and my good friend Derek Tams. I don't like that 'pointy' conversation that people do. Makes me want to just grab their fingers and snap them off, so seeing someone doing it to a mate and a cousin got me riled straight away. I did a double-take but didn't break off from my conversation and, as one of the roid-heads stormed out of the club, I thought nothing more of it. Probably just a 'he called my pint a puff' type thing and he was going to the toilets for a cry. Whatever the reason, from where I was stood, it looked like it had fizzled out. The conversation that actually had taken place wasn't too far from my assumption, but it went as far as the roider asking Derek outside for a fight. They were both pumped up and relentless with one of them needing to prove a point. In the end, Derek said he'd fight him – that's where he was storming off to when I clocked him. In fact, he even ripped his own shirt off as he was leaving. Seriously. He must have been stood outside shivering for ten minutes before realising their straightener was a non-starter. Instead of following him out for a fight, Derek headed to the bar to get another drink. So, with Derek away at the bar, our Tony was left by himself in the same spot. And of course, when the disgruntled meathead returned, it was Tony who took the brunt of his roid rage. He demanded to know where Derek had gone and why hadn't he gone outside. Our Tony told him he didn't know and turned away from him to avoid any further trouble, but this just led to both of the roiders and a few others joining in to give him a hard time, wanting a fight with him instead. Nothing like a quiet night out, eh? So when Tony got sick of their aggravation, he calmly turned to the mug and looked him in the eye.

'I really don't want to fight you, but I know somebody who will,' he said. He then brought the two lumps to the other side of the club where I was stood. As they approached, Tony pointed over to me, 'That's him there, mate,' and stood watching as they headed over in my direction. Of course, I was oblivious to all this, I was drinking and talking bollocks to people when all of a sudden this mug pushed his big finger in my face shouting at the top of his voice.

'Do you want to fucking fight me?'

My first reaction was to laugh.

'Are you fucking kidding?' I asked.

He poked his finger into my cheek, snapping my head back. I've got a little bit of fiery temper, and this fucker may as well have just pressed my 'fight button'. With the force of his finger and that instant of pain, my reaction was immediate. As he shoved my cheek, my head came straight back and butted him straight in the face. I heard the crunch of his nose shattering on my head and I punched the wind out of him with a blow to the stomach. He managed to get me in a headlock and give me what I'd call a crocodile roll – turning me from side, disorienting me and squeezing the breath out of me at the same time. It was like having a déjà vu experience because the next thing I knew he had my nose in his mouth and was trying to bite the fucker off. Is that all people do when they can't put up a decent fight? He started to bite hard on my nose and I punched him in the windpipe and he released me but then managed to bite my arm. I must admit, that *did* hurt. But, fucking hell. Come on! Had he said fight me or bite me? Who calls someone out to just start biting them? His friend tried to get involved by restraining me while he continued with his biting. I know you can fight like a pit bull, but this was taking the piss. It must have looked bad because even our Tony jumped in and tried to wrestle the pair of them off me. He hadn't had a fight since junior school but was as game as a badger and that's what counts in these situations. With nothing to lose, I bit down on the closest thing I could sink my teeth into... which unknown to me, was Tony's stomach just below his ribs. I wasn't letting go for anyone. I felt a few digs on my head and my back, but they just bounced off. I locked my jaw and thought, 'Fuck you. I can bite just as hard as you can.' I was getting one over on the two clowns, but oddly, the only screams I could hear were coming from Tony. I let go but there was no time to apologise.

One of the roiders kicked him in the chest, and Tony grabbed the man's foot but ended up pulling his shoe off. He threw the shoe away, which soared right over to the only place you wouldn't want – behind the bar, taking out a few optics on the way. Talk about slapstick! I can only imagine how this looked to anyone watching. It got worse though. Rather than letting his foot go, Tony proceeded to pull the bloke's sock off and bit down on his big toe. The screams were blood curdling! But it was as funny as it was horrific. I managed to break free from the other bloke and started to boot him over and over again while Tony bit down on that toe for all he was worth. The door staff came running over to break it all up and a few of our mates were on the scene too. We were dragged apart and Tony and me dusted ourselves down and looked at each other and then burst out laughing. It wasn't the most impressive fight I've ever had but it kind of shows how you can go from one serious one with everything to fight for, to something that just evolves into all-out comedy. Again, this would have been a YouTube sensation, but for all the wrong reasons. I'd love to watch it over again... but thank fuck no one can!

Thinking about that really made me smile – all down to the way Legs took a drink. Just like he did on that night out. And it felt reassuring. Any twitchiness I'd had started to subside as I cracked open another can and pictured the scene again. You need insane memories like that to keep you sane, I think.

The plane came to a halt on the runway in Tenerife, signalling to us all that we'd made it: we'd got out of the UK and were free! We'd booked our tickets separately and arranged to hook up once we were outside the terminal. We took our time getting off the plane and headed towards baggage collection before going through customs. There seemed to be an issue at customs before we even got there, with officials running backwards and forwards and one or two of them kept looking in my direction... or was I just being paranoid? Man, you always know when something's up, don't you? Then I heard it: *Sayers*. I heard my name read out in a Tannoy announcement. This wasn't good. It was very fucking far from good. I waited in line trying not to arouse any suspicion or look concerned but I didn't think it was going to end well at all. Again the same announcement came across the Tannoy and there it was again as clear as day; 'Sayers.'

To my left, a group of officials came walking directly towards me. This was it. The game was up. At the back of the group was a female official with a young boy. To my right I noticed a woman in tears running towards the group and the boy broke free from them and ran towards the crying woman and into her arms. It turned out that the 'Sayers' family had lost their little boy in the airport and that's what all the fuss had been about. Christ, what are the odds on that, man? I clocked the lads behind me in the line and we exchanged a few knowing winks and smiles. I mean, there's close calls and there's *close calls*.

Eventually, we all got through customs unscathed and, as we walked outside of the terminal, the sun beamed down on our faces. As the heat hit us, my thoughts were with our John and Ken who were on remand in their stripes in Durham. What I would have given for them to be with us right then. To see that look on your mates' faces when you all know you're free men is a brilliant sight. I could see that we'd all left our troubles back at home. Well, they were certainly at the back of our minds anyway. I don't think you ever fully relax when you're in that situation. You can't completely let your guard down.

We jumped in a taxi and headed straight to the Veronicas complex: it was time to have some fun. We got to the first bar and ordered three large beers. They didn't last long... there appeared to be something wrong with the glasses over there, so we ordered three more to see if the same happened again. The second ones lasted a little bit longer. We started talking to the bar staff and asked if there were any apartments for rent. They were quite helpful and gave us a few numbers to get us started. As we were talking, a group of lairy pissed-up cockneys started shouting over. We were in good spirits though. They asked if we had enough bottle to play them at pool. The leader with the big mouth was about 15 stone and about six foot two, and juiced-up. He was obviously looking for trouble and started calling us 'Geordie Maggots', a term used in the past by John McVicar. So, he's quoting from a film based in Durham nick – the one place we were trying to avoid!

You don't call a complete stranger something like that unless a) you're a total prick b) you're trying to intimidate them or c) you're looking for a good kicking. It seemed that he was all three, but I'm a fair man and always reserve judgement.

He looked at me, still giving it the big one and asked me if I had any money to gamble with. I told him that I only had my holiday money. He said that was good as they were playing pool for £20 a game. He was trying to intimidate me and impress his entourage. I hadn't really reserved my judgement. I knew immediately what kind of arsehole he was; I'd certainly dealt with enough of them in my time to be able to suss them out immediately. I was surprised he hadn't done the same sussing out of me though, but he probably hadn't had enough experience because his intimidation had no doubt worked on many in the past. And this would prove to be his downfall.

He told me to put my £20 on the table. I agreed and pulled it out of my pocket. I'd watched him earlier – spinning a coin to decide who would break and sure enough, as he put his money on the table next to mine he said, 'I'll spin you for the break, Geordie.'

They must have mistaken us for regular holidaymakers, maybe thought we were a bit naive. He was about to realise the error of his ways and discover how a westender deals with a big-mouthed-soon-to-be-fucked-up arsehole.

I walked over to him with the lads watching my back. He took the coin from the side of the table and flicked it up into the air. As he followed the coin up and then down with his head, I caught him with a peach of a right uppercut and knocked him out. As he hit the floor knocking over tables and glasses Legs and Frankie came steaming in with pool cues and started battering his mates. The bar staff ran for cover and the manager was about to call the police when another Cockney lad came over and told him not to. The mug's mates scattered, leaving him lying in a pool of blood, beer and broken glass.

This other bloke seemed ok and must have had something to do with the complex as he got us some drinks and told the staff to clean up the mess. The guy whose name escapes me now was impressed how we'd handled the bully and his mates and it turned out that the bully had been causing him a few issues and the bloke had been waiting for somebody to eventually teach him a lesson. In return, he asked how he could help us. We told him we needed a roof over our heads and he said he would fix us up with an apartment. The mug on the floor started to come round and staggered out of the bar. It was clear that his jaw was broken. What a shame.

With a roof over our heads and a few quid in our pockets we made the most of our new home. We partied hard and life was good in the sunshine. Before we knew it four months passed and the funds began to run out. We all had our own ideas on how to raise some cash, but we went with Frankie Slats's plan after he'd stumbled across a safe full of cash at the car hire place next to our apartment. The place also exchanged money and when we'd been in to hire a car, Frankie had clocked about £30k in notes in the safe and the safe had stood wide open all the time we'd been there, so was likely to be open most of the day. By leaving it open, they made it un-safe. I think that's a French term.

Anyway, the Cockney lads were still on the scene and had started drinking with us most days, so Frankie put the bit of work to them. It turned out that they were a little firm back home in South London and were well up for it. The safe was attached to an outside wall and Frankie's plan was to get the lads to scrape away the cement between the bricks before removing the bricks and then the safe. The London lads had other ideas though and had plundered a few tools including a steel bar and a pick axe from a local building site. I admired their enthusiasm. That night they began laying into the wall with brute strength and the noise started to attract unwanted attention. It didn't take long for a local man to start shouting at them. Then another... and another... until they were surrounded by a crowd of angry locals. The lads panicked and dropped their tools and fled the crime scene. Frankie and Dave (another mate of ours) were sitting at a local tavern waiting for the lads to get back with the wages. Instead, they were greeted with, 'It's come on top, Frankie.' This wouldn't have been so bad, but the lads had also been chased by the group of locals and they were not very happy with Johnny Foreigner coming over to steal their money.

Frankie and Dave found themselves in big trouble. One of the Spaniards nutted poor Dave flush in the face, putting him on his arse. But only for a moment. Dave was an ex-boxer and he got straight back up and got stuck into them. There were around six Spaniards and they even brought a dog with them. It bit Dave a couple of times and Frankie was easy pickings for them; he was overweight and had been partying for four months... not really match fit. They managed to get away from the Spanish Inquisition and ran through a few backstreets and down an embankment to our apartment. When I saw the clip of them and they told me what had happened, I couldn't stop laughing. Dave had a broken nose and had lost a few teeth and was cut and bruised and covered in dog bites and Frankie didn't look that much better. The tears streamed down my face as the young

Cockneys arrived and Frankie started shouting and bawling at them for bringing the trouble their way.

'Why – of all the fucking places – did you fucking run to me to fucking tell me it was on fucking top? Three hundred metres – to me – to tell me it was on top? I could fucking *see* it was on top! I was fucking hiding, watching it all. Look at the state of Dave!'

Poor bastard. He got a right old hiding that night. There were too many of them and he'd been partying way too long to even do anything. And the dog joining in didn't help either. Still cracks me up remembering the expressions on their faces telling me what happened through broken teeth and fat lips. We never saw Dave again after that night. He contracted rabies and died soon after.

We stayed in Tenerife for a total of seven months and I have some fantastic memories of the place, but unfortunately, when it's time to move on it's time to move on. Me, Frankie and our Tony called time on our trip away. It felt right. When we arrived back in the country we sharp realised we wanted the sun on our backs, not the cold wind and rain. It was a bit of a comedown.

Dave didn't really die. He got himself a new set of friends. You can't really blame him, can you? Once bitten, twice shy and all that.

We arrived in Luton, headed to London and booked into a hotel. It didn't take us long to sink into a depression about our situation and, within a few days, Tony and Frankie were going stir crazy and there was fucking murders on between them. Seriously. I even remember passing a cat and dog who were fighting outside and thought they had nothing on Tony and Frankie. On one occasion, the noise got so bad that the manager came to the room and started threatening us with the police. He took one look at us and said he couldn't talk to us until we'd calmed down and cleaned up the mess. He said he'd be back in ten minutes, which meant that he was going for the bizzies so we packed our things together to make a sharp exit. The two of them were still punching the living daylights out of each other in the lift and I just stood there and let them get on with it; I was past caring and just wanted to get out of there with as little fuss as possible. Cue scene from a comedy: the lift stopped and the door opened to reveal Tony biting Frankie's shin. Frankie was screaming – and who could blame him? And both of them had blood all over their faces. The people who were stood waiting to get in the lift took a step back with shock. The lift door closed, next stop reception. Thank fuck.

I managed to prize them apart and out of the lift in one piece. Just, mind. I mean, I was nearly pissing myself laughing in the process because it was the second time that Tony Legs had reminded me of that biting incident with my other cousin. And what with the recent dog attack... it was all too much. *Stop fucking biting each other*! Check-out consisted of running through reception and throwing the keys on the desk. Tony jumped in the first taxi and me and Frankie jumped in the one behind. Both cars sped off in opposite directions. Brilliant.

So, after months together we then lost each other in the middle of London. There was no doubt Frankie and Tony needed a break from each other but not like this. It was sad to lose Tony, but deep down I knew he'd be ok. After a couple of days in London we got talking to a man from Sunderland who was heading up north the next day to make a delivery in Gateshead. He agreed to drop us off at a friend's place in Darlington. After a night there, an uncle of mine called George 'Blow' Shotton came to pick us up and take us back to Newcastle. He got the nickname through the amount of safes he blew in the 60s: top man!

I always get asked how my uncle George got his infamous name. Some people just associate blow with shotgun, which sounds a bit like Shotton. But no, the real reason is a lot more interesting. He was never trained in the use of dynamite so it was all very much trial and error with him. Health and safety didn't really come into it and there were never any risk analysis reports on his mind. He used to boast about his time in the army despite the fact he spent more time in the dock for desertion during his time defending the country. But still, technically, he had been in the army and credit where credit's due.

Blow and his firm were at the top of their game and had slowly worked their way up the criminal ladder. Electronic security was in its infancy and many of the premises they hit were still very secure, but the lads would always find a way in. They also found it easier to peel off the back of these safes and get their loot out than trying to carry the safe away. On one occasion, they found a nice piece of work from a pal of theirs and gained entry through a back door where they were delighted to find not one but two safes. One was huge and the lads' eyes lit up: the bigger the safe, the bigger the haul, they thought. Blow set to work, packing the two safes with some dynamite that they'd nabbed from an old quarry and blow the two of them at the same time. With the fuses, set the lads headed out of the building. They were in no rush. They'd done it many times before. But this time, they hadn't reckoned on the small safe's fuse being quicker than they imagined and there was a huge explosion... which blew the safe right through the window. There were half crowns, ten bobs and two bobs scattered all over the street (that's old money, if you're of a certain age). If the first explosion didn't wake the neighbours then the second one did. It was so powerful that it blew down the supporting wall and the floor above that and all the change in the safe was either damaged or melted... and *that's* how my uncle George got the name.

Anyway, back to our situation. Blow said he was going to look after us and he told me he had a boat on the Isle of Bute on the west coast. He said me and Frankie could stay on it but he also said it needed a bit of a lick of paint. He also gave us a three year-old transit van which was on the hit list for the finance!

We got to work on the van and in no time we had a generator hooked up and a television and video player (that's what we had before DVD players, if you're of a certain age. And DVDs were what we watched before Netflix). One of my cousins had screwed the local video shop and I bought them all off him, so we were like a mobile cinema. We made our way to Scotland with the words of Blow echoing in my mind as he said them that often, 'Make sure the ropes are tight', meaning the ropes that tethered the boat to the shore.

It may have taken us a few months and one or two detours, but we eventually made it to Scotland. Once there, it took us two weeks to sort the boat out. In the meantime me, Frankie and George stayed in a B&B and it was laugh a minute. Uncle George was a really good liar and his stories were always very interesting; he was brilliant entertainment. He didn't have to move up to Scotland with us for those two weeks, but he did it to make sure we got settled in and the right people were there in case we needed help. That was a lovely thing for anyone to do and it was brilliant to have that kind of support around us.

With the boat ship-shape, me and Frankie got settled in and with that came boredom and with it, frustration. It didn't take long before we were at each other's throats and Frankie decided he needed a change of scenery. We both did. I didn't want it turning into another version of the London hotel room – especially after we'd just done the boat up and made it habitable. I took him on the ferry and then to the train station. It was sad to see him leave but he'd devoted eight months of his life to me and for that I will always be grateful.

On my own, I started to get a bit lonely and there was nothing to do apart from drink. I used to drink in the pub on the harbour and I was always one of the last to leave, staggering over to the boat. One night I'd had a good drink and I noticed more and more that I had to jump from the shore to the boat as it was about four foot away.

'Make sure the ropes are tight!' Blow's voice echoed again, like Obi-Wan from *Star Wars*. The rope was as thick as my leg, how on earth was I expected to do that? I couldn't move the ropes at all, so I went to bed and fell into a drunken sleep.

Next thing I knew I was on the cabin floor after being thrown out of my bed as the boat was leaning to one side. With the rope slipping and the tide going out, the boat had moved further away from the harbour and a ferry was just coming in. I had the hangover from hell as I got onto deck, rubbing my head to make the pain go away. What a sight I must have looked! People were getting off the ferry, pointing and staring at the funny man on the boat with no clothes on, scratching his bollocks. I didn't need that kind of attention; I may have had nowt on, but I was still wearing a £75k prictag.

To me, it was more than a wakeup call. I had to get away and I needed some company too, I'd steadily been going crazy and I had to keep it together. I'd been through a lot since I'd gone on my toes, but I'd heard that the lads had been given a trial date and I felt there was light at the end of the tunnel for me.

I made arrangements to speak to my cousin Philip Riley who was living on Hartford camp at the time. Philip is a very loyal and honourable man. I managed to get a message to him and, credit where credit is due, he just dropped everything instantly for me and asked how he could help. A few hours later we were sharing a beer. He was a sight for sore eyes and I was so glad to see him. He told me how the camp had been raided by over 200 police looking for me and our Tony. I stayed with him for a couple of days and then I moved to another camp for a couple more. It was just good to be around people again instead of being on that bloody boat. I moved from camp to camp for a few months but, with the trial date on the horizon, I felt that the time was right to go back home. A safe house was sorted and I headed up the A1 to a hero's welcome. I was pleased to be back home. It had been a long time coming and the time was right.

It was the back end of August 1988. I was 23 years of age, 12 stone and very fit to go with it. I'd been waiting for our John's trial to finish, bored rigid and living in a downstairs flat with one of my cousins. I didn't venture out the house for four months. Four months, man. I was still on the run.

I'd do body circuits and peddle a bike until I was exhausted and at times I would pass out such was my determination. It wouldn't break me – I'd been through worse than that and I knew my mind was strong. One particular day I was sitting in the flat trying to catch my breath after a hard training session. I had the radio on and a newsflash stated that John Henry Sayers and Ken Sanvid had just been acquitted for Britain's biggest ever post office robbery. It sounded sensational to give it such a tag, but it's impressive all the same. Detail about the circumstances of the robbery were read out, saying that it had been done with SAS-style planning with split-second timing.

Fucking hell – acquitted! I jumped up in the air with joy and propelled myself so high that I punched the ceiling.

Man, what a result. I immediately went outside for some fresh air and felt a massive sense of relief and liberty, like the world had been lifted off my shoulders.

I knew Northumbria Police would have no chance of convicting me after they failed to convict my brother and his co-accused. I was still jumping with joy in the back lane, what a sight I must have looked – jumping around in the middle of the day like some lunatic on happy pills. My cousin who I was staying with had also heard the newsflash on the radio and immediately purchased two bottles of champagne. He came running round to the flat with another cousin of mine who was just about to change shifts at work. They arrived as I was still bouncing around the yard and started spraying me in the face and from head to toe with the champagne. The three of us was absolutely delighted... it was brilliant! I don't even know what we were shouting; they weren't even proper words. Just sheer delight!

Word travelled fast throughout Tyneside and the rest of the country. We started off slow with the celebrations because I still had to hand myself in to the police. But that was just a formality. Messages of congratulations flooded in from Glasgow to Parkhurst to my mother's and father's houses and all other family members wishing us the best of luck, love and support. The villains of Tyneside were finally getting national recognition and about time too; it was one up for the Geordies. It seemed like the firm's future was in for the making, but with such publicity there'd no doubt be a lot of heat to follow. After recognition like that, it propels you to a much higher level. And from mentions like that, the Sayers name was starting to spread nationally.

When he was back home and sorted out, we threw our John a huge party at the Balmoral. All our friends from Elswick and the West End were there and a few well-known faces too.

It was a great night. I went down to Zoots nightclub with my good friend Fish Tams, where Viv Graham was working at the time. When we got to the door, Viv saw me and came over and gave me a big cuddle and welcomed me home. With being on my toes for the same amount of time as John had been away, it felt like I'd done time as well. I mentioned we were having a homecoming party for John and that there was around a 150 of us to follow, once they'd had a few more drinks.

A lot of people didn't want me to embrace Viv as they wanted revenge for the liberties he'd taken with people. To be honest, I had my own agenda – just like they did – and I wanted to defuse the situation. He invited us all in as his guests and made sure he bought drinks for everyone. Viv could not have been a better host or more of a gentleman. Viv's sixth sense had served him well… although it wouldn't have taken a genius to see that some of the characters who took a free drink off him that night were there to settle a few scores. I think his philosophy that night was to keep your enemies close. He didn't like any of the westenders and they didn't like him, and so welcoming an army of them into his club was a ballsy move.

Looking back, there were a lot of drugged-up and tooled up psychopathic people who enjoyed violence in there that night. To emphasise it a bit further – this was probably the most dangerous place on the planet to be in at that moment. The atmosphere was fucking dark and not even the music could cut through it. There was a sense of desperation from Viv hanging in the air. All eyes were on him and he felt out of his depth. It wasn't something he was used to. He'd never been intimidated before and that night he felt it in his own club. It would have made an interesting psychological study. *All* eyes were on him, whether it was made obvious or from within the darkness. It would have just taken one person to light the fuse and that place would have exploded; the slightest wrong look from Viv would have signed his own death warrant. He would have got blasted to death by any number of sawn-off shotguns that people were carrying. He was twitchy, on edge, like a caged lion. By inviting them into the club as his guests, he created a sense of peace and I encouraged it. Even though we didn't work together we could co-exist together was my thinking. Newcastle was big enough for us all.

While standing at the bar that night I could see into the eyes of my friends, and I released if I'd lifted my hands in anger regardless if I'd connected or not it would have been fatal for Viv. All the westenders were studying my body language like a pack of wolves... sitting there, snarling, tooled up to the hilt; they were waiting for it to kick off, looking for any excuse, fearless and raring to go but I kept the peace. People who know me will understand I had a fiery temper in my youth but I have always been very diplomatic.

Viv spent a lot of time on my shoulder talking to me about certain things. He was testing the water and obviously sizing me up as his competition. He knew we were the figureheads in the West End; if anyone flew the flag it was the Sayers family and we were tried and tested at the highest level.

He was up and down that night; full of himself, but he also knew that he could not win. He was very uncomfortable and I could see it in his eyes. It was like he was putting on a show – no, make that he *was* putting on a show. But he was fooling no one. He couldn't even fool himself, never mind anyone else in there. He was totally outnumbered in his own club and whoever he was with that night kept a very low profile.

As the night progressed he kept asking me questions: why did some blokes have big coats on, why did he just do that, why's he stood over there? It was quite obvious that people had weapons on them. You couldn't even say they were concealed weapons as shotguns and samurai swords can't really be hidden that well, regardless of how dark the club was.

One person in particular really had him concerned. The person in question was staring directly at Viv from the moment he entered the club.

'What's the matter with him? Why's he starting at me?' he asked.

'Because he wants to do you,' came my reply. I could see by the fear in his face that no man had ever 'diplomatically' put it on him as strong as that before. It was a reality check, not necessarily overdue, it was that he'd never even had one. He was Viv Graham. Even back then he was a legend that feared no one. He'd never been in the sights of another predator until that night. I think he became aware right then that there were people out there who were as big and bad as he was... maybe even badder. The night came to an end without any incidents, which was a miracle in itself. Well, that was until a random big Scotsman and his friend were very disrespectful to my friend's wife and sister. Viv was over in seconds and knocked the two of them out. I think from Viv's point of view, it restored some balance. It meant that he'd flexed his muscles on home turf when he'd been feeling apprehensive all night. There was a sense of a truce for short while. Unfortunately, the truce didn't last; you can't make a dark cloud like that just vanish. It had been obvious all night that there'd been a storm on its way.

A coward and lowlife called Peter Logan Donnelly walked into Santana's restaurant in Newcastle with two of his associates at around 2.30am one Sunday morning to confront Viv. The place was full. Donnelly's confidence peaked when he was drunk and the three of them must have had a few. He had white fluffy socks on his hands and was holding a shotgun and started shouting for Viv.

He found him and pointed the gun at him, telling him to stand up and to go to the back room. Whether this was a personal thing between them or not, it put the frighteners up the other diners in there as there was no telling what might happen next. Donnelly was in control, but once they were all in the back room he was quickly overpowered. During the scuffle, Rob Bell – one of Viv's friends – got stabbed. Viv took a knife and the gun off Donnelly and then proceeded to give him the biggest beating of his life. It was ridiculous, really. I mean, when you're watching a film and someone holds a gun to someone's head, you feel yourself shouting at them to pull the trigger… because you know what's going to happen if they don't. And that was Donnelly's big mistake. You think Viv Graham was going to sit back and take something like that? On hearing what was going on, some of the punters in the restaurant shouted, 'You're going to kill him!' and in Viv's mind, he probably was; only seconds earlier he'd had a shotgun shoved in his face and he wasn't about to show any mercy. He picked up an empty beer keg and started smashing it off Donnelly's unconscious body. One of Donnelly's mates managed to do a runner while the other received a good beating, courtesy of Paul Lister… who just happened to be at the peak of fitness as he'd recently fought for the British Heavyweight title. Basically, it wasn't a well thought out plan at all. If there were two people on the planet not to get drunk and point a shotgun at in a restaurant, it was those two. In fact, it was probably one of the stupidest plans imaginable.

The police and ambulances arrived and they rushed Donnelly and Rob Bell to hospital. Rob had been stabbed through the heart and had a lifesaving operation. He was lucky to pull through. Donnelly was eventually released from hospital, taken to the police station and charged with Rob's attempted murder. If there was ever any sort of truce between the westenders and the city doormen it was well and truly shattered after that. In those days people didn't realise what sort of lowlife Donnelly really was and he still had quite a lot of people in the West End on his side. I was one of Donnelly's close friends at the time; he was my dad's cousin. We had a good bond from our childhood, which would cost me and my younger brother Michael, and good friend Nigel Abadom dearly later on in life, at this point, it had no bearing on my life or anybody associated with me... that storm was building all the time though.

In the wake of all that, there were certain pubs and clubs in Newcastle city centre where you could cut the atmosphere with a machete. One of those clubs happened to be Zoots where Viv had the door. Viv looked down on westenders and he had a real dislike to the westenders; he despised the people and the place because he had no control over either and he couldn't get his head around it. There were a lot of westenders that made much more money than Viv. They had pocketfuls of money and were good spenders with probably 90% of them being a variety of criminals with backgrounds related to serious crimes like armed robberies and murders. Viv was from a different background to us lot. He could not understand the criminal structure of the West End. And he meant nothing to a westender; he certainly wasn't a threat or someone to be scared of, it was just that they were all cut from different cloth and Viv or anyone like him didn't even register on their radar. He was someone who hit people and got paid a reasonable amount, whereas they were people who'd maim or kill for vast amounts – it was two different worlds.

I'll give you an example: we all drank in the Balmoral on

Westgate Road at the time. On a Saturday night you'd get around 150 people in and out of those people, 120 would be men and not one of them would have had a proper tax-paying job. That was the way of life... from cowboy roofers who never paid taxes and lived on the dole to major armed robbers, petty criminals, blaggers – whatever. The majority of us were criminals who survived from the proceeds of crime. When I say criminals this covers a wider scale of criminality. It was a criminal community. You'd see these people in Rea's Café on Elswick Road in the mornings and in the pubs at night. We drank, ate and went thieving together and we were all very close friends – more like brothers and cousins – and there was a bond between us all. We were Elswick Mafia Boys (EMB) and, just the same as in any walk of life, there was a pecking order. In the criminal world the major armed robbers are the elite. They are the Special Forces, if you like because men of action are judged on their merits. If a group of people can repeatedly stop cash-carrying armoured vehicles and successfully rob them, then it makes them a different breed of human being and extremely dangerous. Those vehicles are specially designed to prevent that from happening, so to be able to get in and relieve them of all their cash is quite an achievement. That's where all the would-be tough guys go wrong – they wouldn't know how to put a bit of work together. There'd be more of a chance of them becoming a bit of work... it's that fish out of water thing and sticking to what you know.

Getting back to Donnelly, it seemed to have put a wedge between myself, our John and Viv. John would not give Viv the time of day after that because we were very clannish and loyal to our own. That's how it is and that's how it always will be.

Every Friday and Saturday night, Zoots attracted stag and hen parties by the busload from all over the north east. Even further. You don't have to be from Newcastle to know its party reputation because you've probably been here to do just that! Zoots was a massive venue and absolutely bouncing at weekends with over 1,200 punters, and there was always a guarantee of trouble. It went without saying.

And one time when there was trouble at Zoots, some of us westenders and 20 or so doormen from the club joined together to fend off some outsiders. The lairy bastards had us outnumbered by about 3-1. We were in the lounge part of the club and we had about a dozen or so of these idiots wanting to fight. They threw bottles and glasses when they started kicking off. As I was sat, a bottle just missed my head, thrown by a giant ugly square jawed monster of a man. We got sprayed with glass and alcohol as more bottles and glasses smashed off the wall behind us. It wasn't a *careful you don't put someone's eye out* kind of thing. This fucker was looking to take someone's head off. I stood up from my barstool, took the suit jacket off that I'd just bought that day, folded it neatly and placed it on the table. Glasses were still flying overhead. Then, with the rage building, I picked a stool up, steamed into the huge bloke and swung it straight into his ugly mug. It levelled him and I made sure he wasn't going to get up for a bit by smacking it into his head a few more times. We didn't know the extent of the trouble until we got near the front door and I saw Viv knocking a few blokes out. There's the old cliché of saying it was like a Wild West barroom brawl, but that's exactly what it was like. You didn't have a clue who was who, but people would be running at you with glasses or bottles to stick you and you just hit anything that came your way. Every punch had to count otherwise you got cut to fuck.

'Stephen, we need to stick together. There's fucking loads of them!'

It all spilled out into Waterloo Street with different groups and doormen kicking the living daylights out of each other. There was well over 100 of them – they were everywhere. We used pool balls from the table downstairs to put into socks to use as weapons and doormen were scrambling to their cars to get the tools of their trade out: it was anything goes. We had cars parked up as well, carrying enough gear to arm us all. I think Viv was a bit shocked at how quickly we could spring into action and get ourselves tooled-up.

Hally, a good friend of mine, was shouting, 'Elswick over here!' for us to get stuck in. Fuck what anyone else was doing, we knew how to attack with our style of fighting; we'd spent our lives doing it and it was second nature. We stood side by side grouping together with Viv's doormen as the visitors made their advances. They threw bottles and glasses and bricks and anything they could get their hands on before they started running towards us. Fuck the Wild West... this was *Zulu*! I'm not sure if that would make me Michael Caine in this version, but I took charge and shouted, 'Stand! Stay together and let them run at us.' They were gathering speed and were getting closer and closer. I knew what I was meant to do. I prepared the lads shouting, 'Get ready, get ready!' We continued to stand our ground without moving, never backing down or bolting.

I saw that big ugly beer monster who I'd knocked out earlier. How the *fuck* did he get up from that? I still had a leg from the stool in my hand and was sizing him up for another clump. His mates were all the same build as him – fucking big – and they could definitely fight. Once they were a few feet away, I shouted, 'Charge!'

I had eyes for one man only: my new found friend, the beer monster. For the second time in the space of around ten minutes I smashed him over the head and knocked him spark out with the remainder of the stool. He was coming straight for me as well, with a score to settle. Viv waded in too. He must have taken out at least six on his own. I knew then that the big crowd still fighting in the club was ours for the taking. We had been down this road many a time before, so we stuck together and laid in to these lairy bastards good and proper. We knew how to perform and we did the biggest and best ones first.

I remember someone shouting, 'Take no prisoners!' which brought a smile to my face as that was the battle cry we used when we were in our early teens. In a mass brawl like that you can't give in. You keep fighting and fighting; do the biggest and best first, divide and conquer, hit them until they're finished. Your unity is your strength. There were dozens of men lying on the floor screaming in agony or unconscious. They came for a good fight and they certainly got one. It always feels like it lasted forever, but it was over within maybe 15 minutes. The average fight lasts a couple of minutes, if that. I remember looking down the street and seeing the big beer monster back on his feet giving it what for with a pack of about eight westenders surrounding and attacking him. It reminded me of something from a David Attenbrough documentary where a pack of lions would take down an elephant. He put up a fight but he was no match for them. With ambulances filling the street and treating the walking wounded, it seemed to be over as quickly as it started. I don't think anyone would even remember how it actually did start, other than it being a free-for-all. For us, we'd joined forces for one night only. Although there'd animosity before and it continued after, there was that moment that we can all look back on with fondness.

CHAPTER 7
HOBO'S AND THE AFTERMATH

I was on the drink in Zoots with Fish Tams and Davey Lancaster and we met up with Viv and his good friend, Rob Armstrong. We were having a good drink and enjoying ourselves when a doorman I knew passed a message saying all the Sayers and their associates were barred from a nightclub at the bottom of Bath Lane. The nightclub was called Hobo's. That news was taken by me as a direct challenge, but I thought I would leave it for the time being as the night was still young. Inside I was seething. Barred? Were they for real? As the night progressed, I started thinking about what the doorman had said. First of all, it was not a club we used at the time, but a challenge is a challenge. I sent a friend of mine to the door to test the water and see what was going on and, just as they'd said, the doormen wouldn't let him in, saying the police had barred the Sayers and all of their associates.

This was totally illegal. In the meantime, there'd been an incident at Walkers nightclub and the doorman had phoned Viv for help, so we jumped into Davy Lancaster's Shogun jeep which was parked just outside, and the five of us drove up to Walkers. We went in and Viv was told who was working themselves and he walked over and knocked these two big roid-heads spark out without a word being said; just another night at the office for Viv. We had a quick drink while we were there as it would have been the quickest nightclubbing session in history otherwise. After that, we got back into the motor and drove out the back lane of Walkers, leading us onto Bath Lane. 'Nice coincidence,' I thought, as we parked outside Hobo's. What happened next can be seen on a video on YouTube from a TV documentary called *Viv Graham: A Hard Act to Follow*.

We approached the door and just walked in. I have never paid to get into a nightclub in my life and I wasn't about to start then. When we walked in we walked straight into the dance area and asked the staff who who'd barred us. Then Viv saw a doorman called Stuart Watson and proceeded to punch him all over. To be honest, it was far from a fair fight. Once Viv had punched him about a bit and dragged him through into the club, we kicked him around the dance floor and got nicked for our troubles. To us, this didn't seem out of place (see the David Attenborough reference earlier) but the police thought different. They made it quite clear to Viv and the lads that the reason everyone was being nicked for this was because I was with them and they wanted to make an example of me and my family.

I've heard a few different versions of what actually happened that night from a few other people. The fight between Viv and Stu wasn't *that* impressive. If you didn't know either of them, you'd just see a couple of big lumps having a fight where one throws a few punches. Stu didn't throw any punches back, which was most likely out of fear. His doormen had done a runner and left him to it.

It's also been said that there were undercover police there that night and the whole thing was a setup to get the Sayers locked up. Apparently, Stu was used as 'live bait' and I've heard stories saying we were out to kill him that night. I mean, I've probably said I could murder a pint a few times on a night out, but never a doorman. That's just fucking stupid. There's always going to be rumours with things like this, though. These are all incidents that go to piece together the story of Viv, his involvement with us and any conspiracy theory as to how he met his untimely death. The Hobo's incident is now part of Newcastle folklore and I suppose, whether we knew it or not at the time, we all made history and created a story that would be retold and embellished upon for years to come.

Of course, the next day I couldn't remember any of it. I woke up from a drunken sleep and rolled over to feel the coldness of the tiles. I opened my eyes and realised that I was in a police cell. *Fuck.* I'm sure many of you know that feeling. It's a million times worse than waking up in bed and having a bout of beer guilt. My head was pounding and I had a dry mouth. *What had I done? What the fuck had I done?* My mind raced. I couldn't think how I'd ended up there but my memory started coming back in dribs and drabs. I knew I was in a bit of trouble... then I remembered that I'd led a group of men to a nightclub to basically bash the doormen up, which it has to be said, we did successfully.

We ended up in Newcastle Magistrates Court to face the music. My co-accused were Fish Tams, Davey Lancaster, John 'Nodge' Thompson, Rob Armstrong and Viv Graham. It was unlucky for Nodge because he had absolutely nothing to do with what happened that night. He'd seen Davey Lancaster's jeep pull up outside the club and he parked behind us and followed us in when the fight broke out. When questioned about the sixth person on CCTV footage, I'd said no comment. In my mind, I genuinely had no idea who this sixth person was behind us. He got charged and remanded all the same, poor bastard. As if that wasn't unlucky enough, while I was in Durham nick, Nodge turned up unexpectedly to visit me; slightly different to returning to the scene of the crime, he returned to the scene of the criminal… and that's how he got nicked.

We were in the back of a police van and I was double-cuffed to a fellow prisoner (as you do) and Fish and Davey Lancaster were also cuffed, but not to anyone else, sat to the side of me. Also present in the van were four or so SPG (Special Patrol Group). When I first got into the van a policeman poked me really hard in the side, just under my rib cage and laughed.

'Wait until I get these handcuffs off and *then* try to do that again.'

The van made its journey with the sirens blaring. We were Category B prisoners but we were treated like we were Cat A. There were helicopters flying overhead and armed escorts with blue lights flashing. It was bizarre; completely unnecessary. Had they mistaken us for someone else? It was funny in a way. It showed that they thought we were important enough for such caution, and that was nice. We weren't even over the Tyne Bridge when the policeman who'd hit me said, 'No speaking in the van!'

He was more like one of Hitler's SS Officers, but what this coward did not expect was retaliation. Without hesitation Fish told him where to go. I put a cigarette in my mouth and I lit it. I was inhaling the first draw when I felt a thump on the side of my face that knocked me off the bench. The bastard blindsided me and tried to choke me out from behind. Another copper decided to get in on the action and I had to put up with two of them taking liberties.

Davey Lancaster tried his best to help me and Fish jumped up and put his cuffed hands over the top of one of their necks and got him in a bear hug. I was really distressed at this point and could feel my face going red as he continued to strangle me. Desperate measures were called for and I heard Fish shout, 'Let's see how you like being fucking choked, you fucking dog!' and the sadistic policeman gave the immediate reaction of the coward that he really was and he screamed for assistance. Bearing in mind that I was handcuffed to some other fucker, it wasn't really a fair fight.

We were driving though Birtley Services; the helicopter was directly above us, six cruisers and six motorbike outriders alongside us. The armed coppers amongst them were carrying machine guns. As the fight continued inside, one of the policeman shouted, 'Stop the van. Escape in progress!' into his radio as we rolled around, throwing punches wherever possible. Fish overpowered the policeman and started choking him. Over the top of the action I heard the reply on the radio: 'Do not stop. I repeat, do not stop!'

The closest police armed escort following us positioned its front bumper touching the back doors to prevent them from being opened – quite a tricky manoeuvre from them and there were a few tricky moves being displayed inside.

The policeman who had started it had his forearm around my windpipe and was punching me as hard as he could in my ribs. Fish used his weight to pull him off my back and they fell towards the back doors. In the meantime I was left gasping for breath. The violence seemed to finish as quickly as it begun as we neared HMP Durham. The sadistic policeman who'd started it tried to be calm and told everyone to forget about what had happened.

'Just forget about it and calm down lads, ok?' he said softly.

Talk about Jekyll and Hyde. He probably realised that he wasn't dealing with normal people. The more pain that he was inflicting the worse it was making us. He also probably thought that we'd be the last people on the planet he'd want as enemies once the doors to Durham nick were locked behind us all; he wasn't the only sadistic psycho in that van.

I sat there calmly, as instructed, for ten or fifteen seconds staring at the man but I couldn't bite my tongue anymore. Fish had the same thought and beat me to it.

'When you take these cuffs off me, I don't care what you do for a living, I am going to do a lot worse to you than you've just done to me.'

I was really angry with this man. I was still in a lot of pain and my ribs were hurting. These words were enough to start it all off again but yet again I found myself on the floor of the van getting dragged and pinned down with unreasonable force by the bastards. That time, I was just restrained rather than kicked or punched. The lad I was cuffed to must have taken a good few digs as well. Bless him, he didn't complain though, just went with the flow.

'Let him up! Let him up!' shouted the sadistic copper.

When they picked me up and placed me back on the bench I looked across and there he was opposite me. Calling the others off hadn't changed my opinion of what I wanted to do to him. I looked at his face and it was pale white and he was starting to shake.

I stared him straight in the eye, 'You have just taken a liberty with me, you cowardly cunt.' He couldn't look at me.

We drove into Durham prison but the driver hadn't realised that there was only room for two vehicles. When it stopped, me and the lad I was handcuffed to got dragged out. The sadistic policeman must have rediscovered his bottle and tried to knee me in the ribs. Fish saw what was going on and ran up to him and kicked him straight in the bollocks, knocking the fight out of him immediately.

I heard the riot bell sounding in the prison as the back doors of the van opened and there were 20 screws to welcome us to our new home. With one of them winded and us just getting warmed up, it would have been a good way for us all to get acquainted. The SO (Senior Officer) at Durham was a man called Montgomery; he saw what had happened and he detained everybody, including the police officers and screws, to see what had actually happened; good decision, I thought.

Anyone who has been to HMP Durham will know that there are metal stairs leading up to reception and that they are good old hard solid ones with lots of sharp edges. Montgomery ordered that we should be uncuffed immediately. The police all looked very disappointed at that order. With my cuffs undone, the sadistic copper made his way to the top of the stairs. Another prisoner, who hadn't travelled with us, took a run and jump at him and he caught him sweet as a nut... knocked him flying back down the stairs; couldn't have happened to a nicer fella. The riot alarm, which had just been switched off, was cranked back up and more screws rushed down to reception. The governor arrived to see the copper at the bottom of the stairs being brought round with smelling salts. The governor asked what was going on and, naturally, the officers lied and said we had attacked them in the van and they'd tried to restrain us.

'I want everyone who has an injury to be checked over by the doctor immediately,' he said. When I was checked over, the doctor found all the bruises I'd received. He was shocked at the state of me and went to get the governor. I was standing in just my boxer shorts. The governor took one look at my body and shared the same opinion as the doctor.

'You should press charges and have the police officers arrested for what they have done to you,' he said.

I looked at him and told him and the doctor that I didn't want to press charges against anyone but that I did wish to keep a medical record, just in case they tried to charge me for the assault of a police officer. Davey and Fish looked unmarked compared to me. Bastards!

In reception there are four holding rooms all with clear plastic windows so you can see through. Me, Fish and Davey were sat there for a short while and smoked a spliff that one of the lads sat with us passed around. Over ten minutes passed when the sadistic policeman walked in from the doctor's room. He looked like he'd just had a life-saving operation. Looking back, I still find it funny. It always puts a smile on my face because I know that his injuries were sustained from being propelled down those big metal stairs.

He was placed in the room next to us and sat with his head in his hands.

'Give me two seconds and I'll get that screw to put me in there with you!' I shouted. If they'd let me in the room that day, I promise two things: he would have never worked again and I would never have been released from prison. Once the governor was satisfied with his investigation, the police were allowed to go home and we were given our shower and something to eat and were stocked up with our new prison clothes.

We made our way to our cells. The screw opened the door to mine and Davey's pad and there was Viv Graham. He was lying on his bed which was covered in chocolate rappers and crumbs. Me, Davey and the screw burst out laughing and I shouted, 'Captured you eating all the goodies, eh?! Could you not just have two bars like everybody else?'

He tried to respond but couldn't because he'd crammed a full bar of chocolate into his mouth. The screw locked us in and we embraced each other and I got settled for a quiet night in. I'd be having a few. We were reminiscing on the day's events and Viv was gutted that he'd missed a good old-fashioned punch up.

Three weeks passed by and early one morning the door was opened and we saw some old screw from years back who knew Davey. He came into the cell and clicked the lock.

'Hello, young Lancaster. Back again, are you?'

Davey remembered him immediately. Screws always seem to mellow as they approach retirement and try to befriend you and see if they can help you so they get an easy ride. This must have been the case with this bloke because he told Davey that he and Fish were going to be arrested for fighting with the police. Davey was sat up in his bed and he pulled out a packet of 20 menthols from under his pillow. The packet contained a ready-rolled spliff and £200. Davey lit up in front of this old screw. The screw just stood looking at Davey who blew the smoke directly towards his face.

'Cut it out, young Lancaster.'

Viv was cuddled up under the blankets giggling like a little school kid and, because of the size of this man, it became even funnier. Davey gave the screw £30 and asked him to go and get him 200 menthols. The screw took the money, walked out, and returned ten minutes later.

'Get your stuff, Lancaster. You're late for court,' he said.

Some other screws opened Fish's cell just next door and he came in and said, 'They're taking us to court for fighting with the police.'

Fish and Davey had filled their flasks and were having a cup of tea when another screw finally came to the door to take them out. They left with shouts of encouragement – 'Have a nice day out, lads!' – from me and Viv. We stayed behind the door that afternoon and me and Fish's cousin and my good friend, Tommy 'The Brute' Tams, smoked the day away – Viv never touched any of that. When they returned we were as high as kites. They told us they'd been charged with assault on three police officers. I looked at Viv and he looked at me and then we started to giggle. Fish and Davey were both straight-faced at our reaction, then Fish added, 'If you think that's bad, I'm charged with assaulting two inspectors as well.'

That was it... we both burst out laughing. The cannabis had certainly taken its toll. We couldn't stop laughing for ages! I didn't think there'd been two inspectors to even assault!

Time started to drag on. I was remanded for at least five months with a number of charges that saw me go to court week after week. I played the system as best I could and they were fully aware of it. I was given technical bail on one charge but refused bail on the other charges, so I was going nowhere soon. On our various court visits we would get pre-packed food sent in from Marks and Spencers... meats, peppers, asparagus, sauces and much more. We decided to hold onto the food and see if we could find out who was number one in the kitchen because the food we got in there wasn't up to scratch and we fancied something special. As the kitchen lads came out from work, I asked one of the inmates who the number one orderly was. He pointed to a big man called Jenkins who stood at six-foot-three and was quite thin. I approached Jenkins and asked if we could do some business regarding the goodies in the kitchen. This proposal seemed to annoy and upset him and he started to raise his voice. He was grabbed by the scruff of the neck and dragged into a cell. The two inmates who were sat having their tea were shocked but they knew who Viv and I were and they just sat as if nothing was happening.

Viv had hold of Jenkins and squeezed the living daylights out of him. I pointed at Viv and then pointed at the kitchen.

'You either fuck Viv in a fight or you fuck the kitchen out of stock,' I said, trying not to laugh. It just seemed funny to me, but I couldn't let myself crack up.

'I would prefer, if it's ok with you two lads, to go with the second option,' he replied.

'You want to fight *Viv Graham*?' I shouted. I knew he didn't but I just wanted to shake him up a bit more.

'No, *no*! I'll fuck the kitchen,' he said. I just wanted to hear him say that, really.

Jenkins was not the fool I initially thought he was. It was a wise move. He asked us exactly what we wanted and I told him six fillet steaks. The expression on his face was a picture.

'Where do you think I'm going to pull six fillet steaks from? We're in Durham prison!'

'We need to see more enthusiasm, Jenkins. And you need to improvise,' I said.

'Next you'll be asking me for the joint of meat I'm just about to cook for D-wing's dinner,' he said.

Me and Viv looked at each other and both turned to him and said, 'That'll do nicely.' Jenkins realised he'd dropped a right clanger and tried to backtrack.

'Oh, no... you can't do this to me. What am I going to feed them? There's 147 prisoners wanting beef on their dinner.'

'Fuck 'em! They can have corned beef,' said Viv.

The doors to the kitchen opened and we saw our opportunity and walked straight in. We saw the big lump of beef and grabbed it and wrapped it up in a clean towel. Viv took hold of it, 'Here, I'll carry it back and if anyone asks what I've got I'll tell them it's my dinner.'

The screws were wary of us all, but especially Viv. He could have carried an entire cow to our cell and no one would have mentioned it. We needed some salt and pepper for seasoning so I grabbed some and we made our way back to the cell, thanking Jenkins on the way and even giving him a spliff for his troubles.

When me and Viv returned to the cell, Davey burst out laughing when he saw the big lump of meat. He knew instantly knew what to do. He was an old prison lag and knew all the tricks of the trade. Before bang-up, we got hold of two metal trays for cooking and then Davey showed us the basics of how to cook in a cell. Of course at this stage of the book, due to health and safety reasons, may I add that cooking in your cell is not allowed in any way, shape or form. I don't know if it had been invented then, but we were about to start on our high protein diets.

We waited until the screws had done their count and had gone home so there was only the skeleton staff on for the night shift. Then it was time to get cracking. I was starving and really looking forward to a good feed. The oven was made by placing a metal tray on a hard table. We then got four tins of equal size and placed the other tray on top of them. We then ripped a length of bed sheet and Davey wrapped it up in a ball around his finger. He slowly pulled his finger out leaving a small well and he squirted olive oil into it. He then placed it between the two trays that were supported by the four tins and lit it. The top tray essentially became a frying pan. We used a makeshift knife – a razorblade melted into a toothbrush handle – to slice the meat. With our pan heating up, Viv placed three large slices of meat in and he blocked the door with newspapers to stop the smell of the cooking going down the landing. He was quite nervous about the whole thing, but his stomach kept him motivated. You see, on the outside Viv was a 100% straight man. He was no criminal in any way, shape or form and he was an honest lad who could have a fight. He'd tell you this himself. The nerves were getting the better of him, so Davey come up with the idea that we would do the cooking and Viv would confront any screws that might want to come in. This idea suited us all down to the ground and Viv was back in his element, working the doors.

The stack sizzled away and we opened a tin of beans to go with it. We still had the pre-packed goodies as well... what a fucking feast, man! We had them with coleslaw, some potato salad and bread and butter with a nice hot cup of tea. Well you can't beat a good cuppa, can you? And, as someone had kindly hoisted the kettle from the education block for us, it would have been rude not to put it to good use. We had it wired up to the light as it was the only source of electricity in the cell.

Fish was shouting from next door, 'You'll have the whole jail stinking of your cooking, you'd better be careful!'

I replied by shouting, 'How would you like your steak, Sir?' and he burst out laughing.

'It'll be an hour or so mate, I've still got some more to cook.'

We tucked in, grinning at each other. Such little victories are sweet in jail and that was certainly a victory for us. It felt good for morale and it was very uplifting moment. Cooking in the cell became a regular occurrence for us with no interference whatsoever from the screws. Everyone on the wing could smell it but the screws just turned a blind eye (or nose) to it all. The screws were more concerned about other matters and they certainly didn't want to confront us. It was like that scene in *Goodfellas* when they make pasta in their cell, slicing the garlic and onions with a razorblade.

As time evolved, the bond between Viv and me became stronger. Anyone who has been in prison for any length of time and shared a cell like me, Davey and Viv will understand. We played cards together, cooked together and went to the gym together. We were a good team. We got to really see different sides of each other and see each other's proper nature coming through the bravado we'd only really seen on the outside. That's where real friendship develops.

Back in those days, a visitor could just turn up and didn't need to be approved and the screws would just come and tell you that someone was there to see you. I had a particularly difficult visit one day and I could feel the tears welling up in my eyes. I didn't want anyone in the visiting room to see the tears; man would understand but a fool would see it as a sign of weakness. My eldest daughter had come to see me with her auntie. She told me that her mother was taking her to live abroad with her and her new boyfriend. It meant I wouldn't see my daughter for 12 years. I was devastated.

Every dad would be. I kept telling her, 'Never forget that your dad loves you,' and she kept telling me she loved me. I kept the tears in until I got back to the cell. It was uncontrollable. I was just so hurt inside and I felt defenceless. Viv came in. He knew I was upset He'd been on the table next to me during the visit and probably overheard the conversation. He reassured me and told me not to worry because things would be OK in the long run. Viv had a big heart and he was very family-orientated. We had a little talk and it was nice that he took time out to do that. He was a good bloke and a good friend.

As time ticked by, me and Davey knew we were up for Judge in Chambers but we had no idea when. Our door was always open, which was great if we wanted to go out and see other friends or socialise, but the downside was that we would have every ponce in the prison at the door because Viv was as green as grass and would give them everything and anything if they had a hard luck story. I mean, he was fucking sound and everything, but because of his good nature, he was sometimes like a social worker. I wished he just told them all to fuck off because he didn't have to be so nice to them; it was a prison, not a support group.

One afternoon, me and Davey had just been sat smoking and playing cards with Viv and, when our game finished, we decided to go for a wander. When we came back, I kicked the door closed and it locked to stop any callers. I lay on my bed, stoned and smoked another spliff. It was decent jail weed, which gets you sleepy and chilled while you listen to your music, but I was disturbed by somebody outside shouting my name over and over. Add that to the weedy high and it starts messing with your mind: *Stephen, Stephen, Stephen...* I tried to stand up but was disorientated. The voice was faint, but it was definitely shouting for me.

'Who is it? What do you want?' There was no reply so I decided I was hearing things. The voice started again but it seemed to be closer and more familiar.

I got up from off my bunk and placed the chair next to the window so I could look out and see outside and I heard the voice again. To my surprise, it was my girlfriend Donna! I put my hand out of the window to indicate I was there.

'What's the matter?' I shouted.

She told me that me and Davey had been given JIC bail. I was delighted and had a big smile on my face. I thanked her and told her I'd see her in a couple of hours. Davey returned to the cell and I told him the good news and he was as delighted as me. The mood soon changed when Viv came into the cell and we told him that we would be leaving him the next day. He was really happy for us, but we were gutted for him as well. I didn't want to leave him there. My good friend Fish was next to arrive and the feeling was the same from him. He cheered me up by saying that he was going to put in for it as well. An hour or so passed and the screws came to get us. We said our goodbyes to Viv and I gave him a cuddle then I got the screw to open the cell to say good bye to Fish and Rob before we left. It was a sad moment for us all, really. Given the circumstances that brought us all to be in the nick together, it felt wrong in a way that we were getting out.

In my opinion, it had taken the system long enough. We'd been remanded for over six months for a fight in a nightclub and the injured party wasn't even pressing charges. They released me and Davey on bail and we got put on a curfew. It was a bit shit, but it was better than being stuck in a cell.

We were on bail for about three months before going back to court for our trial. The trial started and stopped a few times when a deal got put to us to plead guilty on a lesser charge of ABH instead of GBH. We discussed it between ourselves and decided it was the best thing to do. Viv pleaded guilty and admitted to being the sole person who beat up Stuart Watson. Me, Fish, Davey and Rob pleaded guilty to ABH on the grounds that, through our presence, we encouraged Viv and we all received a sentence of two and a half years for witnessing the fight. Viv got 18 months for beating Stuey up and 18 months for beating up a doorman at Madisons nightclub.

CHAPTER 8
ROBBING, SHOOTING AND MARCHING ON

Bentleys nightclub in Newcastle was always a decent night out. We all used to go there a fair bit and in the late 80s it was one of *the* places to be. I was there one night with about half a dozen westenders as well as an unnamed bloke from Gateshead and, as usual, the place was bouncing and there was a good atmosphere. Well, that was until Billy Robinson from Gateshead came in with his entourage in tow. Big Billy was, well... pretty big as it happens: about six-foot-three and 20 stone of muscle. He was a former heavyweight fighter who was very agile and nobody's fool; definitely not someone to just ignore. Not that you could ignore the fucker even if you tried.

In those days, Billy was not shy to lift his hands to anyone he came across. He had a fierce fighting reputation throughout the region and was looked upon by many as the best fighting man around. To give you more insight to this big lump; as another string to his bow, Billy was also Viv Graham's mentor. There was an infamous straightener between Billy and Ernie Bewick, the big fucker in Sunderland who used to run the doors. As Viv knew both of them, he was present at the fight and it's been said that he lamped Ernie when he wasn't looking so that he could save Billy from a pasting. In this business, every big tough man is always out to prove himself. Reputations are made in the time it takes to swing a punch and with Billy essentially being anti-West End, saw me and the people I was with and immediately made a beeline for the bloke from Gateshead.

He shouted disrespectful things to him about Gateshead people socialising with westenders. What a racist! He went a bit further though and attacked the Gateshead bloke, but it was broken up quite quickly. As you can imagine, our friend from Gateshead was not at all happy about the attack. Unknown to Billy, our friend also had a 12" blade on him that he could easily have used at any time – during the attack or after – but I'd already anticipated that and took it off him. Thanks to me, Billy got to leave the club without the blade in him. Although he wasn't from the West End, that friend was in our company and we felt obliged to look after him. He was with us and that's how it goes. Fights on nights out were pretty normal. I suppose more so because of our kind of work and the circles by which we move; so something like that wasn't really a showstopper for any of us – it was shrugged off and back to business as usual; more drinks, more laughs and more fun.

We carried on with our night and ended up at a party in Gateshead in a small downstairs flat owned by a lass called Carol. All *back to my place* parties were always heaving; they were just an excuse to carry on drinking when pubs or clubs kicked you out. And this being in a tiny flat, even a few people would have made it seem packed. I was with my friends Fish Tams, Davey Hindmarsh and a few others and around an hour or so later, Billy arrived with his entourage and he was *full* of himself: ladies and gentlemen, the ego has landed. He didn't like the fact that us westenders were at a party in Gateshead... *his* Gateshead. It was plain to see that something would kick off sooner rather than later. The second he walked in, he brought a dark mood and atmosphere over the place.

Billy was in no mood to reason. I knew of his ability for knocking people out, so my hackles were up as soon as I saw him. He approached me and asked what I was doing there in an aggressive tone… it was like he thought we were rubbing his nose in it. There was no doubt in my mind that this man thought that if we clashed he'd come out on top. He tried to frighten me with his size and overpower me with his voice. He was right in me personal space and I was starting to get a bit twitchy. Inside though; I was agitated that he thought he could get away with talking to me like that. I didn't like this one bit. His big face was right in mine and I wasn't intimidated and didn't give a fuck who he thought he was. In an equally aggressive tone, I told him that I was looking for somebody. This got his back up and he asked me who I was looking for. I told him a man called Jimmy Fear. Billy told me he was getting paid for looking after Jimmy and if anyone had a problem with Jimmy then they'd have to go through him first.

'What you got to say about that?' he asked. He was so close that his face was almost touching mine as he spoke. I wouldn't have minded if he was a smart bewer, but he wasn't and I was starting to lose what little patience I had.

He could see by my expression that I was very unhappy with his attitude. At that moment, and unknown to him, I had a firm grip on the razor sharp foot-long blade hidden down the back of my coat. I could have ended the party right there and then.

I knew that whatever I replied with, he was going to attack me, so my response was to look him in the eye.

'My advice to you is don't stand too close to Jimmy, because when we do him we'll do *you* next!'

He immediately waved his bear-like hand towards me and started removing a ring from his finger while telling me to come into the kitchen. I followed him, but it was full of people off their nuts on pills.

'Get outside,' he said.

I obliged; I walked out behind him and closed the door to keep 'our business' between the two of us.

'I know someone is there,' he said.

'Eh?' Who was he talking to now?

I didn't know what he was on about at first, but as I turned to him from closing the door, he was looking the other way. I was expecting him to be ready to fight. Then I saw a man with a balaclava on and a sawn-off shot gun walk out from a shadow. 'Fucking brilliant,' I thought. 'It just gets better... a fight as well as having to dodge bullets.'

In these situations, people tend to say that time goes into slow motion, like in a film. It's only because they keep replaying it back in their head and see it like a film, reliving it as many times as they want. We all know time doesn't slow down. It wasn't *The Matrix* and Billy wasn't Keanu Reeves by any stretch. For me it's the opposite; it happens so quickly you don't really know *how* to react. You're certainly not prepared for it, you just rely on your instinct to kick in and you do your thing and get the fuck out of Dodge in one piece. I suppose there are those of us who are a bit more used to guns and violence, and we have a slightly different instinct by which to rely. But Billy's instinct was definitely a bit different... he grabbed hold of me by the shoulders and pushed me towards the gunman, using me as a human shield! See my earlier thought: *Fucking brilliant*! Again, hardly time to react to it, but I was in the grip of this huge bearlike geezer who was trying to avoid getting shot. He was strong, that's for sure. It was split-second thinking on his part.

The gunman must have been there for a reason though, and his timing was perfect; 'Stephen! Move... *move*!' he shouted.

I was trying to! The last thing I expected was a shotgun-wielding bloke with a knack for stating the obvious. I struggled for a good few seconds before I managed to push Billy away from me and back towards the door. He regained his composure and scrambled his way back into the flat. The gunman discharged his first shot and missed him, but it went off very close to my left side. My hands were raised up high, which had probably stopped me getting hit. If they were by my side, it would have took half of my arm clean off. The blast and the flash of the light was dazzling in the pitch black yard and, for some unknown reason, Billy came back out and shouted, 'You'll never walk in this town again, son,' to the gunman. No doubt the gunman was thinking the same thing and shot Billy in the leg just above the kneecap before fleeing the scene. Talk about a surreal moment! There's a saying about being stuck between a rock and a hard place... here I was stuck between a fighting man and a bad man –

and the bad man had a gun. I could think of better places to be stuck.

Meanwhile, Billy was in no state to make any fast moves. He was on the floor with a very big hole in his leg and was losing a lot of blood, so we would need to act quickly if we wanted to keep him alive. The colour was draining from his face, but he managed to hobble back over to the door. Two of his friends came outside and started charging toward me, thinking I was the shooter. I knocked one of them out and, by then, my friend Davey Hindmarsh was on the scene and he floored the other one. The rest of the party-goers were still dancing in the kitchen, oblivious to what had just happened a few yards from them.

We couldn't get hold of a phone to call for an ambulance or a taxi, so I offered to take Billy in my car. Even though he was in excruciating pain, he was concerned because he thought he was about to be taken away and finished off. Fair enough, though. The shooter had obviously known who I was and Billy would have put two and two together. It probably had looked dodgy, but the shooter turning up was as much of a surprise to me as it was to him. I was only offering to drive him to the hospital; it was the very least I could do, even though he'd just tried to use me as a bulletproof vest. In that amount of pain, I assume your mind would be all over the place; he was in a bad state of shock and wasn't looking good at all. We got him into a car and my good friend Fish Tams took him to the hospital.

Word spreads quickly in our world and when one of our local pubs got word that I'd had trouble in Gateshead, they deserted the lock-in and started arriving at Carol's party by the taxi load. When people heard that Billy had been shot there wasn't many tears shed either. He'd fought and bashed many a westender over the years and people saw it as karma. I've always had respect for the man though. Yeah, he was trying to intimidate me that night and I don't take kindly to that sort of behaviour. I was cut from different cloth.

There are always big names like Billy who come and go. There's always a power struggle, always someone waiting in the wings to take over. You can't do what we do without upsetting people from time to time and I can only assume that one of those people went looking for Billy that night to settle a score. Full respect to the bloke, he'd been there and done it and was always a formidable character that not many messed with in a hurry.

Hello darkness my old friend. I've come to talk to you again...

The winter closed in and the dark nights arrived and Simon and Garfunkel's lyrics seemed fitting as their voices came through the radio speakers. Word was going around that there was a big bit of work in the offing. If it was true then this was going to take the lads who did the job to the next level. This was the big one; a potential retirement fund for whoever had the balls to do it.

The job was plotted up in a bar in Gateshead. The possible haul was in the region of £5m; the region's biggest wages snatch and enough to put a smile on any villain's face. Their plan started to take shape: the money was to be picked up from a depot in Washington and transferred under heavy security to Pritchard Security depot in Gateshead.

Two lads were assigned to monitor every movement the cash van made over a month-long period. Any deviations from route or change in times were noted and recorded. Another meet took place and they shared their information with the rest of the gang. It wasn't good news though. The van was always followed by two undercover police vehicles with three occupants in one vehicle and four in the other. There was also an undercover police motorbike in tow.

Simon and Garfunkel's song seemed very ironic now: *The Sound of Silence...* a very uncomfortable silence. They realised that there was no chance of stopping the van without a massive shootout with the police. The only other option was to do the depot. The two lads were set a new task: find a way in. Another meet was set for a month's time.

And so a month later, the lads turned up at a safe house for a meet. The two lads who'd been staking out the depot were already there and the reassuring smiles on their faces said it all.

'This graft is ours, lads. We can get in.'

The recce mission had paid off. They'd noticed that when the security staff left the building there was no other security staff in place to lock the door after them. Better still, the second door was wedged open and had been every time the front door had been opened. It wasn't a high security door... or, if it was, the staff were not following the correct procedures and this meant the door could easily be smashed open. The graft was on and they were going to go for it. A five-man team meant a million pound payday for each of them.

The graft was put together and the cars were put in place. The cars used for the robbery were a Sierra Cosworth and a big wide top-of-the-range Audi. These vehicles were specifically chosen because of their speed, power and the size of their boots to stick the haul in. Both cars were white to resemble police vehicles, which would help in the getaway.

On the day of the robbery, the firm was plotted up in a car park about half a mile away from the depot. Two spotter vehicles were used and it was them who returned to give the lads the green light.

The Audi and the Cosworth made their way to the security depot while the two spotter vehicles stayed in the vicinity in case of any unforeseen circumstances that might cause problems. Outside the depot, they pulled up and the balaclavas were rolled down over faces and the shotguns cocked. The staff had no idea what was going to hit them as the cars reversed into the car park and all five men got out and opened the boots and back doors. One of them stood on guard with a pump-action shotgun cocked ready and waiting for anyone that dared to challenge them. The other four approached the door and the whole procedure was second nature to them. They were almost clinical in their approach. One of the lads took aim with a sledgehammer, drew it back and smashed it once then a second time before it gave way and was forced open. The lads wasted no time and ran into the building. There were three rooms with staff in.

Three of the gang took a room each and told the staff to get face down on the floor. There were no heroes and all fifteen members of staff complied within seconds. The fourth gunman stood in the passageway with his finger on the trigger. It was enough of a deterrent. There were five big safes in the depot and four of them were already open and full to the brim with boxes of money, around six-feet-high and three wide. The lads wasted no time and started emptying them, grabbing as much as they could and taking it out to the waiting cars then back again for more. When the two car boots were full, one of them shouted, 'Time, *time!*'

Everyone knew what that meant. At the same time, 'Armed robbery in progress. All armed vehicles to attend Prichard Security depot, Gateshead,' was heard over the scanner. The lads jumped into the cars and spun off at high speed over Gateshead flyover with blue lights flashing on the inside of their vehicles. This part of the plan worked to perfection. As it was dark, people who saw two white cars with blue flashing lights presumed they were the police and pulled over to let them pass. As they drove along the flyover they passed the armed police who were rushing towards the depot. *Priceless*. Not even the Rapid Response Unit could catch them!

As they came to the Tyne Bridge the traffic lights were all green. This suited the lads as they'd hit over 100mph coming towards the Swan House roundabout and had no time for stopping. They turned off and headed into an estate in Byker... the appropriately named Blagdon Close. The police scanner went haywire as the lads unloaded the bags into a transit van as quickly as they'd nabbed it. The whole thing had gone like clockwork and the detailed planning had paid off. Big time.

They knew they'd got away with a few quid but they didn't know how much. The money sacks stretched from the seats at the front of the van all the way to the doors at the back. It was the fucking jackpot! With the van packed up, they set off for a safe house in Heaton and discreetly pulled into a back lane and to the side of the adjoining garage where they emptied the van as quickly and as quietly as possible. The garage was a lovely bit smother (secluded) so nobody could see them. Once the van was empty it was taken away and destroyed, leaving two of the lads at the house to count the money up. Typically, the bulb had gone in the living room light so one of them pulled out a torch. This was where things went pear-shaped.

Unknown to the gang, the lad who'd let them use the house while he was away hadn't told his daughter that someone would be there in his absence. And she just happened to be in her own living room – just over the road – and looked out the window at that precise moment and saw the torchlight. Presuming her dad's house was being burgled, she called the police.

The two lads inside were Alan Minniken and Geoffrey Whelans. They tried to escape but were arrested in the backyard. The police walked into the house and were amazed to find millions of pounds in bags lying on the floor. It was the polar opposite of a burglary and a great result for

Northumbria Police. For the lads it was like winning the lottery before realising they'd lost their ticket. Minniken and Whelans and George McFadyen were charged with the '£300k armed robbery'. This was laughable. The card marker was quite clear that the haul would be in the millions – not thousands – and the fact that the haul filled the back of a transit tells a different story as well. They got their money back but decided to claim that they had only had £300k stolen to stop their insurance premiums rocketing. It's not just blaggers that are dishonest!

All this left a bitter taste in the lads' mouth. I mean, talk about bad luck. A few weeks went by and it was no surprise that our John got some special attention from the Regional Crime Squad. At Prime Minister's Questions in the House of Commons, a local MP stood up and said he wished to re-name Tyneside 'bandit country', as per population there was more robberies committed on Tyneside than anywhere else in the country. All this managed to achieve was to pile the pressure on Northumbria Police and they needed to find a scapegoat. And they found one; my brother John Henry Sayers.

At that time, he was on police bail for some minor traffic offence and was due to attend the police station, but when he got there the Regional Crime Squad had other ideas. They arrested him and kept him for a couple of days and then charged him. He was interviewed and then taken to his cell where one of the policemen tried to start up a conversation with him. He told him there had been £3.3m stolen in the robbery and that they'd come close to catching them, but lost them at some point around the Tyne Bridge. He also said that they'd been instructed to shoot the robbers if they caught up with them. That order apparently came from someone high up in the force. These comments got no response from my brother and he went back to his cell. John was hit with a voluntary bill of indictment, meaning that he'd miss all minor court appearances and would be fast tracked to Crown Court, which was unheard of at the time. It left his legal team baffled. They had seven weeks to prepare his defence.

A High Court judge was assigned to the case and the evidence against John was very weak but the police had another trick up their sleeve: a handpicked witness who they'd managed to get to say exactly what they wanted. Philip Bourge was a former security guard who had worked for Pritchard Security (just for the record, he was not the card marker for the job; it was all lies). He was on remand in HMP Leeds and while he was there he repeatedly told anyone who'd listen that he was in for the crime of armed robbery. Northumbria Police said he was the man who was guilty of supplying the inside information about the robbery. In other words, they said he was the card marker. In the exercise yard he seemed to mix in his own little crowd and he would tell his friends that Northumbria Police showed him a photograph of a man he had never seen before and this man's name was John Henry Sayers. They had told him that if he did not pick John Henry Sayers out on of an identification parade and give evidence against him that he would receive a custodial sentence of fifteen years.

However, if he did as he was told he'd receive a two-year sentence.

This must have been on his mind 24/7 because he'd say the same thing all the time – that he'd never met John Henry Sayers before. That was just what our John's solicitors wanted to hear. Three of Bourge's friends all made the same statement to their own solicitors, corroborating Bourge's claim that he had never met our John.

The trial began in 1989 and I went to court to give him my support. It was full of undercover policemen all shaking their heads at any words that John's defence barrister said. This was clearly an attempt to influence the jury, as the evidence against my brother was so poor it consisted of one man and one man only. John called his witnesses and his witness statements were also read out. The judge dismissed John's witnesses and assured the jury that no deal whatsoever had been made by Northumbria Police or Phillip Bourge.

Halfway through the trial there was an application by our John's defence team, led by Mr Richard Louden, to have the case thrown out due to the lack of evidence. Again the judge ignored their plea. The trial came to a close and both sides made their final summaries before the jury was ushered out to consider their verdict. We felt confident. When the jury returned and the foreman was asked if they had made a decision on all of the defendants, he said they had.

Our John and George were found guilty of all charges and were each sentenced to 15 years. They were seen as the ringleaders. Alan and Geoff fared slightly better getting 13 years each, while Fisher got three years for his involvement. There wasn't much reaction in the public gallery but the police were grinning like Cheshire Cats and others were heard cheering outside the courtroom. I was sick to my stomach. My brother and I stared at each other across the court we nodded and winked, but showed no other emotion.

The MPs got their scapegoat and the police got their man. It's not a crime to be a Sayers, but yes, we do get punished for being one!

I will never forget coming out of that courtroom. I was greeted in the hallway by about 15 or so policemen all celebrating as if their team had just won the FA Cup final. Those celebrations went on well into the night I was reliably informed. I headed back to Newcastle and to my mother's house. I parked at the top of York Street and, as I walked to her front door she was pulling up in the car. She got out and started walking towards me. Nobody knows you better than your mother and she took one look at me and she knew straight away. She collapsed to the ground and started screaming relentlessly. I'd never seen my mother like this before. She was inconsolable. She had lost her first child stillborn and this to her was like losing another son. I managed to get her indoors and her friends and family came to show their support. It was a heart-wrenching experience. I felt helpless. I couldn't ease her pain and didn't know what to do. It made me realise that the career we'd chosen did not just affect us personally but it hurt our loved ones at home when things didn't go to plan. The phone rang constantly over the next few days with messages from all over the country sending best wishes and support. I was gutted and my head was battered.

We lost the battle but we hadn't lost the war. We had to do as we always did – stick together; never let them grind us down and carry on through it. There was the appeal to concentrate on and we had to do everything that we could.

Prior to the appeal in 1990, there was a lot of talk amongst the lads about creating some publicity for it. We had a couple of journalists interested in our next move, which was a good start, and we just had to hatch a plan to get exposure for our cause. We all came to the decision to join together and have a march through Newcastle city centre. Why the hell not? Every fucker else does it. We prepared as best as we could, not really knowing what we were doing.

And we found out just how much preparation you needed for this kind of thing; for starters you can't just march through the streets. How ridiculous! That's what a march is! But you have to do it the right way or end up doing more bad than good. We went to our solicitors and he told us that we would have to register the march with Northumbria Police to keep everything legal. We expected problems with this, but we ticked all the boxes and we were granted permission. I was rather surprised by this because I thought they'd want to silence us as much as possible. Next we had to prepare the banners. This was difficult. None of us were budding Tony Harts and it took around six weeks to put them all together. The main reason behind this was that we had to find the biggest, thickest poles possible, just in case anything kicked off during the march – we'd be prepared for anything and we were certainly mob-handed.

On the day of the march around 700 people turned up at the starting point on Elswick Road. The crowd stretched from the Blue Man pub to The Dodds Arms. It was a 1pm start but I had made sure that everyone had arrived by midday. There was a strong, positive and uplifting atmosphere amongst the crowd; a real buzz and you could tell that people actually *believed* in what we were doing. And it would have been a pointless exercise without that belief. I moved the starting point of the march without telling the police due to the vast numbers of people that had turned up. It was more for safety than anything else, but one copper took the hump and started shouting at me to get the crowd back to the arranged spot. There's always one, isn't there? As the crowd was in a good mood, people started booing the copper and shouting back at him, which he didn't find too amusing. It was brilliant – he instantly became a pantomime baddy and I was half expecting someone to lob some rotten tomatoes at him... we could easily have got hold of some! Although Freddy Mills, better known locally as Fred the Head, went one better. He ran past me with one of the eight-foot-long poles that the banners were being held up with. He had it up in the air like a lance as though he was going jousting, then lowered it as he got the outspoken policeman in his sights and chased him around his police car a couple of times. Even though the policeman wasn't hit, hurt or injured, he screamed like a baby at the top of his voice. It was brilliant entertainment!

As 1pm approached, the crowd grew bigger and bigger. Another overzealous policeman decided to act like, well... a typical policeman. He drove past the crowd at high speed and then slammed his brakes on and came to a skidding halt. He immediately jumped out of his car and slammed the door while shouting very aggressively that he was personally going to stop and cancel this march. He was pulled to one side by an inspector who told him in no uncertain terms to stop making a fool of himself. It was all quality viewing and it just made our spirits grow stronger because it unified us in our *us against them*-ness. It was already a march about an injustice and, with the coppers acting like they were, it made it all the more poignant.

I spoke to the crowd using a megaphone and I told them that we were ready to start and told them what the route would be. I lead the march with our John's oldest daughter. We walked along Elswick Road and then down Westgate Hill (which has now become another infamous Sayers landmark. More on that later). The crowd swelled and swelled as we made our way through Newcastle city centre. By the time we got to Northumberland Street, we were over 2,000 strong and most of the town was at a standstill. The police asked us to speed the march up and I politely told them, with the help of my trusty megaphone, to go and fuck themselves. I told them it will be finished when it is finished. You can't put a time limit on a fucking peaceful rally! This didn't go down to well with them and one policeman threatened me. I stormed towards him and I could see the fear in his face. I reminded him man to man that he was powerless to do anything to me. An arrest – especially *my* arrest – on that day of all days would not have been good PR for the police at all. We continued along Percy Street and there was a lot of noise and animosity towards the police. It was obvious that they were trying to provoke a reaction and I'm pleased to say that no one rose to it. We kept our dignity and made our point. I'm sure they were hoping that something would kick off.

We did our best and the march was as successful as it could have been. We finished back on Elswick Road where I thanked everyone for attending and we got a great write-up in the papers the following day. Now it was time to focus on the appeal itself.

Our John hired the services of Michael Mansfield QC who was looked upon at the time as one of the top QCs in the country. He was to look at the PACE Act (Police and Criminal Evidence), which was brought in specifically to prevent miscarriages of justice. We felt John's case fell into that category and hopefully Mr Mansfield would be the man to prove it.

We stayed in a hotel in London the day before the appeal; there were about 30 of us and our hopes were high. Mr Mansfield presented the case like any expert would and proved that the act had been broken on numerous occasions by Northumbria Police, but unfortunately this fell on deaf ears. The judges took no notice of Mr Mansfield and it seemed as though they had their own agenda. The evidence was staring them in the face! It's amazing to think that the law of the land would install a procedure to prevent miscarriages of justice taking place and then totally disregard it. John lost his appeal and it was a very sad day for us all. I was devastated and so was our Michael. God only knows how my mother would take it. John was taken back to prison and we headed home.

CHAPTER 9
MEET LEE DUFFY

Lee Duffy was a young man from Middleborough who was about 17 stone, naturally built, and a good amateur boxer and excellent street fighter. A total all-rounder, Duffy was basically a no-nonsense attack fighter who was as game as any man could possibly be. He enjoyed fighting and would take anyone on and any number of people at a time; nothing fazed him about fighting.

Generally, when you hear Lee's name in conversation or see it in print, the next name to follow is Viv Graham. And then debate as to who would have won in a fight. Who really knows? Would Mike Tyson beat Bruce Lee, would Chuck Norris beat blah-blah-blah, would Ron beat Reg? It's all impossible to know! Everyone can guess with Viv and Duffy, and everyone continues to even now. I had a lot of time for Duffy and a lot of respect and classed him as my friend. Yes, Viv was also a street fighter but he fought on the opposite side of the fence to Duffy; Duffy fought on *our* side.

We first got to know each other on my home leave from Acklington, where I served my sentence for the Hobo's carry on and we had a party at Masters (Tup Tup Palace) to celebrate my return to civilisation. There were about 200 or so of us and it was a really good atmosphere. A lot of my travelling cousins turned up with their friends from up Bedlington and Ashington way – quality lads.

I was in the toilet when one of my brothers walked in with Lee and we were introduced. He first met Michael when they'd both received four-year prison sentences the same day for unrelated crimes and they became firm friends. Duffy got out six months later and their friendship continued.

Duffy went into one of the cubicles and produced a big bag of gak and he and a few others sniffed a line and then asked if I wanted one. I declined, but a few others joined in with him. As they were racking up, three doormen from another venue walked in and when one of them saw what Duffy and his mates were doing he said, 'You can't do that in here, mate.'

I asked him if he worked there. He didn't.

'Well what *fuck* does this have to do with you, then?!'

These doormen didn't recognise my face and I wasn't about to tell them who I was. They certainly knew my name.

'Can you fight?' I asked. I didn't ask just the one I was talking to; it was an open question to the three of them. A Mexican stand-off ensued. It was like a scene from a Sergio Leone film with everyone stood silent, eyes narrowing, waiting... until the silence was broken as Duffy lurched forward, throwing a combination of deadly punches. He wiped the three mugs out in a couple of seconds and I can honestly say I was really impressed with his fighting ability and gameness. Neither of them had time to react, he was *that* fast.

Duffy was on a roll, the red mist had him at that point: 'Go and get Viv Graham and I'll do the same to him,' he told them. They were in no fit state to go and get Viv, but the gauntlet was laid down and a clash was always on the cards for those two. There was no doubt in my mind that Duffy would be more than a match for Viv Graham. Let's not forget, a friend of my called Manni Burgo beat Viv in a boxing match, so he was beatable.

Back in Masters, the bouncers carried the unconscious bouncers out of the toilets and, as they were nursing their injuries, they pointed us out to them. The expression on their faces was priceless when they realised who they'd just ran into. You could see the shock and fear come over and, with Duffy being Duffy, he had to be held back as he was wanting to knock the other doormen out as well. He was shouting, 'Go and get ya fighting men. I'll do the best of them,' but the last thing these people wanted was more trouble. The whole place could have gone up. The 200 guests wanted to fight with the doormen and I had to keep reminding people I was on home leave... for fighting in nightclubs. I defused the situation with the doormen that had been beaten up and they came over and apologised, shook our hands and bought us a bottle of champagne before making a sharp exit. With Duffy being in that kind of mood, they didn't want to be anywhere near him.

Duffy would always say, 'Stephen, a good big boxer will always beat a good little one from a lower weight division.' Lee feared no man, loved a scrap and, when he was out in Newcastle, he represented the West End. He was on a collision course with Viv and we all knew it and Lee was not shy in telling anyone who'd listen that he wanted a straightner with him. This news travelled back to Viv and he was in no doubt that Duffy was different and dangerous to all the others he'd faced and he was wary of him. At the time there was a certain high-ranking policeman who'd taken it upon himself to try and bar us from the city for being Sayers. It was discrimination, of that there is no doubt.

We would always do our rounds of the bars and clubs and finish the night off at Walkers. We also started drinking in a place called Buzz bar, near Central Station. There was quite a few of us out one night and word came round that the bizzies and Viv Graham were saying that we were not allowed in Maceys. We were waiting for something like this to happen. As you know, telling us we can't come in somewhere is like putting petrol on a fire. We were as game as can be and we knew a lot of doormen who fancied themselves as fighters would be drinking in Maceys that night, so we just let it tick along until we were all ready. I looked at my watch and gave my brother and Duffy the nod and told them, 'It's time,' and they new instinctively what I meant. We gathered about 20 of the lads along with six or so special guests. These lads stood back and waited to be called upon, if needed.

We made our way down to Maceys and we just walked up to the doormen.

'Who the fuck says the Sayers brothers are barred from here?' I asked.

There was a lot of them maybe 20 drinking and another five or six working the front door, so it was even numbers. Duffy did four of them in the space of seconds, they went down and there was no holding him back. He was better than me or anybody else for that matter; we hardly had to do anything. He was that good; he could make any fighter on the planet look like shit. It became the Duffy Show and he just knocked them out for fun. You have to bear in mind that some of these lads were 20-stone plus – it didn't matter to him.

In the middle of it all, I heard one of the doormen who was stood next to the window shout, 'Come on, Duffy. I'll fight yer!' Duffy, who at that stage was having a whale of a time knocking anything that moved spark out, reacted to this doorman's challenge by springing forward and sparking him too. He then turned and sprung back and knocked out the other two doormen who were with him. They were like loads of baby dinosaurs lying on the street and nobody would go near him. Duffy shouted that he was with the Sayers brothers and wanted to fight Viv Graham. So, having battered the fuck out of Viv's pals and telling everyone in earshot that he wants Viv next, it became a waiting game. You could imagine the reports that Viv got back that night from his pals.

Viv knew he had a major problem on his hands. The next morning I was awoken by the phone. I answered. It was my dad and he wanted to see me at his house urgently. I headed over, head thumping and, as I walked into his front room, I was greeted by the sight of my dad and Viv. My hangover cleared quickly. Dad explained that Viv had come to see him asking if he could straighten things out between him and Duffy. He could n't understand what he had done to upset him and wanted to make the peace. My dad has always been a fair man and had agreed to speak to all parties. He rang Duffy and, after explaining the situation, passed the phone to Viv. He then pulled me to one side and told me that this should be an end to the issue. Viv looked relieved as he handed the receiver back to my dad. Win, lose or draw, there was no getting away from it: if this fight had taken place, both men would have known about it! Nothing more was said. We all exchanged handshakes and Viv was gone. The fight that many would have paid to see would never take place.

Being in the thick of things gives me a golden opportunity to pass judgement on both of their fighting abilities. The majority of people passing judgement had never seen anyone with Viv's ability before. He was a good fighter in Newcastle. I'm a well travelled man and know of many other characters in the country who could also fight just like Viv... or even better. Alan Wheat from Salford was a very good professional boxer who also got roided up and Davey Ash from Huyton was a martial arts expert. People seem to forget that Viv was a boxer who used to fight people who had reputations, but they never really trained or learned *how* to fight.

So, how do you call the fight that never was? There will always be speculation. Viv had definitely not come across anyone like Duffy before and Lee was just fucking badass. He fought with bad intentions, but I think it's impossible for anyone to predict the outcome. Our family were on good terms with Viv, so it was difficult for us because no one wants to choose between mates having a rick, do they?

The police continued their campaign against our family and started threatening individual doormen, telling them that if they let us in they could lose their jobs. That didn't work, so the next tactic was to tell the bar owners that they could lose their license if they allowed us onto their premises. This didn't work either as we would turn up at the licensee's home and ask them why they wouldn't let us in. That one always seemed to do the trick! The police went back to the drawing board and some bright spark came up with the idea of licensing doormen. They also created a scheme called Pubwatch. Yes, this is when it all started. The only way they could deal with us was to change the law of the land.

I'd been out for five days and the party hadn't even started. Our bond with Duffy became stronger and stronger in a very short time. He was never away from Newcastle and we went down to Middlesbrough a few times too. On one occasion we ended up in a 'blues' – a house on a terraced street turned in to a bar/drug den and a whore house, all in one. I'd seen these types of places before in various cities across England such as Bristol, Birmingham and Manchester and they all had a very similar feel about them: danger. When we arrived we saw a certain firm of men that Duffy did not get along with. He wasn't one for small talk so he attacked them and knocked quite a few of them out.

A week later at the same blues, someone shouted for Duffy to come outside. The man had a Geordie accent. When he got outside to see what was going on, Duffy was shot in the leg. The injury wasn't life-threatening, but this was clearly a warning from somebody. Duffy foolishly signed himself out of hospital within a few days and came up to see us in Newcastle and we insisted he stayed with us.

We put him up in one of our houses and got a Cockney stripper to look after him. Looking back on it that was a bit of a counterproductive move as she had the most perfect body and was running round the house in a nurse's uniform. Duffy was there for rest and relaxation and something like that was probably bad for his blood pressure. We thought she would have lifted his spirits but she seemed to drain the life out of him and he looked in a worse condition after those three days with her than he did after being shot! I'm joking but also being serious. I replaced her with her friend who was, unfortunately for Duffy, not as forthcoming as the stripper and the mother of one of the lads cooked for him, making sure he ate well. And you know what? Plenty of old-fashioned homemade food brought colour back into his cheeks. His mind was certainly on the mend, but physically the shooting took its toll on him.

Despite us telling him he could stay as long as he wanted, he was beginning to get homesick. Lee would not have it; he wanted to return to Middlesbrough. Trying to keep him in Newcastle was very difficult. We were just doing what we thought was best for him, or what we *knew* was best for him. I could see he had the heart of a lion. He was a proud man and he wanted revenge... but he needed to get himself fit first. You can be a lion, but an injured one will never fare well, no matter how big they are. The problem he faced was not knowing who'd shot him because he'd had so much trouble in his life. You know the score – someone like Lee Duffy will have a lot of friends, but also a lot of enemies. He asked me to put the feelers out and to speak to certain people, which I did. Before he returned home he thanked us for our friendship and I gave him a bulletproof vest to wear.

The next time I saw him he had a bag with a couple of guns in: a handgun and a shotgun. I asked him if the guns were really necessary. He was completely paranoid.

'Stephen, I believe my life is in danger and those people are going to come back and kill me,' he said.

He asked for my opinion on his situation; I told him I would rather be judged by 12 then carried by six anytime (12 being the jurors and the six being the pallbearers carrying the coffin). He smiled at that and gave me a wink and was gone.

There was a lot going for us in Newcastle at that time. We had our fingers in a lot of pies and business was booming. Duffy arrived back in Middlesbrough and I received a phone call from my good friend Lee Harrison, who told me that him and his dad Tommy Harrison were going to take Duffy under their wing and look after him until his injuries healed. Lee and Tommy were close friends of Duffy and he always spoke well of them, so it was nice to know that he'd be in safe hands. He looked at old Tommy as a father figure and you could see they had a close bond. I've also got a lot of time for those people. I haven't seen them in many years but I wish them well in all they are doing.

I kept asking Duffy to move to Newcastle but he wouldn't have it. He would say that he'd love to but he couldn't because it would look like he was running away from his troubles in Middlesbrough. He wanted to face things head on. It was the only way he knew.

The next time he was shot, there were three people; two with guns and when Duffy set eyes on them, he knew what their intentions were. He immediately attacked them and knocked two of the three out and then wrestled with the third one. He told me he managed to get his hands on the gun and force gun down from his head, but unfortunately the gunman discharged the gun and shot Duffy in the foot. The gunman should count himself lucky that the bullet hit Duffy that night.

And then it happened. Lee was killed in a street fight in August 1991. Having already survived attempts on his life, getting a blade plunged into him just under his left arm was one too many. He was no saint, as we know. He was only 26. The fight with David Allison started in a club in Middlesbrough and ended up in a car park outside. Apparently Lee was coked up and getting the better of David, and was smashing his head into the ground. Allison also had a duster on him, but it hadn't bothered Lee in the slightest. But it ended when someone threw a blade over to Allison and he stuck Lee with it. I wasn't there, but it sounds like Lee probably wouldn't have stopped that night – it was kill or be killed.

I remember when the news came through. A lot of westenders were devastated. Me, my dad, Manny Burgo and my cousins Michael and Terry Patters went through to pay our respects and speak to his family. His mam and his brother were there and they were inconsolable. While I was down there I made it my business to call in to see our friends the Harrisons; Tommy and his son, Lee. On the day of the funeral it felt like the whole of the West End wanted to pay its respects. I booked a 56-seater coach and a 16-seater mini bus. There was a pickup truck full of flowers and another 20 or so cars that made the journey about 120 in all.

I have been to a quite a few funerals in my time but Duffs' was by far the biggest. It's the first and only funeral I have been to where crash barriers had to be put up for the crowds. The church was full and there was any amount of people outside the church and lining up from the church to the cemetery which was a couple of miles away. There were a few thousand there, lining the streets to pay their respects. The service went off without any issues and we toasted his memory. It was some send off for him. I hope wherever he is, he's found peace.

CHAPTER 10
COULD EVERYONE STOP GETTING SHOT?

In the early 90s I moved back to the West End. It's always a bit strange moving back to your old area. One side of you takes comfort in the familiarity and the sense of belonging, while the other side of you thinks, 'How the fuck did I end up back here?' It's best not to dwell on the negative side of it though. There are worse places to be than back where you belong.

I lived in a two bedroomed downstairs flat in Stanton Street with my common-law wife Donna, and our two children: young Stephen (aka Moe) and Stevie Lee. The flat itself was like most flats – too small – so I decided to buy a house on Grange Road in Fenham; a three bedroomed semi-detached job with two sitting rooms and very spacious. If you had one and you could pick it up, there was more than enough room to swing a tiger. It had a big garden at the back and a car park at the front; perfect. It didn't take us long to get settled in and find our feet and it really felt like it was a good move on every level. To top it all off, there was a pub not far from us in Cowgate called The Ord, which was owned by a friend of mine called Cecil Levy. Cecil was a lovely natured lad and as strong as a bull. I'd known him for a good while and, to give you an idea of his strength, when he was a lad his party piece was to get a six-inch nail and bend it in half. Not bad, eh?

At this time, our Michael was using The Ord as his local. A few of the lads like Tommy Dillon, Richy Hall, Billy

Dixon and a few others were regulars in there as well. The bar itself was not flash or fancy. That kind of bar just wouldn't have suited the locals, if you know what I mean. It was Cowgate afterall, not Knightsbridge. Kick-offs were a common occurrence and I'm not just talking about the blokes. Most Monday lunchtimes you'd see a woman screaming at her bloke outside the boozer because he'd just blown the family's money on a dodgy tip or pissed it against a wall over the weekend. Some lasses wouldn't waste their time screaming and would just attack their man with different things like ashtrays, glass bottles and any other bar paraphernalia they could get their hands on. So, just to reiterate: Cowgate is a pretty rough place. It's that rough, badger's arses avoid it.

A friend of ours Nigel Abadom had just recently been released from prison and he didn't have a place to stay, so we asked Cecil if he could have the flat above the bar for a while until he had got himself back on his feet. Cecil had no issues with that and he gave Nigel a set of keys. Over the years, the amount of mates who have been in that similar situation is unreal. But that's what mates do – help each other out when they hit hard times. The best thing is that you know they'll always bounce back and take you out for a few drinks as well! Win-win! On the day Nigel moved in around a dozen or so of us met up in the bar and went through to the lounge to wait for him while he was upstairs in his new bachelor pad. It would have been rude not to have a couple of drinks while we waited – and we're *very* polite people. There was a group of old ladies in the bar enjoying a game of bingo as well; never a dull moment with the oldies on the port 'n' lemons.

It seemed someone was messing about with the water supply while Nigel was in the shower, with the water going hot and cold. Not at all happy, he came bounding downstairs with his towel wrapped around his waist to complain. As he was talking to Cecil about the situation 'somebody' whisked his towel away leaving him standing starkers in the middle of the bar. The old women were now witnessing a 6ft black man wearing nothing but the soap suds on his head... and then a cheeky grin as most of the old dears started whistling and clapping their hands shouting, 'We didn't know you we putting strippers on, Cecil!'

It got us all in a good mood before starting our night out. Once Nigel was able to get ready we all headed into town before returning after a good drink and coaxed Cecil into giving us a lock-in.

We were all in the lounge when we heard a knock at the door. I looked out of the side window and saw a man who I knew well... Robert Smith, a friend of our Michael. No, not him from The Cure... you could say that this one was more The Cause. Robert was no friend of mine, simply an acquaintance. He was someone who had a reputation for being lairy and he fancied himself as a fighter. He could be outspoken and insulting to people at times and wasn't the kind of person I'd hang around with; I prefer people who are consistent and trustworthy – decent people make decent friends.

Not too long before this, I'd overheard a conversation between him and Michael where he said quite clearly, 'I'll fight your brother Stephen.' I put my drink down, walked over to him and said, 'Get outside, bigmouth!' A silence came over the bar for a few seconds and some people got between us. I made it perfectly clear that any time he wanted a fight all he had to do was to come and see me instead of pulling my brother to one side. People like him never like that kind of humiliation and I knew *something* would probably boil over again at some point. And there he was, at the pub when we were trying to enjoy a lock-in.

I carried on with my drink, not wasting my time thinking about him or why he was there until I heard a voice shout, 'Stephen, you're wanted on the bar's phone.' As I got up to answer the call, I saw a certain individual who I don't wish to name, who became a police informer. Let's call him Mr X. On a couple of previous occasions, Mr X asked if he could be my minder. I had heard a few stories about his use of extreme violence (Xtreme violence?) and he was handy if any incident arose... certainly someone very useful to have on your side. Back in those days, my philosophy on life was to fight fire with fire. I took the phone call behind the bar and, when it had finished, I was making my way back though the bar when I was approached by Mr X, who told me that Robert Smith was in the bar and he was working himself with people. Robert's timing was impeccable... I was just in the mood to give him a good old-fashioned kicking. I made my way through to the lounge where Mr X said he was. As I was walking, Mr X was in front of me and, as soon as Robert saw me, the first thing he did was insult me. By doing this, he gave me the perfect excuse to set about him, but I never even got any words out of my mouth.

Mr X stopped walking, lifted and then lowered his arm, and said to Robert, 'We've had enough of you, arsehole.'

And that's when I realised what the raising and lowering of his arm was. He'd levelled a handgun. I could see his hand clenching the gun which was cocked and directly pointed at Robert's head. Mr X proceeded to slowly but surely pull the trigger. Now, fortunately for Robert, he had a bizarre habit of jumping from side to side spontaneously. Whether it had something to with the high quantity of beak he was consuming or maybe it was due to his mental issues... or maybe both, I don't know why he used to do it. However, the gun went off and the bullet hit him on the side of the head, entering just above the temple and through the side of his head in-between his skull and scalp before exiting somewhere out the back. I was as surprised as everyone else in the bar. I mean, wanted to bash Robert up, not kill him. Someone grabbed the gun out of Mr X's hand and told him to make himself scarce. I looked to see if any of Robert's friends were going to get involved, but those who'd came in with him stayed in their seats.

Miraculously, Robert's injuries weren't life-threatening. Naturally, he complained about the pain in his head. Rather loudly, in fact. As you'd imagine, the bullet had probably caused him a bit of discomfort. The blood was seeping out so I got him a towel to stem the flow and the gun was disposed of. I told Robert he needed a doctor and quickly. In the meantime, I wrapped the towel around his head and we sat him up. He couldn't have been *that* bad, as he asked for a pint of lager before he went to the hospital. Maybe that's just what us mad Geordies do when we've been shot in the head. He downed his pint and took a bag of cocaine from his pocket and proceeded to pour it on his injury, insisting it would numb the pain. One of the lads volunteered to give him a lift to Newcastle's RVI hospital which was no more than a mile away.

With Robert on his way and the mess mopped up, the lock-in continued and I sat and supped a few more pints with Billy Dixon and Tommy Dillon. You might find that a little strange after what I'd just witnessed but this kind of thing was water of a duck's back to me. If there was anything good to come out of that night it was that I never got another bad word out of Robert Smith again. He'd been lucky that night – we all knew it.

I was waiting for our Michael to pick me up one day; he was half an hour late. I kept pacing backwards and forwards to the front door. I hate being late, hate anyone being late – there's no excuse for it. Finally, there was a knock at the front door. 'About time,' I said as I opened it. But it was my friend Yanhal. He told me our Michael had broken down up the street and his car had overheated and asked me for a kettle full of water. Ok, so Michael *did* have an excuse. I went into the kitchen to get the kettle, which my other half had just bought a week ago and she wouldn't be too pleased with me taking it. What she didn't know wouldn't hurt her, though. Unless she's reading this. When I reached the broken down car I could see the bonnet was open and steam was billowing from the engine. I emptied the kettle of water into the radiator to sort out the problem. We gave it a few minutes and Michael turned it over a couple of times before the engine kicked in and we were off.

We started driving along New Mills Road when, typically, the engine made a really loud noise. The car just wasn't happy and it came to a grinding halt outside the Darnell pub; it was going nowhere. We had no other option but to dump it there and go to the pub. I mean, of all the places to break down and we did it outside of a pub. I was too late to get to my meeting by then so it would keep for another day.

The Darnell wasn't a popular bar at that time. It was owned by Vaux Breweries which were based in Sunderland whereas most bars in Newcastle were owned by Scottish and Newcastle. It sounds mad, but that's how territorial we are in Newcastle – no one would drink Mackem beer. The football fans would always swerve the pub because of that link to Sunderland as well.

We were greeted by a man called Charlie and he told me and Michael that the pub was up for grabs, if we were interested. They wanted £18k all-in for the fixtures and fittings and £10k deposit, but I told them it just wasn't worth it. Charlie could see the glint in my eye though... he offered us a chance to take it over and pay the rest as we went. That was much more appealing. Michael and I had a quick chat and agreed to give it a go. We shook hands with Charlie to seal the deal. Maybe that car breaking down outside was fate. It was certainly a novel way of acquiring a new business.

The bar was taking between £500 and £700 a week, which wasn't covering the expenses such as staff wages and bills. Despite this, there was no doubt the place had potential. I couldn't understand why it wasn't making money but I'm sure time would tell. We took over with immediate effect. I'd only popped in for a pint and found myself walking out as the landlord with a set of keys! The staff seemed happy about us taking over and were all happy to stay on and work for us as well. That night we had a bit craic with them and the few locals to see what they felt were the real issues behind the place going tits up. I know it feels like we should have done our research first, but as you can see, it had been a bit of an impulse buy. You know what it's like – sometimes you go to the shops for a newspaper and end up buying chewing gum that's displayed on the counter? Other times you set off for a meeting, your car breaks down, and you end up buying a pub. Same thing, isn't it? Many said that the kids around the doors were waiting to see who went in and were then screwing their houses when they were in the pub. Clever little fuckers, I'll give them that, but I'd sharp put a stop to all that carry on. No one fucks with *my* future customers.

Over the next few hours we plotted how we were going to turn the boozer into a gold mine... over a few pints of course. I headed home just before closing time and left our Michael to lock up. I hadn't got far along the street when my missus appeared asking me where I had been and where the hell her new kettle was. *Fuck*! The kettle! Hearing the noise, Michael popped his head out of the door and shouted that the kettle was wedged under the back wheel of the motor because the handbrake didn't work. Thanks, bro'! That totally pushed her over the edge and we all know that hell that no fury like a woman whose kettle has just been used as a makeshift handbrake. She gave me an ultimatum which I didn't take to kindly to... it was all just a storm in a teacup, really. She threatened to kick me out. The situation had been brewing for some time and Michael had just stirred it too far. It was pointless trying to sweeten her up and I knew instantly that it was too late to turn over a new leaf. I had a couple of other properties and now I had a bar to run and errrrr… money to urn.

Word spread like wildfire that we'd taken over the bar and, during the first month, we managed to get the takings up with the assistance of good match day trade and some major overnight lock-ins. Most of the time we were open later than nightclubs and we loved every second of it. Well, we never really closed the bar and were averaging £8k a week. It was mental how it all fell into place for us. In one lock-in alone, there was around 100 people or so and we'd been partying for one of the lads' birthdays: Tommy Dillan, a very good friend of mine who's more like family – one of the Dillan brothers from the West End. There was a brilliant atmosphere in the bar that night and we certainly had a big celebration. Before we knew it, it was 9am and the area manager from Vaux Breweries had come out to see me to say that, because of the large amount of alcohol that we'd been buying from them, they'd decided to offer us a deal. They told me to scrap the idea of paying for fixtures and fittings on the bar and that they had another two bars and wanted to know if we were interested in running them as well.

He put his cards on the table and told me straight: 'Head office can't believe how much alcohol you have been buying.' He continued to tell me that we had ordered a £5k dray beer order for delivery on the Monday and got another £6k order only days later on the Thursday of the same week... and those kind of figures were second to none. It certainly had created a big impression and got us noticed for doing something right for a change.

There were stables at the back of the bar which hadn't been used for years but they were still suitable for horses. And then, as luck would have it, one of my travelling cousins gave me a horse as a gift (as you do); he was drunk that night (my cousin, not the horse) and had it in the back of a horse box, which I think was becoming an inconvenience to him. I happily accepted the horse and put it in the stable. It became a bit of a novelty act during the lock-ins and you could guarantee someone would get drunk and offer to take one of the girls to see the horse... and off to the stable they'd go.

Anyway, getting back to the area manager. If we took on the other two pubs as well as the Darnell, he assured us we'd not have to pay any bills: no rent, no gas and no electric... just our alcohol bill. He told me he was going to spend £70k on the Darnell but the refurbishment had to be done by the people from the brewery so there was no earner on that part for me.

I took it all in and then told him that I'd take the three bars on but I wouldn't need £70k spent on a refurb, as the place was perfect the way it was. Instead, I told him that I wanted a reduction on the price of beer I'd buy from them for all three pubs. The area manager went away, made a phone call, and came back and a deal was struck. I was very happy indeed!

As we were signing the deal, the area manager looked at me in quizzical manner and asked me, 'Stephen, what's your secret?' I sat back and savoured the moment. I looked at him and said, 'To be honest, there is only one way to describe it.' I let my words hang in the air for him to cling onto. 'What? Please tell me. The suspense is killing me. What's your secret?'

I'd just opened my mouth and the word 'Respect' was coming out when door to the bar lounge swung open and in wandered the horse with a girl sat on its back wearing nothing but a pair of high heels and cowboy hat (the girl, not the house. That would just be weird). We just sat open-mouthed and I felt speechless for the first time in my life... that was until the horse slipped on the wet floor and knocked all the tables over. The girl went flying and landed on the floor. The area manager didn't know where to look first, and tried to help this beautiful naked girl up. She thanked him and asked who he was. I told her he was the horse owner. It brought a smile to his face and he shook his head in disbelief. It was a classic; all in a day's work!

In the space of a few months the Sayers brothers had three pubs and we were buying in cheap drink and turning over good profit. The Darnell was our main bar though and the parties were relentless. The atmosphere was always the same in that place: plenty of laughs but a few ricks as well... some really good fights, as it happens. We tended to let people sort out their disputes and clean up afterwards. It was that type of place – all self-contained and no funny business. Hand-shakes at the end and a round of drinks – just how it should be.

On one evening in there, I arranged to meet a lady who was working for a local newspaper at the time. She was very down to earth, well educated and a genuinely nice person. Doesn't always happen that often!

When she said she was going to do something, then she would do it. She stuck by her word and had done a good write-up on the march that we held for John Henry. Typically, that night a fight broke out between two men in the pub who'd been out on the drink together. The two of them proceeded to punch the living daylights out of each other. It was so normal for something like that to happen that punters hardly bothered looking up from their pints.

The young lady in question looked concerned. 'Aren't you going to break the fight up and stop them?'

'I most certainly am not,' I replied.

'Break it up, Stephen. They are really hurting each other.'

'Don't be alarmed. This is not unusual. They fight better in this bar, I said.

She looked shocked, 'Why is that?'

'Because in this bar, winner stays in!'

This educated lady did see the funny side and looked concerned and confused, but she knew she was safe.

Night became day in that bar. All the lads would come and use the place and we'd put a lot of free food on for the pensioners and the people from the estate. People would come for hot food, a warm environment with good company and in a safe place. If anyone came in drunk, working themselves and looking for a fight then they'd end up unconscious after a right-hander from me or Michael. We were fearless and nobody could take one of us on, never mind two of us. It was the perfect formula.

We were hitting the beer hard partying every night and doing what red blooded males do. One night I was lying in bed at my just round the corner from the bar when my phone rang my missus (the one with a brand new kettle that she never let out of her sight) answered it and she started screaming.

I immediately jumped out of bed and took the handset off her and placed it to my ear. I just remembering hearing the words, 'He's dead, cuz. He's dead.'

'Who the fuck is this and who's dead?'

It was someone calling me from the bar and all I could hear was screaming in the background, it sounded like complete chaos... like a fucking disaster movie. Once he regained his composure he told me that our Michael was dead as well as a couple of others in the bar. It was a horrible feeling. 'Please, God. Do not let this be right,' I thought. I got dressed straightaway and put a bulletproof vest on, coat over the top, got in my car and headed for the pub. As I arrived, there was a lot of police activity and people nosing around. There air was full of sirens and flashing blue lights – it was fucking mental. The chaos had not subsided and there was so much confusion.

About half a dozen policemen shouted, 'Stop him! Stop him!' as I got out of my car and legged towards the pub. I was stopped dead in my tracks by armed police with guns pointing at my head.

'Show us your hands!'

They asked who I was. I told them I was Stephen Sayers and I explained that I'd received a phone call about my younger brother. They told me he'd been taken to hospital but they were not sure if he was alive or not. I turned around without hesitation and jumped in my car and drove to the hospital at high speed. My mind was racing and I thought to myself that they'd not take him to hospital if he was dead, so there was still a flicker of hope in my mind that our Michael was alive.

I felt myself getting emotional and, before I knew it, I was at the hospital and screeched to a halt and just jumped straight out of the car with the lights on, the keys in and the engine still running. All I wanted to know was if Michael was alive and if he was going to be OK and, of course, who was responsible. As I ran through the doors, I was stopped by two armed policemen who pointed their guns at my head. They searched me and found that I was wearing the vest. One of them put his machine gun right on the temple of my head and shouted for me to slowly raise my hands and drop to the floor. I lowered to my knees with my head forced against a wall. He pointed his gun to the back of my head and they slowly took the vest off me. They asked who I was and what I was doing there, so I explained it all for the second time. I got nowhere fast with these two mugs and, despite having a gun pointed at my head, I'd just about lost my patience with them. The situation was defused by a sergeant who was walking past and felt that their behaviour was uncalled for. He spoke to them and they allowed me to stand up... and even removed the machine gun. I mean, a *fucking machine gun*. The sarge then gave me permission to go on my way. I left carrying the vest under my arm.

I ran down one corridor and then another until I reached A&E and heard a familiar voice. It was our Michael's! I made a beeline to the cubicle and barged my way in. To my amazement he was sat up and actually looked perfectly normal, considering he had been shot four times. It sounds mad, but I nearly asked what all the fuss was about! He didn't seem bothered in the slightest, he was laughing and was even cracking jokes with the nurses. *I'm worried about you – look hurt or something!*

I looked him in the eye and asked him if he was really ok and, with a smile on his face, he said, 'Apart from my bullet wounds, I'm perfect,' and laughed out loud.

'Poor Harry though,' he said.

'Who the fuck's Harry?'

'Poor Harry Orange. Our dad's cousin. He was mistaken for you, Stephen. He was shot five times and they have him on the operation table now fighting for his life.'

Fortunately for Harry, he was a big strong 18 stone man and survived. He was lucky, but not as lucky as me for not being there. Once I'd established that our Michael was OK I asked him the million dollar question.

'Did you see who it was?'

His reply was short but simple: 'Yes.'

Before I left the hospital I saw a good friend, Richy Hall. I got him to one side and asked him if he'd seen what happened and he told me he had: when people were arriving or leaving the lock-in at the pub, for some reason Michael was letting them in and out which he didn't normally do as we had someone employed to do that. The bar had been quite full; around 30 people. There'd been a group of girls sat right next to the window just moments prior to the gunman's arrival, and fortunately for them, they'd moved and sat elsewhere. Hearing someone tap on the window, Michael had lifted the curtain up and saw the gunman stood on the opposite side of the window. He fired at point blank range, hitting him in the shoulder and knocking him over. Michael being the kind of person he is and not wanting to shy away from a bit of trouble decided to get up and charge at the gunman. He shot Michael twice more, again knocking him to the ground. Amazingly, he got back up and charge at him again before getting shot a fourth time. The gun was then pointed at its second target, who he believed to be me, but as I now knew, was my dad's cousin, Harry Orange, who took five bullets to the core of his body.

When I left the hospital I immediately went home where some of my friends were waiting for me and checking the house over to see if my partner and children were safe. I moved them all to a safe house. My head was buzzing. The gunman was still on the loose and the question was: would they come looking for me? The answer in your head in this situation is, 'Well, probably. Yes,' and then you go into survival mode.

My cousin lived over the road from me and had a caravan which was parked just outside his front door. It was what we would call the perfect smother as it blocked the view brilliantly for an ambush, if anyone appeared. I jammed the halogen light to stay on and opened my front door. It was about 3am and it was a deliberate attempt to draw attention to the fact that my front door was open and the passage lights were on as well. There was a car at the top of the street with a few lads in and a car full at the bottom of the street as well. They were ready to ram their vehicle if they showed up. There were also people in the caravan and in the house and everyone was tooled up. The instruction: show no mercy. Everyone knew what I meant by that.

Hours and hours went by and cars went back and forth... but not with the occupants we were looking for. People have a saying about living by the sword meaning that you'll die by the sword; that can be true, but to live by the sword doesn't necessarily mean you will die by it... but you might get cut occasionally.

A police informer and heroin addict called Lee Shaun Watson is prone to making a lot of allegations. Amongst them, he said that the would-be assassin ended up getting murdered. He said that our Michael picked him up and threw him out of the window of a block of flats. As he landed on his head eight floors down, there's speculation that the people who threw him said something like, 'If you like shooting people through windows, why not fly through one!'

❋

I've been arrested for a lot of unsolved murders on Tyneside, which, to be honest is too much to put into this book (the next one will go into them in more detail). Some of it was just in bad taste though, like getting dragged in for the murder of Viv Graham. We've all been questioned over that. Our relationship with Viv was always a bit up and down: he chinned some of our friends, westenders had a go at him and his lads... but then we did time together, bonded, and it was our family who intervened when the biggest challenge of his life came along. Like everyone else I've seen buried way too soon, Viv's murder saddened me because he was a mate. There's a man later referred to as *the jealous grass* within these pages. He did his best to frame us for Viv's murder by telling another grass to confess to being the getaway driver. All that achieved was making sure that more police time was wasted, more money was wasted and more hopes were dashed. I can't shed any more light on the subject. Everyone has their own theory; no one will ever know for certain and I doubt the police ever will.

Fucking guns, man. They're a part of life as much as having a cup of tea on a morning. Part of *our life*, I should say. I don't mean that in the sense of we sit around all day discussing them and dismantle them and put them back together like that mentalist in *Full Metal Jacket*. What I mean is, as people of power and reputation, there's generally someone who won't like seeing you with all that and will try to take it. And guns... well, they're a tool of the trade, aren't they? What we had to factor into our daily lives as so-called 'career criminals' was that some fucker somewhere might try to shoot us. We'd seen it happen and we'd survived it: been there, done that, got the bullet proof t-shirt.

In 1995, my dad John Brian Sayers was approached by a man by the name of Robert Stokoe. Robert seemed to know a lot about our John's trial; so much so that he'd personally seen evidence on a computer which indicated that prosecution witness Phillip Bourge had been shown photographs of our John prior to his identity parade.

Phillip Bourge was a security guard who was employed by Pritchard Security Limited. Bourge was the one who'd told people in HMP Leeds that he'd never met my brother but he had been shown photographs of him. Stokoe told my dad that he'd not only seen this on a computer but he could get this evidence downloaded. If that was true, then it would tie up a lot of loose ends and possibly help clear our John's name and sway the judgment in his next appeal. This man had convinced my dad that he was going to download a statement made by a member of Northumbria Police, stating that he had personally witnessed Philip Bourge being shown pictures of our John prior to the identification parade. He was very convincing.

He'd downloaded information off the Police National Computer and, when the paperwork was obtained it was handed over for legal advice to see if it would be useful in John's forthcoming appeal. It went on for a couple of months; back and forth with more paperwork and more convincing stories from Stokoe. He phoned my dad at 11am when I was there and asked if they could meet down in Birmingham later that day. I looked at my dad and instantly shook my head. He asked if Leeds was easier for us and I shook my head again. He said he'd turn up the following afternoon with the vital information which we needed.

After the call I sat with Dad for around half an hour and we discussed Stokoe and the statement. I remember asking if he trusted this man and my dad replied by asking me what I thought Stokoe had to gain out of it. We came to the conclusion that if this man produced the paperwork we'd be extremely happy and he would deserve a few quid for his help: couldn't say fairer than that.

I left my dad's and made my way to Hartford camp to see my cousins Frankie, Phillip and Joe. When I arrived, our Joe was just pulling away. He had a horse box on the back of his van and he asked if I'd go with him. We went to his stables, got the horse out, and we harnessed it up to the cart. That day me and our Joe went for a lovely relaxing couple of hours on the cart and it was brilliant. We eventually made our way back to the camp where Aunty Sylvia made our tea and, as I left, I said my goodbyes. I drove back to Newcastle with a smile on my face. I honestly believed that the couple of hours I spent with Joe on that cart refreshed my mind and recharged my batteries.

I picked up my cousins Edward Lennie and Tony Sayers and we went down to my dad's hostel in Newcastle, just on

Westmorland Road. The building, now derelict, was a huge tall detached building and it had a large cellar that we'd converted into a gym. We'd been in the gym for an hour or so doing pad work and a bit of circuit training when I heard someone shouting my name down the stairs.

'Stephen, get to the phone! Something's happened to your dad.'

I got to the phone, picked it up, and the line was dead so I placed the phone back down into its receiver. *Fuck*! About five minutes later it rang again. It and it was my uncle, Thomas Kelly, who told me my dad had just been shot. I asked how serious it was and Uncle Thomas told me he'd been shot in the face, but he'd drove himself to hospital. He said to get to Newcastle General Hospital immediately.

I paused for a split-second. When I'd gathered my thoughts I went straight into action mode. I ran back down to the cellar to get my cousins and tell them to come with me. We got straight into our Edward's Mercedes and drove directly over to the hospital which was probably only a mile away. We arrived at A&E, where we came across my dad's BMW with the driver's door wide open and the keys in with the engine still running. Talk about a déjà vu experience! I didn't even have time to consider the fact that the crazy bastard had driven himself to hospital after getting shot in the face. I quickly had a look inside and all I could see was broken glass and blood: it hit me that someone had tried to kill my dad.

I ran into the hospital and I was pointed towards the operating theatre. Within seconds I was there and I burst through the doors to find Dad lying on the trolley bed, waiting to be pushed in for an emergency operation. He had trouble speaking because the bullet had gone into one side of his face and lodged itself to the opposite side of his lower jaw. I could see it wasn't life-threatening and was relieved. I held my dad and I looked at him and I asked him two questions: the first question was, 'Are you OK?' The second was, 'Who did it?' Even though he had difficulty speaking, I knew *exactly* who he meant.

My dad had his mobile phone under the pillow. He shuffled around a bit before passing it to me. And then it rang... I answered, holding it between my dad's and my ear: it was Stokoe. He was crying down the phone begging for forgiveness and he kept saying things like 'special branch' and 'the police' and saying that they'd made him do it. He also said they had supplied him with the .22 handgun and it was their instruction to get my dad to go down to Birmingham or Leeds.

Was there any truth in these allegations? Well, if you didn't believe anything this man had said in the past, then how could you believe him in the present? Was the man a Walter Mitty, as many have described him? I didn't know, but I did know that the shooting was out of character for this man. Why he did it we will never know and, to be honest, I wasn't interested. The conversation carried on between him and my dad. As I listened my blood boiled and there was only one thing in my mind: I was going to settle for no less than revenge. I got myself into the conversation and I let him know I was there listening.

'Stephen,' he said. 'I still have this paperwork here. What shall I do with it?'

I could read him like a cheap newspaper. 'How much do you want for it?'

He asked me to meet him in a public place as soon as possible and he wanted £10k to leave the North East. In return I'd receive the paperwork that would release our John from prison. This mug thought I was brand new and I knew that this was his weakness. The main advantage he had was surprise, but not anymore. He carried on doing what he did best; talking and trying to convince me that meeting him was my only option.

I told him I was worried in case he came back and killed my dad. As far as I was concerned this fool needed a little reassurance, a tickle under the chin so to speak. All I wanted to do was to get within eyesight of him. I had to be careful not to alert him too much to this and it felt like a game of cat and mouse. I increased the amount to £20k saying that I'd give it to him that night if he promised he'd leave my dad alone. I could feel the confidence grow in his voice as we spoke. My acting must have been spot on because the fool thought I was frightened of him. He agreed and said he would meet me in two hours in Leazes Park, next to the lake. He also insisted that I come alone.

I made the calls I had to make and some very close friends of the family attended without hesitation. I trusted nobody but them at that stage; I needed my own around me but also it had to be people who knew the magnitude and the possible outcome and aftermath of such a situation. Around

20 of my family arrived at the hospital for support, protection and revenge, and the conversation and atmosphere was rife with it all. We talked in the waiting room for a bit, but for me it was time for me to leave.

First and foremost, I spoke to my friends and explained to them how we had an hour and a half to prepare for battle. After a brief conversation we came to the same conclusion: if Robert Stokoe turned up that night, it was for the sole reason to kill me. Deep down, I can honestly say the thought of it excited me. I couldn't wait to get there and see him. You know when people talk of tasting revenge? Well, I almost could at that point and I needed to get closer to it.

My friends reassured me that they'd be there and would be prepared. Make no mistake: there would be no mercy shown to this man and any of his accomplices. Little did he realise, I had some of the North East's finest blaggers, psychopaths and dangerous bad bastards watching over me like guardian angels. To them, extreme violence was just a way of life.

The time arrived. The lads had already done their homework and checked the area out. They arrived early and were ready for work. I saw two of them plotted up with fishing rods at the lake. I approached the meeting place from the opposite side near the docking area where people pay to ride on the small boats. As I walked round the lake, I saw a few people night fishing, which was a common thing then.

The sun had set, it was dark and my watch showed 9pm. There were a couple of people sat at a park bench near the lake. I was a bit concerned but I was wearing a bullet proof vest concealed by a baggy top. I'd have to walk past with only a few feet between the lake and them wearing hoods. I pulled the walkie-talkie from out of my pocket.

A message came over. 'Two suspected bogies, 100 yards ahead on bench.'

As I got closer and closer my heart-rate increased as the adrenaline gripped me. I am nobody's fool though. I certainly didn't turn up with a bunch of flowers to congratulate this man; that couldn't have been any further from the truth. As I approached them, I heard a familiar sound – once heard, it can never be forgotten – the sound of two shot guns being cocked from the bush behind the bench. I knew it was my guardian angels. With the two people only feet away from me, one of them turned towards me as I approached. It was on! I steadied my breathing and gathered pace readying myself for the start of my revenge.

Then one of them lit a cigarette; it was just a young girl in her 20s, sat with what appeared to be her boyfriend. Fucking hell. False alarm. It wouldn't have looked too good me going on a killing spree and wasting a couple of Emo kids and some fisherman witnesses out of spite for my dad being shot. I knew my guardian angels' eyes were firmly set on me and the couple. Also knowing they posed no threat; I carried on with my business and walked calmly past them.

I looked at my watch and, as planned, I was exactly five minutes early. I was fully aware of the circumstances and the large possibility of having my life taken. As far as I was concerned it was about survival. As I stood there I wondered, 'Does this fucking idiot think he can come into our lives, try to murder one of us and then try to kill me?' I mean, he must think he's untouchable. No matter what happened to me that night, that fucker would not leave Leazes Park alive.

I've been asked on numerous occasions: how is a man's power judged? It's quite fucking deep that, isn't it? My answer is that the power of a man is judged within the justice of his brethren's revenge. My guardian angels are more than willing to prove their loyalty through revenge, if need be. It's always been that way – always has, always will be.

The clock ticked away and it was a no-show from Stokoe or any of his associates. We waited until quarter-past and rang his mobile phone but it was switched off and went straight to voicemail. I didn't know at the time, but he'd handed himself in to the police and admitted to the shooting of my dad.

I discreetly left the park by a different route and was shadowed by my guardian angels. I made my way straight back over to the hospital. By then there were TV cameras and press waiting outside, so used a different entry point for maximum privacy. I met up with a lot of my family in one of the waiting rooms, about 30 of them in total. The doctor kept coming back and forth reassuring everyone that my dad was going to be alright and that, although not life threatening, he was still in the operating theatre. I suppose I'd already talked to him and knew he was OK – they'd all rushed there hearing that he'd been shot and was now in an operating theatre. I'm not playing down his injury by any stretch; to be shot in the face, you imagine instant death. It shows what a tough man he is to go through that.

The rumours were rife. We were still not clear on the reason he had been shot but we knew who'd shot him… but we also knew that there'd been talk of the police and Special Branch. The only hard facts we had was that someone had tried to take my dad's life and there was a high possibility that they'd return to finish the job.

While he was in hospital it was standard procedure to have an armed police presence at the hospital and there certainly was: six of the fuckers with sub-machine guns. I suppose you know my opinion of them by now, but it was reassuring to know that they were there for him. It never stopped us having our own protective circle though. Me and my cousins Joe, Philip and Frankie Riley, Tony Sayers and Edward Lennie remained by Dad's side throughout the night and the following three days and nights to ensure his safety. The days passed in the hospital and my dad was released to go home. Prior to release the doctor told to us that my dad had to give permission to have the bullet handed over to Northumbria Police, but my dad had refused this permission. Later that night, someone broke into the office where the bullet was held, forced filing cabinet open and taken the bullet. What sort of people do things like that, I'm left to wonder? Who is at the level of seeking out such evidence and is able to steal it without suspicion? I assure you I'm not pointing fingers at anybody, but the plot certainly thickens.

My dad finally got discharged from hospital and the bedside vigil was over. We got him home and I was happy to move in with him. I was there as a loving son but I was mainly there for my dad's security. I would not hesitate to give my life for my most loved ones. I stayed by his side for over ten weeks until he felt comfortable enough and I knew it was time for me to leave. I had a family of my own to look after.

On numerous occasions I've been asked by many people if I'd comment on the wedding... or should I say, the *aftermath* of the wedding between my cousin and one of my very good friends.

It was the mid-90s and there was a bit of an atmosphere, with a lot of bad blood going about. It's difficult to quite put your finger on, just that these times were a bit unsettled, not between the Sayers and my friend's family but amongst other families and individuals from the West End. It seemed things were kicking off all the time: not just 'he said, she said' stuff, but things where people were getting seriously hurt.

For example, on one particular Saturday night, a cousin of mine was on a night out down the Bigg Market when he was approached by someone. For the sake of this person's liberty, we'll call him George. George seemed to be full of himself and was trying to lay down the law, which was totally out of character. *Oh, come on George! What are you playing at, George?* He started telling my cousin that Charlie 'Harra' Harrison (son of big Trevor Harrison from the scrap yard) wanted to see my cousin and he'd better get his arse up to the Half Moon pub, which was just up the street.

My cousin didn't take George's attitude lightly and told him directly to go and fuck himself: 'If Charlie Harra wants to see me, tell him to come down here and see me,' he said as he supped his drink. It's at this point that I should go into a bit of high-level detail: you know I come from a big family. If I say 'my cousin', there's dozens of them, but it gives a bit of anonymity and I don't drop them into anything.

Looking back, I remember asking if he'd had any trouble with Charlie and he told me that he hadn't. Something didn't add up though. George left the bar and immediately headed straight up to the Half Moon to tell his tale. Whatever George said to Charlie it was enough for Charlie to put his drink down and head straight to Circus Circus where my cousin was still drinking.

And that was where my cousin caught a glimpse of George from the corner of his eye. He was with Harra, pointing over in his direction, whispering in his ear and generally getting him wound up. They approached him and there was a confrontation. It escalated. It got heated. Words were exchanged and the next thing you know, Harra got shot in the leg. He fell to the floor and was rushed to hospital. Luckily for him, the injuries were not life-threatening and he was patched up. Unfortunately, a few weeks later as he was making a recovery, he was involved in a high-speed chase and there was a car crash which took his life. I mean it when I say I hope rests in peace. That kind of 'situation' seemed to be happening way too often so, when I say the atmosphere seemed a bit unsettled, it gives you more of an impression of just how unsettled it was.

The wedding: it took place at Newcastle Civic Centre and my cousin looked a million dollars. Our good friend was suited and booted and he scrubbed up pretty well. It was a good ceremony, and from there we all headed to the venue where everybody enjoyed a good celebration and a big party. This was the official coming together of two rather well known families, so it was always going to be a massive night for us all. The drinks flowed and the atmosphere was really good, but on these occasions, there's generally always someone who spoils it.

Inside, you could access the same toilet from the bar or the lounge... and who came waltzing in? George, our friend from the backstory above. George entered the toilets from the lounge and my cousin, accompanied by another cousin, entered the toilet from the bar. They all set eyes on each other inside the toilet and words were spoken. When he saw how quickly the last confrontation had escalated and ended, you'd think he'd just fuck off somewhere else for a quiet night. But George didn't seem to understand the circumstances he'd found himself in; his aggressive attitude on his previous meeting with my cousin had led to a bad result and it was very far from resolved. Now he'd just walked into the lion's den. And, unfortunately for him, it was packed full of lions. Big fucking hungry ones. Rule number 10,863: don't come into our bar, to our wedding and try to pick a fight with us.

Obviously, George was a bit confused and he managed to find himself lying in the piss trough on the floor. The situation was defused quite quickly but George didn't learn his lesson and, as he pulled himself together and staggered to his feet, he began making threats towards certain individuals. You see... George, the uninvited party clown, was also a fool. Which sort of *is* another word for clown, but just go with me on this one because I'm on a roll. Whether he was drunk, whether the situation had got to him, whether he was just a total fucking idiot... only he knows. It was like the bang to his head when he hit the floor must have triggered something in him because his whole character changed. He started to act like a gangster. Yes, he was now going to 'gangster' his way out of it. All that was missing was the bad Al Pacino accent.

Unfortunately, he was out of his depth. He had made a life-changing decision by underestimating the wrong people. Word spread quickly of this man's threats. I know calling him a clown added a bit of slapstick to the situation and made light of it, but trust me... his threats were serious and were made to people who'd take them seriously. When you issue something like that to the people he did, you need to factor in that you either carry it out quickly or they do worse to you.

George left the pub at about 3am and returned home to bed. An hour or so later it was him who had an uninvited guest. Make that three. The sound of a loud bang as a sledge hammer smashed through his front door was the first indication that all was not right that morning. When three masked men in boiler suits armed with various weapons burst into his bedroom shining a bright torch in his face,

George probably knew that he was in a whole world of shit. He found out that you don't make threats and then go to sleep.

Once they'd confirmed it was George, one of the men shot him. George let out an almighty scream and he was squirted in the face with ammonia and then shot again for good measure. Fortunately for him, the second bullet went through his shorts and narrowly missed. He was then pistol-whipped by one of the attackers, which bizarrely saved his life. As he was hitting George with the gun in the head and face, it must have dislodged the bullets, so when the attacker pressed the gun into George's chest and pulled the trigger, the bullets jammed.

He wouldn't have thought so at the time, but that was the luckiest day of his life. And maybe it was the kick up the arse George needed – he never played the gangster card again, never threatened anyone and he just got on with his life, keeping himself to himself.

For the record, this incident had no bearing on the wedding or divorce years later.

I pulled up at the traffic lights on Stanhope Street and noticed my cousin Stephen 'Gun' Shotton with his brother-in-law, a lad called Stephen Rice walking by. It was quite dark at the time, but still ok to recognise them. I told Gun that I wanted to see him and he replied saying he'd follow me up to the house. 'No,' I told him. 'I'll see you at your house now and don't be long.'

They walked round the corner to one of the back streets off Stanhope Street and got in their car when a man wearing a hoodie rode up to them on a pedal bike. He dismounted, approached them and then pulled out a handgun and started firing at them into the back window of the car. He emptied a full magazine and miraculously hit everything in there apart from Stephen and Gun. Fuck me – was he blind or what?

In a state of shock, they drove to my house in their damaged car. I was smoking a spliff at the time and was in a giggly mood, if you know what I mean. I looked at my hidden camera system and I could see it was my cousin and Stephen. I was pleased they'd came round as quickly as I'd told them to, but they were acting very strangely. I went down and opened the door. They were both white as sheets and sweating.

'What's up with you two?' I asked.

'Look at the fucking car! Someone's just tried to kill us!'

There it was on my front drive. I took a look at it. It was riddled with bullet holes and you could see where the bullets had deflected off the support for the headrest. If that support hadn't been so solid, then these two would have been goners for certain. They were asking lots of silly questions because their heads were all over and they were certainly on edge. It looked worse than that time when we attached window poppers to carwash rollers and messed that bloke's Jag up! I mean, imagine a car that gets shot to fuck in a film. That's exactly what they look like... I'm surprised it still moved.

However... I must say, I found the whole situation quite amusing – probably because of the spliff – and couldn't resist winding them up a little bit more. It was just such a serious situation, but the way they were going on and the way my head was, I just wanted to laugh about the whole thing! Just so you know, I was only laughing because of the situation and the fact that they'd survived it. I headed back indoors while they leant against their car looking up and down the street for the would-be assassin to return on his BMX. The kids over the road pumped their music up a bit, which gave me the opportunity to put my plan into action. I went to my trusty cupboard under the stairs and pulled out large box of fireworks. I picked out a couple of bangers and went back outside. The lads were too busy talking to even notice me (so much for them keeping a close eye on the street) so I lit the two bangers with my spliff and chucked them under the car. *Bang-Bang-Bang*! Tears streamed down my face with laughter as I watched them run for cover. They were not amused – their nerves were shattered. I couldn't stop laughing for ages. But they did look rather shaken up, so I invited them in for a cup of tea to calm them down. I even offered them a bite to eat as it was teatime… 'Bangers and nash, anyone?' Again, I appeared to be the only one laughing. Tough crowd, eh?

I asked them if they had any idea who the gunman was. They told me it could have been anyone. They stayed for an hour or so talking through any possibilities, but they were right the first time: it was impossible to know. They had a little safe house to go to, to get their heads down for a bit and let the dust lie on what had just happened. The car was taken away and scrapped and no police were involved.

Two weeks later, on 30th November 1995, I was arrested

on a blackmail charge and remanded to custody at HMP Durham.

CHAPTER 11
DID THE CRIME, DID THE TIME

There was a lot of illegal activity going on throughout Newcastle and the outlying districts. I was an active criminal with my finger in plenty of pies. I used to look after a lot of people whether they liked it or not. Some call it blackmail some call it protection, but I called it a living. My reputation was well and truly established by this stage and I would go as far as saying that there was not a businessman on Tyneside who did not know the fierce reputation of the name Sayers which, if I'm honest, I took full advantage of. I used to get approached all the time with problems, debts and people trying to tax people and a lot of people would approach me and my associates to assist in their matters and stop whatever illegal activity was going against them... mostly taxing.

I was approached by a certain individual who I will not name for obvious reasons, but let's just call him Jack. Jack told me about a friend of his; a successful businessman who'd bought himself some licensed premises and was terrified in case any so-called gangsters approached him. So Jack approached me on behalf of the businessman and asked me how much I would charge him to use my name, if necessary, on his premises. I told him that if he gave me a monkey a week (£500) and a drink when I called in, I would do it. Sounded like a fair deal for us all. He told me he was going to make a phone call and get back to me.

I met up with Jack again in a restaurant on Stowell Street in Newcastle's China Town later that night. He told me there was good news and bad news. The bad news was he wouldn't give me the £500 and my drink but the good news was he would give me £1,000 a week to stay out of his establishment and a little lump upfront. I was pleasantly surprised and of course I accepted.

There were a lot of incidents happening like this for me at the time. If I was called upon for such a service, then it was nice to make some money from my name. On another occasion, I decided to put it on (ask for money) with a successful businessman from Newcastle who I cannot mention due to legal reasons. Prior to me approaching this man, two or three masked gunmen had recently gone to his home and shot out his windows with pump action shotguns. I'm not sure if they were in or not, but it couldn't have been a pleasant experience for the family. This, I thought, was a golden opportunity to make a few quid and put whoever was responsible in their place (but not in jail)... let's not forget, I'm no sheriff either.

I approached a man called Malcolm Barmer who was a straight working man. He wasn't a criminal, but was a tough guy in his time who had served a sentence for manslaughter. I asked him if he was still looking after this successful businessman. He said he was and that he was still a good friend of his. I asked him to go and have a word for me. This became counterproductive as he immediately told one of his other friends, the lowlife Peter Donnelly. Malcolm didn't do this to cause trouble he was just naive to the situation. His lowlife friend Donnelly wasn't. Donnelly had his own agenda. Remember, this man is my dad's cousin... who happened to be insanely jealous of me and my brothers. Wouldn't you expect a bit of loyalty from someone who is related... even if distant? Donnelly arrived at the house that had the windows shot out, the parts here I am placing together though tape recordings of the victim (the businessman) talking on his phone to his friend recorded by Nothumbria Police.

The businessman phoned his friend and explained that Farmer and Donnelly had just been to his house. Despite a heavy police presence, the two men made themselves at home and told him that we were responsible for shooting his house up and that we were going to demand money from him over the next few days. Donnelly then told him that he should not stand for this in any shape or form. His motive was not money, but revenge: I'd fallen out with Peter a few weeks earlier and we had a fair fight where, after a roll around on the floor, I broke his hand and his heart. He didn't fancy a rematch and we both walked away agreeing that was an end to the matter – in short, a straightener. We straightened out our differences and that was that. It turned out that Donnelly was not a man of honour though. He had carved what reputation he had from attacking people who were either mortal drunk or off their heads and by digging people from behind. What Donnelly lacked in basic intelligence he made up for with jealously. Looking back on it, his motive was quite clear to me; he wanted me nicked and by any means necessary. This whole twist in fate gave him the perfect way in to manipulate the situation to his advantage and see if he could achieve his wish. So, Donnelly and his former partner, a registered police informer called Joe Hunt hatched their plan (Joe was on remand at the time for discharging a firearm on a security van robbery in Birmingham. I will discuss that slag later on in this story).

With the trap set, contact had been made with the businessman and a fee of £50k was arranged, which he'd agreed to pay. The next thing I knew, I was arrested and placed on remand in Durham with 'The President' Nigel Abadom. The police were still looking for my brother, Michael. Nigel had been released from prison six weeks earlier after serving an eight-year sentence for supplying heroin. The Abadom brothers, Philip, Nigel and Stephen made a name for themselves in the 70s. Their father was Nigerian and their mother was English, which Nigel told me was a rare thing in those days. They were the only black family from Birtley in Gateshead. When they were in their early teens, their father took them back to Nigeria. He was a very intelligent man and was the personal dentist to the Queen for a while. During our court case, the Judge even mentioned that he knew of Nigel's father and said that he was five years ahead of him academically. It amazed me.

Me and Nigel were sat in B-wing in HMP Durham. It wasn't all bad as there were droves of people who brought bags of goods to my cell door: tobacco, dozens of phone cards, shower gel and pretty much anything of any use that you were allowed in prison. Every morning it was like the doorway of a charity shop with more bags and donations appearing throughout the day.

A screw came to the door and I heard him making a lot of noise asking a couple of inmate cleaners what they were doing hanging around as only those in uniforms had access to the wing. To the screw's surprise, the cleaners had been given permission from another screw to come to my door. Rules don't always apply when you're the biggest name in there and a lot of these screws knew me from way back.

The screw came in and shook our hands and told me that his nephew had been threatened by an idiot from another wing. He was very concerned about his well-being once this inmate was released and asked if I'd have a word with him. I told him it was possible and I'd see what I could do. It was a two-second job. I sent Nigel to take care of it and give the kid the heads up and a warning about the allegations. The young lad was very impressed by it all and wanted to return the favour; he said if there was anything he could do for me inside or outside of jail, he would. I thanked him; good lad.

We went down to the canteen to collect our food and a couple of newspapers and went back to the cell with a couple of joints. I was looking forward to going on exercise the following day and just relaxing for the rest of that evening. I remember waking up the following morning to the sound of screws screaming on the landings. That's the kind of alarm clock you have to get used to in there. I got up washed and ready, breakfast done and waited for exercise. I heard a screw scream at the bottom of the wing, 'Ring ya bells for exercise,' which I did.

I don't know how many hands I shook outside that cell door but I had a lot of friends in there and a lot of people had respect for me. I went on exercise and was

211

immediately greeted by a group of familiar and unfamiliar smiling faces. Peter Beaumont Gowling, Richy Hall, Michael Alsop and plenty of others. They were all full of questions about how I was feeling about my case.

'Always remember, lads, it seems bad at the beginning. But if there was a way to get you in, then there is a way to get you out. The show's not over 'til the fat lady sings,' I told them.

Durham jail was always on the edge. There were slashings and stabbings almost every day and that's just how life was in there. I'll probably say it at every opportunity when talking about prison life, but it really is survival of the fittest in any nick. If you go in there soft, you'll not come out. You've got to be tough or you're fucked.

Our Michael got captured and arrested and was also remanded at Durham jail.

One day me and Nigel were sat in the cell when a screw came to get us. Strangely, there was another screw with him, a senior officer, who I knew from old.

'Stephen, I don't know what you've done, but there are a few governors downstairs and they all want to see you,' he said. How very ominous! We were intrigued as we were taken down to see them. We entered the room and I remember looking over at Nigel who was a little worse for wear after a night on the prison hooch. Come to think of it, the Valium and spliffs couldn't have helped either. It was like he was in the Bigg Market, not the big house.

In the room were three prison officers, three principal officers and three senior officers; it was like the who's who of the prison. The governor came forward and told me he had just got off the phone to the Home Office where he'd had to explain why Durham jail had become the most violent in the country. It really was weird. Why he told me that, I had no idea, but he continued.

'We know it's not you, Stephen, but these young inmates are so impressed by the Sayers' reputation that they are doing this to impress you and your brothers, John and Michael.' I still didn't reply.

Realising that the speech was falling on deaf ears, another screw piped up.

'We should just bend him up and take him down the block, Sir.'

I looked at him and told him to come forward and give it a try. Needless to say, he was a man of words, not action. His arse dropped immediately. 'If you can't say anything constructive, keep your mouth shut,' I added. He didn't seem to like that either.

The governor made it quite simple; unless these slashing and stabbings were stopped then me and my brother would be made Category AA prisoners and moved to another nick. He knew it would be a massive inconvenience for us and make it more difficult for our family and friends' visits. Either way I stood my ground; bullying doesn't work with me.

His final piece of advice to me before we were led out the room was to get the situation sorted. My advice to him was to not make it too personal. He asked what I meant by that and I didn't answer. Who the fuck did this fool think he was, threatening me? He was a grafting peck, a straight-goer, a creature of habit with a set routine. He was getting confused. What he did for a living and what I did for a living were worlds apart and he didn't bother me in the slightest. My brain was racing but, pushing my temper to one side, I thought about how I could take advantage of this situation.

I stopped and turned back to him and calmly explained that I could defuse the situation, but not from behind my prison door. He asked what I meant and I said that if there was trouble in the gym or the education block then I could not defuse it sat in my cell tapping messages on the pipes with Morse Code. If he wanted me to be active, then I had to be able to *be active*. He agreed. It just so happened there had been a slashing that morning in the education block when someone went mental in the cookery class which, at the time, was very difficult to get on to. I told him I'd need access to all the wings and the gym in case a situation like that arose. I knew I could defuse the situation, but if he thought I was going wing to wing at his beck and call he had another thing coming. I wasn't going to be his puppet. I was going to use the situation to my advantage. Once I took up my new post, there wasn't a stabbing or a slashing for nearly four months. The governor was happy and I was happy.

One Thursday I was sitting in my cell gathering my thoughts just after dinner. The prison was on bang-up until 1.30pm and after that they opened us up for work. A screw opened my cell door.

'Stephen, your solicitor's visit has been cancelled. You need to phone them up.'

I went downstairs to phone him and I will never forget his words. He told me that he had spoken to the businessman's solicitor and the businessman had instructed his solicitor to pass a message onto my solicitor that he was dropping the charges on Tuesday in court and I would be released on Tuesday. That was the best news I'd heard in all the time I was there. It was unreal, in fact.

On the 23rd of December 1995, I went to sleep around 10pm. I woke up at 5.30am and it was still dark and there was that eerie silence that you only get in the nick. I'd had the strangest of dreams; that vagueness and familiarity at the same time. I couldn't remember anything at all about it, but I could remember my cousin Frankie Kelly was in it and I was a bit freaked out by it. I couldn't put my finger on what was bothering me about it though, that's what was making it worse. I got out of bed, put the light on and woke Nigel up. He was in a heavy drug-induced sleep and took a fair bit of shaking and prodding before he opened his eyes. I told him about the dream and I couldn't really settle for the rest of the night. At 7.30am Nigel's Iman (Muslim priest) knocked at our door, surprised to see us awake so early. He came into our cell and Nigel told him about my dream, but the priest was unable to offer an explanation either.

A screw came to the door.

'Stephen, I need to see you alone,' he said. I could see by the expression on his face that something was up. He told me I had to call home and he couldn't say any more than that. I called Donna, my common-law wife at the time, and she told me that our Frankie had been shot dead in the Bigg Market the previous night. My eyes filled up and the tears were ran down my face. I couldn't speak. Frankie was my cousin, but we were so close that he was more like a brother to me. When we finished the conversation I kept my head down in the phone kiosk until I'd dried my eyes and managed to compose myself. I returned to my cell and the Muslim priest was still there. I told them both my news. It was then that the priest asked me to recall my dream again. He listened carefully and, realising that the person I had dreamed about was the same person who had been shot the previous night, told me that he believed that his soul had come to see me after he'd died. I found this comforting but still could not quite comprehend the whole thing.

I made some enquiries and found out what had happened: Frankie and his brother-in-law David Armstrong aka Army, had fallen out with Ricey (Stephen Rice) who was our cousin Gun's brother-in-law. Gun and Ricey had trouble with Army.

Two days before Christmas and the Bigg Market was absolutely rammed. The Prince Naseem fight was being shown on the TV as well and a fair few bars were screening it, including Maceys – a very popular place with loads of people out to watch the fight, including Gun and Ricey. A lass called Ann-Marie Kelly saw them and headed over the road to a public phone box outside the bar. The phone box was covered by CCTV and she was clearly seen putting money into the phone. She called Army, her boyfriend, to inform him that our Gun was drinking in Maceys with Ricey. Army was not too far away with our Frankie and a friend called John Thornton, aka Ginger Lugzy.

Fuelled by drink and drugs, they went straight to Maceys to confront them. Ann-Marie had arrived from the hone box and walked up to Gun who was stood next to Ricey, kissed him on the cheek and said, 'It's got nothing to do with me, cuz.' The judge later described this action as 'the kiss of Judus'. No sooner had she walked away when a gunshot rang out followed quickly by another. The noise came from behind the two, with the bullets flying past them. The second bullet actually went through Ricey's jacket and shirt and grazed his shoulder. He pulled a gun from his pocket and fired back. It was all split-second timing and he connected with his shot. Unfortunately it was our Frankie. He was shot through the chest. The bullet went straight through him and ended up in Army's arm. Our Frankie staggered a few feet then dropped down and collapsed into Lugsy's arms where he drew his last breath.

I was very close to Frankie. We were brought up together as brothers. I was absolutely devastated about what happened. If this had gone down in any other way I would have kicked up a massive fuss, but how can you blame Ricey and Gun for being armed? For the second time in six weeks, someone had tried to assassinate them. For me, Anne Marie Kelly and Army have to answer for their actions. It was Army and Anne-Marie's actions that led to the shoot out. All the evidence was shown to me in Durham jail. You could clearly see Ann-Marie making the phone call then kissing Gun and speaking those words to him. I saw her looking out of the windows, waiting on the arrival of her boyfriend and the trouble that he was about to cause. My blood was boiling watching that scene. I felt powerless – it was all in the past and there was nothing I could do about it. But it had only just happened and it was painful watching it evolve because it was real.

What happened next was unbelievable. Anne-Marie and Army jumped into a taxi and rushed back to her parent's home. She saw my Uncle Frankie and Aunty Anne and decided to tell them that Frankie had been killed. Who'd do something like that? His body wasn't even cold at that point. Naturally, they were distraught and wanted answers. As if that wasn't bad enough, they also decided to blame totally innocent people – namely those who'd been stuck in Durham prison for the past six weeks. They told my uncle and aunty that me and my brothers were responsible for giving Ricey a gun and, of course, that it was him who had shot Frankie.

I'd like to send this little message to Anne-Marie: what you did that night was despicable. You deliberately misled your two grieving parents with malicious lies at our expense. Never in a million years would I have condoned anyone doing anything like that to our cousin Frankie and I know my brothers John and Michael feel exactly the same way. There are one or two other things I could say, but for now I have said enough and would like to leave this matter closed. I've tried to resolve the situation on many occasions with my aunty and uncle, but it has fallen on deaf ears. I've always been as respectful as possible, under the circumstances. We loved our cousin Frankie. We are innocent. Why should we get the blame? To be able to put this into writing gives me closure after 30 years of hurt. Rest in peace, cuz. May God have mercy on your soul. Love you and miss you.

The following Tuesday I arrived at North Shields Magistrates Court for an old-style committal. We were sat in cells below the court and they shouted Nigel's name out and took him to see his legal team. He returned five minutes later and was the colour of boiled shite. He never got a chance to talk to me but he quickly shouted from the passage that the charges were not getting dropped. The police had said that, even though I was in Durham prison at the time, I was responsible for having a Crown Prosecution Service office burned down and having a retired police sergeant's leg shot off by Bob Morton – a man I'd never even heard of. This was just Northumbria Police up to their old tactics. Every time they can't solve a serious crime they blame the Sayers brothers and their associates. Talk about relentless persecution... and as for going home that day, we had to wave goodbye to that as the businessman had a change of heart. Little did I know at that point, there was a grass working flat out in the background; a registered police informer from Durham named Joe Hunt, who I mentioned a bit earlier.

This is where he comes into the equation: Joe Hunt was a Category AA prisoner who was on remand in HMP Birmingham in Winson Green. He'd been arrested with another man called Tony Weldon, who had nothing to do with this situation. After Hunt found out the businessman was intending to drop the charges against me, he allegedly wasted no time in ringing the businessman and telling him 'Not to weaken' and to, 'Get the bastards lifed off.' He had various conversations with him to pressurise and to not drop the charges and keep us locked up. It seemed obvious to me that he was doing the bidding of his handling officer.

Hunt got his way, as did Northumbria Police. When I saw him in Frankland Prison years later, Tony Weldon told me that Joe Hunt's handler had gone to court in Birmingham, stood up, and asked for Hunt to receive bail. This was the same police officer from the Regional Crime Squad who'd just happened to be on the front page of our local newspaper six months earlier after finding a machine gun in a rubbish bin on Newcastle's quayside. What are the chances?

Bail was refused for Hunt and he went back to Winson Green, where a good friend of mine called Gary Bingham from Birmingham was in for the robbery of over a million quid from a security van. He was also a Category AA prisoner, next door to Hunt. Gary told me he couldn't understand how Hunt was allowed regular telephone calls because no one else in that category was allowed them.

My friend Big Bud Armstrong was also placed on the same landing as Hunt. He went directly to Hunt's cell door and told him that he was a lowlife grass for assisting the police in putting the us and Nigel in jail. Bud also put it right on him saying he was going to do him when the doors got opened up. During bang-up, Hunt put his bell on for the screws to come to his door and put himself on protection away from Big Bud.

Hunt only got away with it for so long until his co-accused Tony Weldon attacked him over the situation and exposed what he was doing. Tony was devastated to have been connected to Hunt and that he'd be associated and tarred with the same brush. Hunt screamed for screws to get Weldon off him and they eventually pulled him out of the situation. A letter from his solicitor appears on the next page, where he tries to discredit me and my brothers as police informants. On the following page is a letter from Stephen Richards, a writer who investigated the ridiculous claim.

attempted to blackmail ███████ precisely because they knew that ███ was off the scene. My own view is that they had a great deal to do with him being off the scene and my information is that they are responsible for both of you being in high risk Category A security at the present time. The Sayers brothers are controlled by D.C. Henderson of N. C.I.S. They inform to him regularly and through him they had your security categorisation changed. It was not aimed at you, but you were caught in the crossfire.

I am sure that if the police want you to co-operate, they will at some stage want you to give evidence against ███ because their case is not that strong against him. It is far from a certain acquittal, as you seem to think in your letter, because of the forensic evidence, which, on the face of it, looks as if it has been manufactured.

The police are, however, likely to want you to inform on the name of the person who is presently at large. I would like to have that name as well, but unfortunately no one will tell me it. It would do my client a great deal of good if I had it and, if he knows it, certainly he will not tell me it. The point quite simply is that the police know that there were two people outside the security van. You have admitted to being one of them and the other person is still at large. We both know that it was not ███. The question, therefore, is, who was it? I make no bones about the fact that if I had that information, I would supply it to the police and I would make sure that whoever gave it received credit for it, but I am not likely to obtain it, because certainly if my client knows it he will not tell me, or anyone else.

That should really answer your point that he is responsible for getting people locked up. That is entirely false and, no matter how much it hurts him, I doubt if ███ will ever cross that line.

I do not see anything wrong, however, with him handing in firearms to the police in the current climate. In fact, it is welcomed by them and if it does do him some good then so be it. The police have said to me that, even though he will not give any names, the mere fact that dangerous weapons are off the street is a matter of great importance to them because that weapon cannot then fall into the

MIRAGE PUBLISHING
www.miragepublishing.com

15 May 2015

FAO: Steve Wraith

Dear Steve,

Matters relating to Stephen Sayers

Please find enclosed copy pages 267-274 from typescript for paperback book *Viv Graham: The Final Chapter Vol.3* published 5 November 2001, of which I am the author

The enclosed pages relate to the then solicitor (Clive M Hindle of Hindle Campbell Solicitors, North Shields) of convicted criminal Joseph Trevor Hunt, in which he made claims in a letter to Tony Weldon (who at that time was on remand facing serious charges for robbery) on 21 June 1996 that the *"Sayers brothers were controlled by D.C. Henderson of N.C.I.S."* (National Criminal Intelligence Squad).

The letter made some unsubstantiated remarks that *"They inform to him regularly"*. Having fully investigated these claims made by Clive M Hindle I can advise that there was no such evidence, either anecdotally or documented, to substantiate such claims.

Certainly many career criminals have done deals with the police in order to secure less severe prison sentences or even to escape conviction, but none of my findings during my investigations revealed this to be the case in relation to any of the Sayers brothers of Stephen, Michael and John.

In fact I came to the conclusion that lengthy prison sentences passed on all three Sayers brothers over the time of their criminal careers were of a lengthy enough nature to substantiate that they could not be informants due to severity of prison sentences imposed on them.

I also discovered that the alleged named "handler" (D.C. Henderson of N.C.I.S.) of the Sayers brothers did not exist and was seemingly concocted to add depth to the untruthful letter Clive M Hindle sent to Tony Weldon.

Best wishes ever,

Stephen Richards

Enc.

Back in Durham, a screw gave me a look at Hunt's letter list, so I could see the people that he'd been writing to. One of them was a man who comes into this story a bit later. This man is a notoriously jealous grass who, for some bizarre reason, thinks he's a criminal mastermind. But more on him later... Hunt had been writing to him twice a week for the previous four months. When confronted about this he tried to twirl it saying he had all of the jealous grass's letters and that he'd kept them for me.

I read them and was amazed by the shite this man was talking about. It was not hard to see this man had suffered a mental breakdown of some sort or was suffering from a mental illness. I showed Mickey Lang, a very good friend of mine, who also came to the same conclusion.

I saw my friend Eddie head back from a visit and he told me he had a nice little bit of draw in, back over in his cell, and he invited me and our Michael over that night for a smoke during association (time for inmates to shower, get a haircut or use the phone and whatever... definitely *not* a time meant for smoking weed). It could be a very sociable place, prison.

Later that evening, I was walking along the landing when I saw Mickey Lang. He told me that the boys had the hump with the jealous grass's spy. I understood their feelings very well. The screw shouted out that it was tea time and for the different landings to come and collect their food. That didn't bother me because my door was always open. I strolled down when I felt like it, no rush, and got my food and returned back to my cell.

224

Me and our Michael had our tea together before going to visit Stuie Henderson upstairs in his cell, armed with our cups, for some decent hooch. As we were getting settled we heard a disturbance come from the landing below; it was two people having a fight... or so it seemed. I realised with one glance what was going on. They were just going through the motions of a fight, but neither of them was getting hurt; just rolling around the floor shouting and bawling creating a scene, which was their objective as they were there to create a diversion.

About 20 screws headed over to break them up leaving only three screws to handle about 180 inmates. Radios were turned up loud as inmates tried to silence any screams. I could tell that these actions had been coordinated by a large group of people; ones who were prepared to suffer the consequences. I'm not brand new in this department; I knew what was going down and I had a good idea of who the intended victim would be.

Whatever other people were up to on the wing was not my concern. I was sat with my pal Stuie having a drink and then Eddie brought a nice bit of weed with him. We continued getting drunk and stoned until the riot calmed down, then refilled our cups and made our way to our cells.

As I walked down the stairs I saw a man come from the direction of the shower, his face beaten to a pulp with blood coming out of every orifice. He just collapsed to the ground. I looked across the landing and saw my good friend Mickey Lang, who gave me a nod. A nod is as good as a wink, so they say. Even though I had not asked for this to happen, I have no doubt that Mickey took it upon himself to put right what he saw was wrong. The beating was a little too much for HMP Durham. The screws shit themselves after seeing such a bit of work take place.

A screw came to see us and said he'd worked in prisons across the country for over 25 years and had never seen such professional violence behind bars. There was a slight pause for a few seconds, then I asked him what he wanted. He produced a quarter ounce of cannabis from his pocket and threw it on the bed next to me and told me he that he'd found it when searching someone's cell, who he believed was a friend of mine. He told me he was not going to nick him and he most certainly did not want any trouble with me, my brothers or associates. I was quite happy with this, if the truth be known. The tough screw was shitting himself, and he'd come to see us to make sure there was no further trouble... along with a nice little present. The screw may have taken it lightly but the governor didn't, and he was as good as his word.

We woke up in the morning to find the governor and around 20 screws outside our door. It was 7am and it wasn't a spin. I looked over at our Michael, who was just waking up as well.

'Did you order me a strip-a-gram?' I asked.

I think we were still a bit hammered from the previous night and started laughing as the governor approached.

He told me us that our security categorisation had been changed and increased to double category A of which there were only 30 or so out of 60,000 prisoners. Our John was also being upgraded from Category AA to Category AAA and there was only three of these in the country. We were starting to sound like a fucking packet of batteries. I'm glad we haven't got ginger hair, or they'd have started calling us the Duracell brothers.

There were what we called 'dog' screws that were always barking at someone and who would try and belittle inmates by calling them by their second name. I'd met many dog screws over the years – just pathetic excuses, really: pond life. They were the ones who got pleasure from being sadistic.

There was one in particular I'd come across before who'd turn into Superman when he put on that uniform and went to the segregation unit. Although this man never had a go at me he most certainly had a go at everyone else in the block and was nothing than a bully, using his uniform to hide behind. The segregation unit was used as a dual-purpose for the screws: one purpose was to house people who'd been put on punishment for misbehaving on the wings, where they would be served with a piece of paper which was classed as a nicking sheet. The other purpose was to house Category AA prisoners; us lot.

Being 'on the book' as they call it is no advantage if you're hoping to be set free. It does give you an ego boost in prison, however, so it does have some plus-points. We were already pretty notorious though, so it didn't mean that much to us. What it did mean is that you have screws watching your every move, waking you up with a torch every hour and generally play games with you to mess with your head. They have psychologists listening to every call you make, looking though your history, childhood application forms, they look though everything to find out what your state of mind is and look for a weakness and they to try to break you. Let's not forget here the majority of double Category AA prisoners are terrorists that have stood against this country, so in many ways, it felt a bit ridiculous that we were there... a bit excessive, you know?

We carried our belongings down to the segregation unit accompanied by 20 or so screws. I'm surprised they didn't put us in orange overalls and wheel us there, because the whole Hannibal fucking Lecter treatment was well over the top too. They separated us from each other and put us into single cells but it didn't take us long to adapt. I mean, the food was pretty bad and the cells were in a disgraceful condition with windows smashed, bodily fluids all over the walls and they smelled disgusting. I bet there's inmates now who'd end up getting put into a five-star hotel because their human rights had been breached in the block. There was many a time we'd get woken up by some smack head screaming in the middle of the night cold turkeying. They wouldn't stop until they got a fix and it could take the screws hours to finally make the decision to place them elsewhere and, generally, there wouldn't be an elsewhere. They'd lie on their backs and kick the cell doors for hours along with the screaming. I can understand their problem and all that, but it was difficult to have any sympathy for them – especially when the howling and pleading would just go on forever and a week... the place was bad enough and that going on all the time just added to the sheer insanity of it all. And when you have a trial coming up and you're trying to concentrate on your deposition papers, it was even more of a fuck-on.

A ten-year sentence was nothing to be sniffed at. We got our perks and everything but it's still a long time to do bird. Me, our John and our Michael were serving 37 years between the three of us and we were all on the book at the same time. The whole 'on the book' thing became a fucking pain in the arse as well: gym visit recorded, class recorded, breakfast, lunch, tea, shower, shit, shave... all of it. I personally thought it was inconvenient and found it a hindrance. I hoped that one day I'd get off the book but it never happened. I was kept at that level until the day of my release. I loved getting letters sent in and my sons Moe and Tommy's mates Mark and Paul used to write and Chantelle Connelly used to keep in touch as well. Letters always used to keep me sane in an insane environment.

One day I was taken back from the gym by a couple of screws and was about to go on the wing when one of them stopped me for a routine rub down and told me that I had someone waiting who'd been making enquiries about me. I looked up to the landing and saw about six screws standing outside my door and an old man who I recognised... Charlie Kray.

The screws were worried sick in case it kicked off, for some bizarre reason. He seemed to look down his nose at them. They called him Mr Kray, which was nice and respectful. I didn't know him, but he seemed like the kind of bloke who got respect not just because of his name, but because he was a genuinely nice bloke with it.

The screws turned and left us to it and wandered off down the landing to kill time. I turned the music on low and asked Charlie if we needed to go to the exercise yard and talk.

'No. What I am about to tell you has already happened in my court case. I've come here to mark your card, Stephen.'

He told me how my name had been mentioned repeatedly in his court case where he'd recently been convicted for his part in a £78m coke scam.

He told me he'd arranged a meeting with two men in some flash boozer in London. There was a big showbiz party taking place. The Spice Girls were there celebrating another number one hit and All Saints were also there celebrating signing a record deal. The two men arrived and it turned out that they were from Newcastle. He didn't know it at the time, but somebody had slipped the old bill in to him and those two Geordies who befriended him were undercover officers.

Charlie told me he was taken aback by the fact that these people were Geordies and their conversations went stale for a short while until he decided to test the water with them and, believing they were cut from the same cloth, asked if they knew the Sayers brothers. He said the expression on their faces was priceless. They looked at each other and then looked at Charlie and sheepishly said yes. Charlie told them that when they got back to Newcastle to tell the Sayers brothers that he was asking after them and to get in touch. He said that this was recounted in court by one of the officers when he was in the box. He told the court that on his return to Northumbria Police HQ, he informed his superiors of Charlie Kray's request for the Sayers to get in touch. They found it amusing. The judge struggled to come to terms with this and asked them why this was so funny. The officer would only say that it was a North Eastern joke amongst themselves. I wasn't overly concerned about this revelation, but I thanked him for coming to find me and for letting me know. He didn't have to do that.

Charlie didn't belong in prison. He was too old and should have been in a nursing home, not banged up like he was. I mean, I've since read *The Krays Behind Bars* by my mates Steve and Stu and the way the police went after Charlie as the last Kray was a fucking disgrace. Steve is a close friend to us and was mates with Charlie – always spoke highly of him and I could see why. Frankland was to be a short-term stay for Charlie so we tried to make it as comfortable as possible for him. It was nice to see that the Kray name still carried respect in the system and rightly so.

Our Michael started doing a bit of cooking and there were three of us on the food boat together, which meant three of us cooking together and getting our food together. There was me, Michael and our good friend Paul 'the wee man' Ferris. I got introduced to Paul by a good friend of mine and Paul said to me, 'We are neighbours, so if you need me to be neighbourly, just let me know.' I knew what he meant and I thanked him for that, the feeling was mutual. We became good friends and I gave him the nickname, 'the wee big'un'.

One night we invited Charlie Kray over for tea. There was me our Michael, Charlie and Paul Ferris. We had a great night and it was nice to have such a good friendship with people like that – they were a much better class of criminal than the usual vagabonds and ruffians that would call by!

Being Category AA meant I wasn't allowed to work during the day, so the screws would let Charlie out of his cell and he'd automatically come to mine and we'd have a cup of tea. They'd open the door from 2-4pm and I had the chance to spend a bit of time with him and get to know him better. He would tell me stories about London and the night life and I found them all very interesting. I told him that my family originated from Stepney in the east end of London. He knew the manor well and it was great to have some common ground like that. With meeting so many villains over the years, a lot of it can be a kind of 'false friendship' and you get wise to it from the off. To spend time with someone like Charlie who'd been there and done it was different altogether. Sitting two hours at a time where it's just the pair of you drinking tea and eating biscuits, well, you get to know someone properly.

He'd been in Frankland for about three and a half months and was due a visit from his brother, Reggie. We were having our usual cuppa and natter when a screw popped his head round the cell door. He told Charlie that he had to go with him as Reggie was on the phone. It seemed a little strange and when he returned he looked shattered. Reg had been diagnosed with cancer and Charlie took the news badly. His own health was also deteriorating and this news seemed to speed up the process. Doctors were called into see him and they advised that he be moved to a more suitable prison.

On his final day at Frankland, Charlie requested the screws open my door so he could say his goodbyes. I'll never forget his last few words of advice.

'Stephen, don't let what's happened to me and my brothers happen to you and your brothers. Don't let them get you. Don't die in prison. God bless ya, mate.'

Charlie knew he was dying and we knew we'd never see each other again. He passed away three weeks later.

They knew plenty and used their strengths to become very influential people in London in the 60s. When I was a kid and I heard stories about the Krays and their like it wasn't the infamy and reputations I was interested in; I was more interested in where they had failed because I had no intentions of making the same mistakes. Although I liked him as a person, there was nothing glamorous about poor Charlie Kray in his latter days. He died a sad and lonely man in prison with nobody to support him and I can honestly say, hand on heart, that if this is where a life of crime leads to then I'm glad I've retired. Because of their crimes but mainly because of their name, the authorities were able to make examples of them. If there are any similarities between us and them, I'd like it to end with crime and name only.

I'd been locked up for a good while when I had a special visit from the girl of my dreams; my Geordie Princess, Cheryl Ann Fernandez-Versini-Sayers. I don't know how I managed to wangle it, but there she was, wearing a kind of sexy female prison officer uniform. Again, no idea how she got hold of something like that, but it was amazing; *I* was amazing.

Right up until I was awoken by a fucking riot bell going off outside my door – probably some lowlife smackhead caught passing some gear around – had spoilt the best dream a man ever could wish for!

The bells were deafening and the screws ran around screaming for everyone to clear the landings and get behind their doors. *Bang-up, bang-up, bang-up...* what a way to get woken up, but what can you do? That's prison life and I was an inmate. The majority of screws from the wing bent some fool up who was screaming to high heaven for his mother. I shook my head wondered what his could mother possibly do to help him. Maybe give him a clip round the ear and tell him to grow some bollocks? They restrained him and carried him down the block and F-wing fell silent again. It was a pain in the arse to get woken up like that (to be woken up and told you're banged-up, even though you're already asleep and not out on the wing anyway!) but one of the first rules of prison life is never break down and never cry for your mother. You need to keep some dignity, man.

I looked at the gab of my cell door and saw my newspaper. I bent down to pick it up and, as I did, a stiff came under the door (in prison there are two kinds of mail delivery. One is legal and by the prison service, helped along by the royal mail for the price of a stamp and the other kind is illegal and run by the inmates. In the case of 'internal mail', someone with a trustee's job, a red band (a letter) is passed by an inmate for an inmate on a different wing and is called a stiff). I looked through my spy hole to see who'd sent it. The lad showed his face and I recognised him from doing previous time in Frankland years earlier. We briefly spoke and I asked him who the stiff was from and he told me it was from a doorman from Newcastle who claimed to have known me, but he wasn't told his name. I thanked him, he wished me luck for my forthcoming trial and off he went.

I used to get a lot of these types of letters in jail. I'd receive ten letters or so from inmates in Durham jail a week asking for various things, help or advice in one way or another. Whether they were being bullied or had an incoming family member or friend who they wanted me to look after. I'm not being big-headed here, simply stating a fact. The Sayers name was the biggest name in North East prisons and if people needed help then they would turn to us.

I sat down and opened the letter and began to read it. I felt like I was reading the words of a man who was struggling with pain and clearly felt wronged and victimised. This man asked me for advice, it was clear he was hurting. I read the letter a couple of times throughout that day and I have to say that the tone and words within the letter concerned me. I couldn't decide what to do and needed a bit of time to consider my reply, so I sleep on it.

The following morning was a Friday and my friend's son, young Riggers, arrived on the landing. He was inside for a one-punch murder. He'd been in Newcastle one night and ended up in some sort of altercation with another reveller. A punch was thrown and the man who got hit fell to the floor and bumped his head and unfortunately passed away. Riggers never intended to do anything like that; it's not in his nature to kill. Yes, he liked a fight, but he was not a killer. There's even things like the One Punch Can Kill campaign that kicked off in Durham recently and adverts on public transport because it's happening too often. I'm surprised there wasn't more of it back in our Wild West days. I'd pulled a few strings and managed to get Riggers on the wing with me and in a cell just opposite where I could keep an eye on him. I grew up with his dad Michael 'Rig' Ridley in Elswick and, like me, he was an Elswick Mafia Boy. Even though the street gang didn't exist anymore there was and still is a strong bond between us all. The screw brought him over and opened the door so he could put his stuff in the cell and I thanked him. I had no problem with showing young Riggers the ropes. We both got called to reception so we dumped his stuff and headed up.

Reception is a busy place first thing on a morning; organised chaos with people being released and others heading out to court for the day. It's a place for flashpoints where cons who don't get on pass each other and can end up kicking off. In amongst all the hustle and bustle that's going on, it was always easy to get your point across quickly if you had the urge.

As we approached reception, I saw an off through the holding room window: three were punching the living daylights out of someone, who seemed to be giving it what for back until he ran out of gas. There were no screws in sight. We were still in the passage way and hadn't been put in the holding room at that point.

The first screw arrived on the scene, saw what was going on and hit the riot bell and screamed, 'Staff! Staff!' and around 20 more appeared within seconds. They burst into the holding room, which was full of around 30 inmates who were on their way to court. Seconds later, around 30 more screws arrived – I'd never even seen that many in one place – and charged in our direction. Me and Riggers were stood watching it evolve, careful not to look like we were participants. The last thing I needed as part of Riggers' initiation was to get worked over by 50 screws!

The inmates in the holding room were being severely restrained and carried out one by one to the holding cells. The brother of a lad who'd been beaten up decided to wade in, which was fine, but stood right next to me when he started throwing punches. Fucking hell, man! We were trying to keep our noses clean! A load of screws charged and were on him in seconds – and in the process fell into me. I had to get out of the situation and fast or I'd be hauled away as well.

Suddenly, a big pair of arms got me in a bear hug from behind, lifted me up and spun me in the opposite direction. Whoever it was distanced and shielded me with his body against the screws and kept me away from all the trouble. I was 16 and a half stone at the time and this person lifted me up with the greatest of ease. I didn't really know what was going on; it was so bizarre. Stuff like that just doesn't happen. When he turned round and released me, there was no aggression in his face and no malice or badness whatsoever.

It was Raoul Moat. He gave me a friendly cuddle and I could see he was genuinely happy to see me. As the screws restored order we were ushered into the holding room together and he asked me if I'd received his letter. I told him I had but that I'd not had time to reply and as I was aware he was being released. I said I wasn't comfortable writing him a letter that he may not get a chance to read and what I had to tell him was better said face to face.

We managed to grab twenty minutes together in that holding room and the words we exchanged between each other that day will remain that way… between us. I don't have to go into why I don't want to broadcast it all. A screw shouted for Raoul to leave and he gave me another cuddle and wished me well. I told him that if he couldn't be good, be careful. We all know what happened next.

CHAPTER 12
MORE MURDERS

On a dark night on the 20th of September 2000, a group of assassins were plotted up around the perimeter of Freddie Nights' mother's house in Longbenton in Newcastle. The occupants of the house were startled by a heavy knocking on the living room window. Freddie was called and arrived within minutes to see what the disturbance was.

He drove directly over to his mother's in a transit van with his wife Grace, and parked up near the house. As he got out, he couldn't see anybody lurking outside, and followed Grace to his mam's front door. With Grace through the door, a masked gunman jumped out of the bushes and shot Freddie twice in the head at point blank range with a shotgun. Grace instantly started screaming, which was quite understandable under the circumstances, and Freddie's mam, Ella, phoned the police in a total state of shock.

She screamed for help as her son's life ebbed away. The assassins escaped in a car which was later found burned out, destroying all traces of evidence. The ambulance and police arrived at a pub named The Rocket, very near to the house. They waited at the pub while the helicopter and armed police made a swoop of the estate to make sure it was safe for them to enter. It took around 20 minutes. They closed and cordoned off all the roads leading in and out of the estate. After that time, there was no chance for Freddie, but nonetheless, they arrived at the scene to try to revive him before rushing him at high speed with blue lights and sirens blaring with an armed escort to the hospital. Unfortunately for Freddie, he was pronounced dead shortly after arrival. A heavy presence of armed police started combing the area for evidence and suspects.

A year later a man called Lee Watson – an alleged heroin addict and dealer – was driving through Gateshead one night with Dale Miller when they passed a couple of policemen who were also in a car. The policemen must have thought they looked suspicious because they decided to turn round with the intention of stopping and questioning them. Watson and Miller were having none of it and a chase through Gateshead ensued. During the chase, Watson threw nine ounces of high grade heroin out of the window, but the policemen saw what had happened.

After ten minutes, the police managed to box them in and pull them over. They arrested Watson and Miller, and it didn't take them to discover Watson was a heroin addict as he started cold turkeying. He was put under close observation by the Regional Crime Squad, and they decided to use his addiction to their own advantage and questioned him over more serious matters. Watson started saying everything but his prayers.

When I spoke to one of one of Watson's family a few years later, they told me the reason the police manipulated Watson so much was because they were feeding Watson the heroin to not only encourage him, but to also put words in his mouth. This is something I wouldn't take as the gospel truth, but I certainly didn't dismiss it. Whatever the reason, he did what he did and told lies. All the excuses in the world don't justify taking innocent men's freedom.

Watson was well and truly on the police's payroll and they didn't let him off the hook. Northumbria Police, like many other police forces in this country, know exactly how to manipulate a drug addict with a heavy habit. He became an informer and he sung like a canary, but the only problem was that he wasn't singing the right tune. The words that came out of Watson's mouth were not his words. I've read his statement; it just wasn't him – totally out of character and not words that he even used. He'd been manipulated and he just threw as much mud as possible, hoping it would stick: crazy accusations all over the place regarding murders and shootings... it's just as well the shooting of JR Ewing had already been sewn up because he'd have squealed about that one as well. Watson allowed the police to put his name to any unsolved major crime up in the north east and he pointed his finger at us and our associates.

These allegations were so severe that it makes up a 70,000 page statement called Operation Insight, which I mentioned earlier. Watson mentioned our John, Michael Dixon, Dale Miller and Edward Stewart, claiming that they were the masterminds behind Freddie Knights' death.

Along with Watson they were all charged with his murder. All the lads were made Category A prisoners, apart from Watson who was living the good life courtesy of Northumbria Regional Crime Squad. They were all placed on remand in different prisons until they eventually ended up in HMP Doncaster together.

John, a Category AA prisoner, was placed in Full Sutton High Security Jail in Yorkshire; the only remand prisoner to be held in a high security jail, as all the other inmates there had been convicted. Fortunately my younger brother Michael was doing his 12-year sentence in the same jail. For our John and Michael it was time for them to have a catch up and John used the time wisely and prepared Michael for his trial by helping him get mentally and physically fit. He had him training twice a day; fit body fit mind.

The trial took place at Leeds crown court, during which, Watson's girlfriend Vania Allen was called up as a witness. During her cross-examination, our John's barrister, Jonathan Goldberg, asked her how she'd met Watson and if he had acted in anyway different with her compared to any other boyfriends she'd been in a relationship with. She explained that, on her first date with him, Watson took her out for a couple drinks in a local pub in Gateshead. Everything seemed normal until they finished their drinks and Watson stood up and abruptly said, 'Come on. We're going now.'

They left in Watson's vehicle where he drove to a farmer's field and insisted she took heroin with him, which she had never taken before. Unfortunately, that was the start of the young girl's addiction. Watson then decided to have some fun with her when she was warped out of her mind. He drove around the farmer's field, herding the majority of the sheep until he had them boxed into a corner. Watson, high on this power trip, got out of the car and produced a fully loaded pump-action shot gun from the boot and blasted the innocent animals until the gun was empty. He killed four instantly and severely wounded three or four which bled to death. This gave Watson some kind of cheap thrill and a feeling of control and power but for him the night had just started. From there he drove them to a street in Gateshead, reloaded the shot gun and went to some innocent family's home where they were gathered round their TV. Watson thought it would be a laugh to shoot their windows out before doing the front door. Only Watson will know why he did it, but in his deranged mind maybe he thought he'd impressed the young girl. She continued seeing Watson for only a short while after that incident, but sadly her heroin addiction got the better of her.

In court, legal arguments were taking place centring on telephone calls made. Surprisingly, some evidence had gone missing which would have proved John and his co-accused's innocence. The police claimed that the records could not be retrieved. Convenient, as the original copy would have been on their master computer, they'd have had to delete them on purpose, surely.

The police were not afraid to stoop low to gain a conviction. One of them who took the stand claimed that he, 'Had a clear and unobstructed view of John Henry Sayers who was standing next to a gate and talking to his fellow co-accused, Michael Dixon.'

The judge allowed the jury to be taken from Leeds Crown Court to the place where it had allegedly taken place just outside of Newcastle Racecourse in a car park. When the jury arrived there, it was quite clear yet again that this police officer was lying through his teeth as the gate from where he said he'd had a clear and unobstructed view was actually around a corner and was covered by a six foot wall and trees. It was unreal. The jury saw right through the lying bastard and, at times, were sniggering at him it was that blatant.

Any person who goes in to court and deliberately perverts the course of justice by telling lies should be arrested and charged, but this wasn't the case on this occasion. How very odd.

Next up, the star witness: Lee Shaun Watson's turn to face the music. Watson was in the box for a total of two days; two days of hell as far as he was concerned as Jonathan Goldberg asked numerous questions like why he'd jumped up at Gateshead Magistrates Court and said that he was the man responsible for killing Viv Graham. This had been witnessed by three or four policemen, as well as members of the court, who all heard and made statements. Goldberg asked directly, 'Did you kill Viv Graham?' Watson's reply was, 'I do not want to answer that question.' Then, when Watson was asked, 'Are you responsible for the murder of Kicker Milligan?' he also refused to answer the question, saying that he didn't want to incriminate himself.

There were a lot of people who'd been in Frankland Prison with Watson, myself included. He was a racist violent bully, but only to those weaker than him. One particular lad had come forward to me and asked me if I he could have a word in private. We sat down and closed the door to a friend's cell. This young man went in to detail and broke down uncontrollably. I'd never seen such heartache as this vulnerable young man told to me that Watson had violently raped him in his cell on numerous occasions. This is the calibre of the degenerates that Northumbria Police dragged out of the gutter to use against me and my brothers. I was sad to hear that this young lad had tried to take his own life. If I could have got my hands on Watson when I heard that story, I would have castrated him myself. I have always wondered what happened with the young lad and I hope and pray he got his life back together.

The trial lasted a few more weeks. Mark Rowe and I were there every day and we travelled up and down each morning. The judge finally dismissed the jury and sent them out to make their decision. They were out a couple of days as they were uncertain about some legal points and sent notes back and forth to the judge.

To us it was all a bit tiring as it had been a long haul with all the stress on the family and the travelling. Our John got found not guilty on murder and not guilty on manslaughter. The case was then adjourned until the following day and the jury returned to their secure locations. We travelled back up to Newcastle for the night and prepared ourselves for the next day. Even though our John had received a not guilty for murder and manslaughter it was still possible that he could receive a life sentence for GBH.

We arrived the following morning at court as planned, but that day turned out to be different to the others. There was a long queue to get into the court. I spoke to Richard Haswell and his junior barrister Andy Rutter and wished them well. Armed police were searching everyone on arrival more than usual. When we were finally allowed to enter the court buildings, I could see all the legal team together talking with very serious looks on their faces. I asked one of the juniors what was going on and all he could tell me at this present time, no family or friends were allowed into the Freddie Knights murder trial. I spoke to Toby Hedworth QC and I asked him what was going on. He told me that someone had contacted a jury member that night and had tried to knobble them. Naturally, the prosecution pointed their crooked fingers at the innocent party: me and my associates.

We took this with a pinch of salt because our attitude was if you're going to nobble a jury then you'd nobble the jury at the start of the trial and not at the end, wouldn't you? As John had already received two out of three not guilty, it wouldn't make sense either. The trial continued and after the jury were called back a couple of times: 'Have you made the decision on John Henry Sayers for the charge of Grievous Bodily Harm with intent?' and the foreman of the jury replied, 'Yes, we have a decision on John Henry Sayers.'

'How do you find John Henry Sayers... guilty or not guilty?'

The foreman replied firmly, 'Not guilty.'

The courtroom erupted with cheers and screams of delight. The noise was deafening. The judge shouted for order, but we took no notice. We had big smiles on our faces as we waited outside for our John to come out, then we saw him, walking down the street coming towards us with my dad and Uncle Thomas Kelly. All three had big grins on their faces and it was such a pleasure to see this after the stress everyone had been put under.

We made our way back to Newcastle, arriving at 6pm. I went with our John to see his children and then to see our mam. My phone was like a call centre that day, maybe a hundred or so congratulating our John. We stayed at our mam's and had a cup of tea and she had tears of joy streaming down her face, she was so overwhelmed with happiness. Many family and friends were waiting to see him in the Prince of Wales in the West End. This was one of our pubs at the time and was run by a good friend, Mark Mennim.

We parked up outside and, as we were parking we saw so many people going in it didn't seem like there would be enough room in there; at least 300 people, including my co-authors Steve and Stu. We walked in the big swing doors of the pub where we were greeted with an enormous roar. It was one hell of an atmosphere. I could hear the lads whistling a tune from the corner of the bar: the one they whistle in *The Great Escape*. The music was turned off in the bar and everyone whistled along with them. It was very emotional and I could see grown men with tears in their eyes. It was one of those moments in life you just want to repeat over and over again.

The drinks flowed and people came in all night to greet us and congratulate us, even though our John had been found not guilty it was a sad night for some of his co-accused. They all got found not guilty of murder but Dale got 16 years, Eddie received 13 years and Michael Dixon received a nine-year sentence. The degenerate Watson, who the prosecution decided not to charge, received 11 years but, may I add, when he arrived at court to be sentenced he'd previously pleaded guilty to murder. The judge asked him if he'd like to plead to murder again and he replied he would. They allowed him to re-plead, so Watson changed his original plea and went with not guilty to murder but guilty to manslaughter.

Watson put in an appeal in against his sentence and expected his friends at Northumbria Police to get his sentence reduced, but Watson had served his purpose and they had no need or intention in doing the degenerate any more favours whatsoever.

I never really heard of Watson much more after the court case, apart from when he got out. I heard he had received an IPP sentence for violence; no doubt again some harmless person and, as for his admission in open court that he was responsible for the murder of Viv Graham, no action was ever taken against him for the crime. Although there have been other people admitting to it over the years; in particular, one reported in *The Evening Chronicle* in 2014 when a police informant claimed to be the getaway driver on the night. Apparently though, he just regurgitated information that was already in the public domain, so it was plain to see that he was trying to fit someone up for it.

For a while, there was a lot going off in Newcastle. There seemed to be high profile shootings being covered in the press quite often. It elevated the reputation the city had for gangland activity because they were labelled as 'hits' or 'contract killings'.

Peter Beaumont Gowling was an associate of mine who served almost five years of an 11-year sentence for laundering £2.5m worth of drugs money. My involvement with Peter consisted of taking care of much of his debt related problems, which were nothing to do with drugs. We'd been on remand together and he was just as flamboyant inside as he was on the outside.

Peter was a wealthy man; he sold property in Darlington and was worth well over a couple of million at the time. He felt secure having me around him and it suited me because he was a brilliant bloke to be around and it was a pretty easy job to do. I chased a few people who were trying to shake him down and also one or two who were trying to bully him. In that sense, people like Peter could be an easy target; he was very generous and sociable and I suppose that made him vulnerable to those on the take. Basically, he was a decent bloke and there'll always be people around to take advantage of decency. After the way I dealt with the bully who'd targeted him, Peter knew that the bully was not going to return, and he regained his confidence and felt good about himself again.

After a night's drinking it would always be back to his place for a party. He loved the 'Champagne Charlie' lifestyle and never wanted the night to end. Although, by the amount of toot he had, the night never *did* end. Peter could quite easy spend ten grand on beak and put it on the table for everybody until it was gone... just like Jack Nicholson in *The Departed*. Every time I went on the drink with him he would always insist on trying to give me money. He wanted to pay me well for my time and I'm talking grands at a time

249

without me even asking or hinting for anything. That's how nice he was. It was like when you try to take your dad out for a meal and they keep insisting on paying almost to the point where you have to leg it to the till to pay first rather than waiting for the waiter to bring the bill over. It was just him, his generosity; how he was. 'Here you go, Stephen. Keep it. I insist.' It was crazy, thinking back.

He phoned me up one day and asked if I would do him a favour. He told me he'd heard a whisper that he was going to be tied up and he gave me the name of the person that was going to do it. It turned out that it was my cousin and Peter insisted I should give this man £20k to not tie him up. I told him I'd do better than that and said I would have a firm word in my cousin's ear. I was sat in Peter's front room; a lovely downstairs flat on Osbourne Road in Jesmond, Newcastle. He came in and handed me a briefcase containing £30k and asked me to deal with his problem. He was so frightened he had tears in his eyes. This kind of situation wasn't the sort of thing Peter needed in his life. He only had money to pay his way out – it was all he knew to do. He demanded I took the money and sorted everything out for him so I phoned my cousin and asked to make a meet.

My cousin told me he'd been drunk in the pub one night and saw Gowling drinking there as well. Knowing Gowling had been tied up previously, my cousin would torment him; he was a right workie ticket after a few drinks – it seems to run in the family – and he yelled across the bar, 'I'm going to tie you up!'

My cousin had no real bad intention; he was just drunk and being daft. I asked how much it would take for him to leave Gowling alone and his reply was 'nothing'. He asked if I was looking after Gowling and I told him I was. He phoned Gowling and apologised; he said it was just drunken banter and this gave Peter the peace of mind he was after.

Later that night I went to my cousin's house. He was feeling a bit down and told me he was finding things hard and his car had been stolen. He had no insurance and had paid £4,500 for it. I told him I was going to cheer him up and told him, his girlfriend and their kids that I would send them on holiday to Spain. You could see the delight on their faces immediately. They were over the moon! I gave him ten grand so he could afford to buy a new car and book the holiday, with a little to come back to – all is well that ends well.

I went back to see Peter and told him my cousin had accepted ten grand of the money he'd given me and that I would take the same. He just wanted me on board and knew I could be relied upon. He knew my reputation. Everyone did. Everyone still *does*. He knew I was loyal and, of course, he knew my capabilities.

It was back to normal: partying back at Peter's on the famous Osbourne Road. Peter had a sky blue Bentley that was only six months old; a lovely car, definitely what you'd call a head turner. I couldn't get a taxi one Saturday night so he told me to take his car, which I did. He said he'd phone when he needed the car back, so I was up sharp on Sunday morning and got Donna and our children in the car... and off we went for a day out in Edinburgh! Well, what else could I do? It was a beautiful car and I wanted to be seen out in it and enjoy it a little bit longer. No harm done, eh? When we returned, Peter was at my door with a big smile on his face. I guessed it was because he saw his car back in one piece. He asked for the keys and immediately went to the boot where he proceeded to remove a sports bag with £100k inside! That's why he was so happy to see the car again! He'd left it there as he wouldn't leave money in the house anymore. If it was me, I'd have thought of a less conspicuous mobile bank... Mainly one that didn't draw the attention of car thieves. I mean, imagine the feeling if you'd nicked such a car *and then* found the jackpot in the boot! It was scary how reckless he could be at times. I'd been driving around in his car for three days with no idea the money was there. If I'd found it, I would have given it back to him immediately. Not just because he was a mate, but in case the law clocked me in it and pulled me over for a search! I doubt I could have talked my way out of that one very easily.

My involvement with him just kind of fizzled out soon after. It was a shame to lose out on the work as well as his friendship, but with a character like Peter, I always thought I'd hear from him again when he got into the next scrape or some other firm tried to put the squeeze on him.

Unfortunately, the next time I heard his name was on the news. He was shot dead in his own home on Valentine's Day and it was his girlfriend who found his body. He'd been shot several times in the head, the chest and the back at close range. Poor bastard. This is what I meant earlier about guns having an effect on everyone concerned... discovering that kind of scene will stay with you forever. Not only because he was dead, but shot in such an excessive way and there must have been a fucking horrible mess. It was reported that he must have known the killer or killers as he'd opened the door to them.

You know, Peter was a good bloke: very generous and down to earth, despite all his money and connections. Anything he'd been involved with in his past, as far as I could see, was just used to fund his champagne lifestyle. He loved parties and coke and that's what he was about. He wasn't a gangster or a hardman or wanted any involvement with guns or violence. There was a quote in one of the local papers where he said: 'Irrespective of how I felt in relation to my sentence and an excessive fine of £1m I have conducted myself very gracefully throughout. I believe that my debts to society have now been paid in full. I'm determined to leave the past behind me and am looking forward to continuing my life in a productive and sensible manner.'

Again, it's an unsolved case and I've heard a few rumours over the years: some of them have been plausible and others laughable. One thing that is certain is that Peter lived his life to the full – maybe not always as sensible as he said he was going to, but it was what he was about – and no one deserves to come to such a horrible end like that. Just to thicken the plot a bit more, *The Journal* reported that a letter was sent to them as follows:

'It seems that someone is going to have to explain why BG had to go. He thought he could walk straight back into the business. He was special once and made us lots of money but he couldn't keep his head down. He had to be seen with the birds and play the big spender. It was all bad publicity. When he went down it was bad news for both producers and investors. We had to fill the void. Confidence had to be restored. Sacrifices were made. Whatever plans he made couldn't be allowed to happen. We couldn't take the chance. The decision in the end was easy and best done quickly. Who was going to miss him. Just his women. No loss really. And by the way the police are wasting their time doing forensic matching. That really is insulting our intelligence.'

The police were apparently looking into it further, but nothing has really happened.

Guns went from being something you feared and respected to being something that any skip rat could get their hands on very easily. You only used to see a gun in an armed robbery or something else high profile. We used to think it was just the Americans who had guns, then we used to think that it was just those London folk who had hold of them... surely we wouldn't have guns in the North? But we do and they've been around for ages. Forget any misconceptions about levels of criminality in the UK and any North-South divide in that respect. They've been all over for as long as I can remember. I think the media has played a big part in it all. First there was all those LA gangsta films where people would brandish handguns at a 45-degree angle, which I suppose looked pretty cool to the kids and made guns seem like a good accessory for all the hoody lot to carry around. And maybe that's why we tend to associate guns with all those types – they'd shoot each other up because they wouldn't have a clue how to fight. Fucking hell, in Newcastle people had been getting shot for years – it's just that you didn't always hear about it.

CHAPTER 13
THE JEALOUS GRASS

Okay let's get this straight; the only reason I am mentioning the jealous grass in this book is because, in my mind, we have a right to reply for the first time to 20 years of slander and outrageous accusations that this pathetic excuse of a man has made against me and my family. He does not belong in this book otherwise. He has never committed what I and other criminals would describe as a criminal act of bravery in his entire life. He's laughed at by other criminals the length and breadth of the British Isles. I'd heard that even his plan to steal candy from a baby was foiled before he got anywhere near the pram. He commands no respect. I am an old-fashioned man with old-fashioned morals and I am going to set the record straight once and for all. Why has this man chosen to discredit me and my family? He is incapable of doing anything psychical to us so he has chosen to use the tactics of character assassination, and what better way to do that then to call the opposition 'grasses'. He even came a bit unstuck when things didn't quite go so well for him on Westgate Hill during a run-in with 'the Sayers firm' where he maintains 14 of us did him over. Luckily for him, he managed to knock six of us out in one go (cough) before he was taken down. Surely a man like the jealous grass would have came out on top, no matter what.

I was introduced to a wise old man once who described himself as a historian amongst other things and he told me that he knew of both the Sayers and the grass's family and also their respective criminal backgrounds. He compared the two families to football teams: Newcastle United being the Sayers and the Bedlington Terriers being the other family. He also said, 'Just bear this in mind; when the managers of Newcastle United and the manager of Bedlington Terriers have their team talk, both will sound very convincing and both will sound very similar, but when the two teams go out to play the quality of the football played by Newcastle as opposed to Bedlington is so superior it's leagues apart.'

I found this wise old man very interesting and accurate. He also went on to tell me that history has a tendency to forget the quiet ones. I asked him to explain himself in more detail and he told me that people like myself, my brothers and our associates are a dying breed due to advances in technology. He said that there were no records of us trying to defend or clear our name against the slander and outrageous accusations that this man has used to deflect attention away from himself. So in years to come our name would be blackened with no way of clearing it and the only records of us that would be out there would be extremely inaccurate. In telling the truth within this book, I can at least start to address some of that.

The jealous grass is, without doubt, a police informer and a coward who is driven by jealousy and hurt through failure and he uses the Sayers' name to portray himself on par with us. There's been a lot of blood spilt and a lot of prison sentences served and a lot of tears shed for us to bow to him or anybody. This fool has got us so wrong.

It was 1995. After the failed attempt on my dad's life the hitman Robert Stokoe drove himself directly to Gateshead police station and made a full confession and statement and that he now feared for his life. He handed a .22 handgun in. Stokoe was charged and and was remanded immediately. He was so scared that he felt he'd be safe behind bars. Stokoe arrived in HMP Durham prison fully aware of the situation he had willingly or unwillingly placed himself in. He didn't fancy his chances on the wing and he requested protection and put himself down the block in the segregation unit which was also used to hold Category A prisoners. He was put next door to the jealous grass who, at that time, had no bad feeling towards us apart from his jealousy of our success. While Stokoe was being moved into the cell his new neighbour was taken on a visit. This was when he came across Stokoe and they made their introductions as they passed each other.

The grass's brother made it very clear that his family were indebted to the Sayers family for a major favour we'd done for them, which them and their associates were incapable of doing themselves. It was a bit of work out of their league but it was sorted by a member of my family. This was not a financial debt in any way; it was a debt of honour and the older brother specifically told his younger brother that he must attack Stokoe on sight for their family's respect. But the grass had never been a violent man. He would always handpick his victims and he never fancied his chances with violent men. The older brother left the prison and drove immediately to my home on Grange Road, Fenham, with a big smile on his face and I invited him in for a cup of tea.

He asked to talk with me outside so we went into the garden where he told me the man that shot my dad had arrived in Durham prison and that they had placed him next door to his younger brother. He assured me that his brother was going to beat Stokoe up and leave him in a really bad condition. He always had a high opinion of his brother, but my opinion was totally different. I knew he was just an aggressive schoolyard bully with no brain and a child's temper. The older brother left and told me he would give me a phone call later when the job was done.

His final words were, 'This is the least we can do for you. We are indebted to you and more than grateful for what you've done for us and we're only too happy to help.'

I believed those words that he spoke to me; it's just a shame that his brother didn't share the same morals. He was clearing something in his family's name and it meant fuck all to him. Time passed. A week went by and still no call. Instead of giving him a hiding, the jealous grass befriended Stokoe! In fairness, Stokoe was a convincing liar and he had a way of getting people to like him. He was a half-educated man and the subjects he talked about he seemed knowledgeable in. A man of low intelligence like the grass was very easy prey for Stokoe, who wrapped him around his little finger and he hatched a plan that only the jealous grass could fall for. He told him that he had discs containing records of all paid informers and transactions involving our family. He said he was willing to hand these over to him in exchange for £10k. He had his victim eating out of his hand.

In the meantime, the jealous grass had been told he was facing a sentence between 20-22 years for the charges he faced. He was involved in an alleged torture and subsequent armed escape from the prison van he was being transported in. You have to wonder what deal he made with Northumbria Police to get his sentence reduced to less than half; bearing in mind that we got ten-year sentences on guilty pleas for charges that have guide lines of three to four years?

About two weeks passed by and the news we were getting from our friends on the wing was that the jealous grass had been shouting that he had discs on the entire Sayers family and every one of their associates, claiming that we were all grasses. He also sent letters to people in jails up and down the country saying that people were getting arrested everywhere in the UK because of the Sayers family and he had discs to prove it. The fact is that not a sinner had been arrested. Talk about counting your chickens before they hatch. This was the fool trying to deflect the attention of shame away from himself for failing to carry out the job he should have done for his family.

As the months went by, nobody could get to him or Stokoe because they were separated from all the other inmates and the jealous grass was still ranting and raving saying that he had proof that my dad had positively identified Stokoe on an identity parade and made a 20-page statement about Stokoe, but this could not have been any further from the truth. The problem the jealous grass has always had is that he's always judged others on his own low-life morals and degenerate standards. This was his weakness yet the fool couldn't see it.

A very good friend of mine arrived in Durham from Winson Green; Tony Armstrong (Big Bud to you). He'd been placed on the same landing in the unit of HMP Durham prison as the jealous grass. How convenient! He immediately went to the jealous grass's cell door and put it directly on him, demanding to know where the evidence was about the Sayers being grasses. The jealous grass told him that he was getting the evidence in the next couple of days and he was going to show the world and its dog and it was going to go viral. Bud had little option but to walk away as the cell door was locked and there was no way the jealous grass was going to ask for it to be opened.

Two days passed and Bud was lying in his cell. He heard the jealous grass's big mouth on the phone talking. Soon after, he heard something get pushed under the threshold of the door. It was a lump of dope. It was the jealous grass saying that he had the disks and that he wanted no hard feelings, so here was a smoke on him.

By that time, the grass had arranged for a meeting to take place between his older brother and Stokoe's wife to exchange the cash for the half a dozen discs. The meet was made for a Wednesday. Once they had the discs the plan was to sell them back to the government to make a deal for the jealous grass to be released. I think he'd watched a few too many films, or had smoked a bit too much gear.

The older brother made arrangements and turned up with his brother in law, who was also a friend of mine. There were also three legal representatives and a half a dozen top-ranking civil servants from the Home Office in London. The meet was made for 6pm in Newcastle and it was to be a straight hand over, or so they believed. The two parties turned up and the woman had her hand in the bag as though she was about to take the discs out and the older brother passed her the cash payment of £10k. In turn, she pulled out a key. The older brother asked what was going on and where the disks were. She told him that, for security reasons, she'd placed them in a locker at Central Station and that was the key to open the locker. Sneaky fucker, eh? There was a keyring attached to the key with a number engraved into the metal. The older brother took the key and let the woman leave instead of getting her to take him to the locker. Had he not watched *any* crime films?

He took the key and, along with the people from the Home Office and the jealous grass's legal team, straight to the Central Station to open the locker and collect the disks. After months and months of calling us and our associates grasses and swearing he had the evidence to back it up, it all hung on the turn of this key. He must have felt like a low-rent Noel Edmonds... and in this case, it was No Deal. All eyes were on him as he put the key in the lock and turned it and opened door to find.... absolutely nothing. Fuck all, in fact; just empty space which, ironically, is what you'd find in his younger brother's head if you opened it up with a baseball bat shaped key. There were no discs, no evidence. For safe measure, he tried the key in every single locker that was there but the key only fitted one locker. To say the people from the Home Office were a little upset would be an understatement. They shouted at the grasses legal team for being amateurs and time wasters saying they were the victims of a confidence trick and had been swindled out of £10k.

I spoke to Bud and he told me it was absolutely hilarious as there were only four people in the unit and the grass had not shut up about these discs and how he was going to be released in the morning. He was that so certain of his imminent release that he'd given all his belongings away including his radio and tobacco. All of which now resided with Bud.

The jealous grass was like a cat on a hot tin roof. He got a screw to allow him out of his cell to make an emergency call.

Seconds later:

'Where the fuck are the fucking discs?! I'm supposed to be getting released today! I want to go home!'

Hearing this, Bud was close to death by laughter. The jealous grass was screaming so loudly that the screw terminated his phone call, which only took his childish temper to the next level; a stamp-your-feet tantrum.

'I should be going home today! I want my fucking discs!'

The screws had no choice but to restrain him and force him back into his cell. Bud had never seen or heard anything so ridiculous coming from a grown man in his life. This from a man who claimed he was running Newcastle! Then it suddenly dawned on him that Stokoe was still in the cell nextdoor to him, so he screamed, 'Stokoe, where are my fucking discs? I want my fucking money back!'

Stokoe, always thinking on his feet, pacified the clown (probably gave him a toffee or entertained him with a lullaby) and somehow convinced him that he'd put everything right the following day.

When Stokoe was up for sentencing at crown court, all of the jealous grass's family and friends attended. My dad attended with his solicitor to try to assist Robert Stokoe as he'd not made a statement; all he'd said was that he didn't see who'd shot him. Even though my dad was a victim of the crime, he said 'no reply' all the way through.

The prosecution stood up and told the judge that Robert Stokoe was pleading guilty to GBH with intent for shooting my dad in the face. It was also stated that he'd been a police informant for over 15 years and that he'd been helpful to Northumbria Police. Gasps of disbelief came from the grass's family as reality sank in. Their brother had been conned out of £10k through his own stupidity. The older brother, being old-fashioned and respectful in his ways, approached my dad and shook his hand and apologised. He explained that his brother's head was gone and he kept apologising. Reporters from newspaper, TV and radio were there and they all repeated that Robert Stokoe was a police informer and told of his massive assistance to Northumbria Police.

Bud and everybody on the wing were tuned into their radios for the 2pm news. Well, everybody except the grass who'd given his away. Bud turned it up for his benefit though. It was the top story and explained why they were only giving Stokoe a four-year sentence for shooting my dad in the face. The grass shouted and screamed at the top of his voice saying, 'They are all grasses and they work with the Sayers!'

Bud laughed at him. 'Who are all grasses? Who's working for the Sayers?'

The jealous grass shouted back really aggravated, 'All them mugs in court; the judge the defence team and the CPS. They're all grasses!' Bud could not believe his ears. It seemed that the man's mind was shot... I guess he's taken his obsession with 'grass' a bit too far these days.

After my dad's court case the cat was out of the bag as far as Stokoe was concerned. Everybody was 100% certain that he was a grass and they were correct. A week or so later, the jealous grass got moved from HMP Durham to HMP Full Sutton. In the meantime, our good friend Bud Armstrong saw an opportunity and seized it with both hands. They would never put Stokoe on association with him, but because Stokoe would always ask to be with the jealous grass and vice versa, they would end up together all the time. One day on association, Bud was watching a bit of boxing on the TV when Stokoe just appeared and started talking away to him like he was his long lost friend. Stokoe asked what he was watching as there was a wildlife programme about to start that he wanted to watch.

'Watch what you want, mate, I'm going to take a shower,' he told him. Bud made his way back to his cell and improvised by melting razor blades into his tooth brush handle, then he came straight back for the unsuspecting Stokoe. Bud grabbed him by the scruff of his neck and said, 'The Sayers brothers say hello,' and carved him up like a Sunday roast.

Stokoe screamed for the screws, 'Armstrong has a knife! *He has a knife*! He's cut my face. He's slashed me,' he screamed! The big wufter.

The screws took Bud back to his cell and took Stokoe to the hospital. He required 58 stitches and Bud was later arrested and charged and eventually ended up with another four years on top of his 14 that he was already doing for violent robberies.

During the time the jealous grass was in Durham unit, he remained in contact with Stokoe and he'd not have a bad word said about him. This annoyed a lot of people, including his family who found it shameful. Bud eventually ended up in HMP Full Sutton and got put on the same wing as the jealous grass and it seemed he was like he was vast becoming the Angel of Karma. Keen to shut the grass up once and for all, but not keen on adding anymore bird onto his sentence, he bided his time. One day the screws shouted Bud up for a visit where he necked a nice little parcel. To cut a long story short, he ended up needing laxatives for a week-long bout of constipation and, when his seven days of prison food finally arrived, he stored it up in a newspaper, walked straight over to the grass and, from behind, forcefully rammed the newspaper into his face and scrubbed him with putrid shite. After crying and vomiting, he ran back to his cell screaming and didn't venture out again that night. Instead, early morning before the cells got opened up, he put himself down the block on protection, which he was known to do in most places he served his time.

It's not difficult to work out that I've been a criminal all my life, as have the majority of my associates. It stands to reason that as criminals we associate with other criminals. Every profession works in the same way. Myself and every other criminal in Newcastle upon Tyne are amazed and flabbergasted why this man could contemplate even passing any sort of opinion on crime, as he's never committed any or experienced any at major level. The biggest job he's ever done is probably shoplifted from his local Farmfoods. If he went on *Match of the Day* and commentated on football, people would ask what he was doing there and why he had the right to talk about a subject that he has no knowledge of; he same goes for crime. People have asked me what crimes he's ever committed and the honest reply is nothing. Absolutely nothing. He's never worked on the pavement (blagging) nor fought on the cobbles (straighteners), but in his mind there is nobody quite like him and he has become a legend in his own kitchen. The jealous grass has always been obsessed with men that have reputations for violence and Psycho, who I gave that terrible beating to in Raffles, was his hero. I bumped into the jealous grass about two weeks after I'd beaten up Psycho, at the Citroen garage on Elswick Road. As I was driving along I caught a glimpse of him, I immediately stopped my car and put it straight on him, 'Do you have a fucking problem with the fact that I did your hero? Because if you do, I'll do you now. Get down the back lane!'

Being his usual cowardly self, he bad-mouthed Somerville to try to get on side with me.

'Fuck off, you fucking coward. He was your friend, man! Get down this back lane with me, now!'

He knew better. He has only ever liked violence with people who are not violent. The jealous grass immediately jumped in his car and wheel spun away, only daring to shout idle threats from his car window when he was a safe distance away. He can talk a good fight but not a person alive has ever witnessed him stand up to any man that was not weaker than him. He's always been impressed by violent men and has always been impressed by criminals. He has an unhealthy obsession with the Sayers' name and reputation. At any and every given opportunity whether it be on TV or in books, online or in newspapers and even in general conversation with any fucker who'll listen, he thrives and jumps at the opportunity to mention us.

This impressionable fool has now become our biggest fan and tries to link himself to major crimes and robberies that are not only completely out of his league, but that he has nothing to do with whatsoever. He has even invented a mass gangland feud between the Sayers and his family in Newcastle but it could not be further from the truth! The fact of the matter is this is a complete one-sided affair. The feud has only ever existed in his own big, empty head. It's quite sad and pathetic, really.

During the Freddie Knights trial I had a lot of support from friends and family. My friend Mark Rowe, my travelling cousins Frankie and Phillip Riley, Jason heels from Bishop Auckland and my good pal, Boss Kal, Javid and Mumtaz, and many more. They all made their way to Leeds to show their moral support for the family.

We decided to go for fish and chips during a break, so about 25 of us made our way to a chippy. We were all enjoying our food and sitting in the sun when we received a call to say that the jealous grass had gone and sat in the courtroom to point and laugh at the lads that were stood in dock. He was holding his stomach and mocking them with exaggerated signs of false laughter. He stayed for no more than five minutes before leaving, knowing full well that we were on our way back for him, and he got out before we arrived. I think what he did that day was an act of a man with no morals; gloating at the possibility of another man facing the rest of his life in jail. A man of such low morals who can find amusement and pleasure in another man spending the rest of his life in jail would surely have no problem in putting him there.

The jealous grass had already decided in his polluted warped mind of bitterness that our John was going to receive a life sentence and the jury's decision was just going to be a mere formality. Little did he realise, we're from good stock and we don't give in or crumble under the first bit of opposition we come across... unlike him.

The end of the trial came and our John was acquitted on the charge of murder but was waiting on charges of manslaughter and GBH with intent. Either one of these charges was enough to give him a life sentence and the jealous grass was fully aware of this. He'd arranged for about 30 of his family and friends to have a barbeque in his back garden to celebrate the outcome, and apparently spent over £1,000 on champagne and fireworks for the party to celebrate the news that he'd been craving.

The phone call came through that John was found not guilty and my friend's sister, who attended the family get-together told us how his happy mood descended like a lead balloon, or even like an over-grown child who'd just been told his party was cancelled. He smashed the phone off the floor and he ran over to his fireworks (that had taken him over an hour to assemble) and kicked into them, screaming and shouting at the top of his voice. Needless to say he called off the barbeque, but still there were fireworks!

During his mission of discrediting us to draw attention away from himself, me and John were approached by David Glover senior, who told us that the sad excuse for a man had pressured his son to turn police informer and make a statement to Northumbria Police saying, in the idiot's words but through Glover's mouth, that me and Michael had been responsible for the murder of our friend Viv Graham. It turned out that Davey Glover junior made a deal with Northumbria Police to be the main prosecution witness in the case, giving evidence against me and Michael.

Unfortunately for the jealous grass, this did not happen as he had planned. Old Glover also told us that if any harm was to happen to the jealous grass that me and my brothers were to be immediately arrested because the jealous grass had sent a letter to the CPS, the Home Secretary, Northumbria Police Chief Constable and the Lord Chief Justice and any other person in a position of legal power. And probably the Prime fucking Minister. No doubt his handlers got a copy of the letter too. Each letter stated that if any severe harm came to him or if he was killed, the people responsible would be the Sayers brothers and their associates. I have to admit this did amuse both me and John.

I asked Glover Snr if the jealous grass would fight me to put an end to this farce and his reply was, 'Stephen, this coward will do nothing but mouth off from a distance.'

So basically if any harm comes to him, we'll get arrested and remanded off the back of a statement that he cobbled together. There is not a chance in the world this coward will turn up for a fight with anyone that will hit him back, so my options are very limited. I was brought up with old-fashioned morals and, before I retired, I was an old-fashioned villain. I am not an attention seeker; as a villain it is not a good asset.

You may ask me why I'm on social media websites and publicising a book that you're now reading, when it's out of character for me to draw attention to myself? It's very simple: it's to set the record straight.

In 2005 I was drinking in Newcastle with a load of my friends who I had grown up with in a pub called The Mill, a very busy bar that I was involved with. There were a lot of characters good and bad that used to frequent the place including my dad and a lot of my family. Our Michael's kids Michael, Anthony and Camille would always pop in to see their granddad. Good mates like Tom Brayson and his twin's son Thomas, my young namesake Stephen Maurice, Hezzy, Rig, young Riggers, Tommy Dillon, Billy Dixon, and John 'Mario' Cunningham to name a few. There were a lot of good nights in that bar, but unfortunately it was all going to come to an end. One quiet afternoon about 20 drug squad officers burst in and ripped a certain area of the bar to pieces. Everybody found this strange as it was not a bar that sold drugs. They found nothing and were very upset. The bar had to be repaired and was closed for a couple of weeks, but it was eventually re-opened.

I called in with Michael to see my dad and have a couple of drinks when we were approached by this man whose face was black and blue. He told us that he was one of the reasons why the bar was raided. We took him to a quiet table so he could explain himself. He said that the jealous grass had given him a bag containing smack, crack and coke and told him to hide it in The Mill in a certain place and, if he didn't do it, he was in for a good hiding. Credit where credit is due this lad did not do what the jealous grass wanted. Instead he went round to his mate's house and they consumed the contents of the bag.

The next day the lad left the house and bumped straight into the jealous grass who demanded to know why the drugs had not been planted in the bar. The lad made a good enough excuse and convinced the jealous grass that he still had the stuff and it would be done in half an hour. I later found out that the jealous grass had been nicked with two or three knives on him when he was still on license and due up in court, expecting jail. With the effort he had put in to get us nicked, all he got was a slap on the wrist for his crime.

On his release, he continued to launch his tirades against me and my family, but his tall stories had worn thin. Shame he hadn't as well. People started to wise up to this fool and his TV appearances and attacks in the local newspapers have all been for nothing. He was famous for four minutes, but ultimately he has mugged himself off. His family have disowned him and the self-proclaimed King of Newcastle's Underworld lives in caravan on his ex-wife's drive, smoking dope, ranting and raving about me and my brothers on Facebook. He even tried to grab some publicity in 2015 by wanting to go on *The Jeremy Kyle Show*. There'd be a multitude of reasons, but my guess is that he wanted to confess his love for the three of us. His eagerly-anticipated book (cough) ended up with someone else's name on it. I've heard he's planning another one now. I hope he's got plenty of photos to accompany the blank pages. Maybe a dot-to-dot or a colouring book would be easier for him to complete. He's tried his utmost to disrespect our family; a family that has been tried and tested at the highest level and, despite his humiliation, he still has his agenda and that is why I have had to set the record straight. You see, I might be as loyal as an old mongrel, but I'll not be treated as such.

CHAPTER 14
WASTING MORE TIME

I was living a single life in an upstairs flat in Grace Street in Byker with Angie and Brooksey living downstairs. Angie and her two twin daughters Shauna and Jamie aka Wor Fizz, used to cook and clean and do other household chores for me. Not that I couldn't do it myself or wasn't domesticated, it was just nice to have an extra helping hand and some company. Brooksey and Angie were like a comedy duo with their constant dysfunctional public arguments. They were as functional as they were dysfunctional – just like watching a sitcom. Joking aside, Angie and Brooksey have always been there for me and my brothers over the years.

Angie had made tea for me and Brooksey one night; lamb chops with onion gravy, mashed potato, and loads of veg and homemade triple chocolate cake and custard just like you used to get at school. It was proper food; the kind where you have to loosen your belt and have a snooze in front of the TV after it. Most of the meals she cooked were like that. She used to be a school dinner lady, so we were never going to go hungry. I was a bit worried I might fall through the floor into their flat if I wasn't careful. Rather than falling asleep in front of the TV though, we finished our slap-up meal with a couple bottles of wine each while the twins washed and cleaned up. Can't get better than that, eh?

My youngest daughter, Stevie Lee, would always be there; she practically lived at Angie's. I remember Brooksey and me finished up drinking around 3am. I staggered upstairs smoking a freshly made spliff before bed. I fell in to a deep sleep and was rudely awakened by a group of armed policemen braying on my door. *Why was it never just the fucking postman?* My head was still all over the place. I looked out the window and, as I rubbed my eyes to try and remove the previous night's drink and sleep, I saw a much heavier-presence of armed police in my back garden than previous visits. They were shouting and trying to intimidate me and most of them had machine guns. Machine guns, again?! I'd been down this road so many times before and knew their routine.

I got dressed as they continued to hammer on the front door, screaming for me to open it. I was neither impressed nor intimidated by any of this and I decided to take my time. Maybe a bit more time than usual, just to prolong their wait. I noticed there was half the spliff left from the previous night and they'd probably have me for supplying drugs if I wasn't careful. So, being careful, I sat down and disposed of the evidence before putting my socks, shoes and fleece on. I strolled to the kitchen, opened the fridge and finished of half a carton of freezing cold fresh orange juice. Then it was time to face the music and I opened the door.

'Stephen Maurice Sayers. I am arresting you for perverting the course of justice in the trial of Freddie Knights.' And then he read me my rights.

Take heed in what I am about to tell you: when arrested, silence is the most powerful weapon you possess. I didn't need to give my name or address as they clearly already had it. They handcuffed me and took me downstairs. On the way out I saw Angie, Brooksey and the twins. They all had a tear in their eyes for me that day. I looked around and gave the twins a wink and assured them I would be ok and told them to contact my solicitor, Richard Haswell.

The police took me to Etal Lane station in Blakelaw to mess me about for an hour or so as I wouldn't give my name. I wasn't there for conversation and they knew exactly who I was and why they'd picked me up. It seemed like a pointless charade to me.

'We are not bothered. We'll keep you here all day.'

They placed me in a cell and told me if I gave my name they'd let my solicitor in. OK, then. I told them my name and they let Richard in and he explained that they were going to interview me and possibly charge me for perverting the course of justice on the Freddie Knights murder trial.

As we entered the interview room, Richard give me some professional legal advice which I took notice of. Naturally, I used my right to remain silent and sat there and listened to the allegations against me, emotionless with a poker face. Actually, I listened to the accusations in disbelief and wondered if this was some sort of sick joke. It was difficult not to react to it all; like their lies got more and more outlandish just so I'd crack. I was half expecting them to ask me where I was on the day that JFK was assassinated.

It turned out that the allegations were made by Errol Hay; against me, our John Henry and our good friend, big Mark Rowe. Errol told the police that we'd contacted two of the jury members on the murder trial from two separate phone boxes in County Durham.

I've mentioned the calibre of witnesses that Northumbria Police have used against us over the years and this man was no different. Errol Hay was a registered cocaine addict who was living in Thailand with his prostitute wife who was selling her body to support him and his drink and drug addiction. What a lowlife! If he wasn't a degenerate, I don't know what one is. On the word of this degenerate – and with no corroborating evidence whatsoever – me, Mark and our John were charged with perverting the course of justice and remanded in custody at HMP Durham. Fucking hell, man.

When we arrived, they immediately made our John a Category A prisoner. The governor looked at me and Mark and told us firmly that John was getting moved to be put on remand in HMP Frankland and we were lucky we were not going there ourselves. Personally speaking, I would have preferred Frankland as you're allowed to cook food and there's a better class of criminal to mix and socialise with. I spent four and a half years in Frankland and, as far as prisons go, it's a good jail with a proper 'no riff-raff' policy. I didn't tell him any of that though.

They put me and big Mark in the smallest cell they had with next to no natural light coming through the tiny window. It was a real *Withnail & I* 'We've came on holiday by mistake' moment. We turned to each other as the door slammed shut behind us and we didn't need to discuss the finer details of how shit it was. Our expression said it all. Our new home had clearly been a punishment cell in its day. Yeah, yeah... it's prison and it's supposed to be shit, but this was a whole different level of shit. It was enough to put you off prison for life! No home comforts – nothing.

I looked at Mark. 'This is not for us. I bet you I get us out of here when the door opens up tomorrow.'

The next day I went for a wander, which was against the rules but since I don't live by those people's rules, they simply didn't apply to me. My philosophy was *if you don't like what I'm doing, try to stop me*. And no one did.

I made my way up to the fours; the top landing of Durham jail. I was on B-wing and at the top, at the far corner, was what's called a 'listener's cell' which is two cells made in to one for people who have problems of some sort. No sooner had I found the cell when I heard a Senior Officer shout, 'What are you doing on this landing?'

He looked up and saw it was me he greeted me with a smile.

'Hello, Stephen. How you doing?'

'I'm in prison for starters, you fucking stupid cunt. How the fuck do you think I am and what's with the fucking stupid questions? Fuck off out of my fucking face. And get me some biscuits, you mug!' is what I could have said if I was that way inclined. But I'm always polite. It helps get what you want.

'Not so bad,' I replied. 'But that all depends on you...'

I explained the circumstances to him and he said, 'Leave it to me.'

With that, he walked over to the cell and evicted the two inmates who were in there and told them they were getting moved. It was impressive. I returned to my cell and the SO gave us a knock a few minutes later.

'Stephen, pack your stuff. I've got you a cell move.'

It took moments to pack our stuff and make our way to our penthouse top floor double room with big double windows that we could open and experience fresh air. What a contrast! The sunlight was beaming in and all we were missing was room service and a TV. You can't have it all though.

We got settled into our new routines and, as time went by, we had a couple of visits from our solicitor and I suggested to Mark that he should put in for a bail application. We'd been remanded for around three months at that point. He agreed and, on the morning of his bail application, there was mixed feelings in the cell. Nothing was wrong though: I was happy and he was sad. I was happy for my big friend getting bail so he could spend Christmas with his family and friends and deep down we knew I had no chance of bail. He felt sad leaving me because he's a very loyal person and even offered to forget about the bail application and stay there with me. It was a really nice gesture and I know he meant it, but we also both knew he belonged with his wife and children – especially at Christmas. I knew I'd be fine. It meant more to me seeing him get out than losing his company... and it was a little victory, for one of us to get bail.

The door opened for dinner time and, as we went down to get our food, I told Mark I thought he'd be released after dinner. I asked a screw who confirmed it and the look on Mark's face was priceless. I saw he was still unsure, but I gave him a wink and a smile broke through. We got our scran and returned to our cell where we sat and had a short chat before a screw came in.

'Mark, are you ready, big fella?'

'Aye, I am,' he replied. And he was. I could see it in his face.

I was sad to see my big friend leave, but it was for the best. We hugged and wished each other well. As for me, I hadn't put in for bail and thought I'd give it a go. There was nothing to lose. I was up for the bail application by the 18th or 20th of December just before the courts closed for Christmas. I got refused. I'd kind of expected it, but you still have to hope. You get no favours from the CPS if you have the name Sayers, quite the contrary, as they have the hump with us.

I felt a little bit down in the dumps with the news. Not for myself but for the kids. I'd been in prison over the Christmas period on numerous occasions before. What seems to happen is that the atmosphere in the prison changes for the worse. As the prison routine is disrupted and the inmates' thoughts are on the outside with their loved ones which made them very short-tempered and the riot bell would constantly go off. So in there, Christmas for me was a time for extra food that would not be available any other time through the year: Christmas cake, sliced turkey with stuffing, roast potatoes... that was my Christmas shopping list to the number one lad on the kitchen staff. I must remind you this is certainly not the normal prison procedure and, as I said before, I do not always live by prison rules. With Mark back home, I only had me to look out for.

I saw two lads tormenting a young screw. Being an opportunist and not being able to let this opportunity pass me by, I went down and spoke to the two lads and asked them what was up. They told me they used to go to school with the screw that they'd been tormenting. They explained to me how the screw's mother still lived in the same house that he was brought up in. Interesting. The conversation ended and I made my way directly over towards the young screw. He was leaning against the landing and he looked as sick as a parrot with a harelip. I told him I was his Santa Claus and that I was there to cheer him up. I asked him if he would like me to defuse the problem with his two school chums and he knew exactly what I meant.

'Stephen, what will this cost me?' He asked me with no hesitation.

'A change in your attitude for starters,' I said.

He was known to be quite a bully with the younger inmates, so it was a chance to even the score a bit.

'Is that all?' He asked. How would that be it all?

'Of course not. Put your school chums in the same cell together. You know, like they already asked you but you said no,' I continued. 'You've brought all this trouble on yourself with your attitude.'

I told him I had a bag of goodies waiting to be picked up from the kitchen and that I needed him to take me there. On the way we were going to bump in to his two school chums. The young screw had no problem with agreeing to this, as long as I could keep the lads off his case.

I saw them standing in line to use the phone.

'Listen, lads. This is the deal; I have sorted it for you to be padded up together.'

They were more than happy about it. I told them that all

they had to do was get off that certain screw's case and they'd be in there. They weren't daft. They knew the score.

The screw was over the moon and took me down to the kitchen to collect my bag of Christmas goodies. The kitchen was a hive of activity. It was Christmas Eve and the kitchen was full with everyone preparing for the big day. The screw had a reputation for being a bully and a dog; I found it comical as everyone was on edge at the way he was talking to them. He asked out loud to them, 'Who's the number one orderly in here?' And a concerned-looking inmate approached to be told to make a special goodie bag up for Mr Sayers right away. When it was almost full, the screw looked at me.

'Is this OK for you?'

I instantly replied, 'No, it is not.'

The screw then looked straight at the inmate and barked, 'More!'

The orderly asked 'More of what?' and the screw just said, 'Everything.'

He was a total cock, but what the hell; it was Christmas. Seconds later and the bag was bulging; it really was the ultimate Christmas prison feast. I had everything that was worth having from the kitchen along with extra turkey sandwiches with stuffing and extra Christmas cake. On my way back to my cell the screw asked me, 'Are you happy with that, Stephen?' I told him I was.

On the way I bumped in to my good friend Keith Loxley. I asked him if he fancied a pad change. Keith took seconds to agree and it didn't take him much longer to move into my big double cell. He came and joined me for The Feast of Stephen.

The weeks flew by. Keith was a good pad mate as far as pad mates go. I knew Charlie, Keith's father, very well and I have a lot of respect for him. Keith and I would do a lot of trading together to while away the hours. Yet again the time flew and the weeks passed very quickly.

One night we were sitting there watching the TV when a note came under the door saying they were shipping me out and moving me to HMP Hull. There I was in the reception of Hull nick the next day and it absolutely honked of piss; the smell was putrid. A screw came through and told me that the jail was full and they might have to move me to HMP Leeds. I was sat there with three strangers for half an hour when the screw came in and told us they had found room for me and the two others and then our names got called out. They placed the other two in a cell and put me in a cell next door to them by myself. The three of us were to be moved to Doncaster prison first thing in the morning, so it was just an overnight stay.

I was in the cell for a short while when a screw told me to head down to the server to collect my food. Everybody else had been fed and was locked away separate from us three on the wing which, I found strange at the time, but I found out why later on.

I was stood in line at the counter with the two other inmates waiting to be fed when I heard a Geordie accent. It was one of the inmates serving food; he fancied himself as a bit of a comedian, I think. He asked me what I wanted: choice one, two or three. I picked my choice and he asked, sarcastically, if I was from the toon and said it in a ridiculous voice. He then sniggered. Was this cunt for real? If he'd been within punching distance he'd have been on the fucking floor in a second. Then he proceeded to try and take the piss out of me with his full audience of screws and kitchen staff witnessing.

He lapped up the attention and asked where in 'the toon' I was from. I'd had enough. I looked him straight in the eye and told him I was Stephen Sayers; one of the Sayers brothers from the West End of Newcastle. He stopped laughing and his face turned a shade of white. The joke was on him, only he didn't get it. He screamed at the top of his voice for staff to help him and then ran over to the prison riot bell and pressed it frantically. His reaction was so over the top and his audience undoubtedly thought he was a total fucking idiot.

A screw walked over to me and I was already foaming, knowing that the idiot had landed me in shit for no reason whatsoever. It almost made me wish I'd jumped the counter and smashed his skull in with his ladle. As the screw got closer, I recognised him from when I was young'un in HMP Frankland.

'Stephen, what are you doing on this wing?' I explained the story and it turned out that the only three beds that were spare for overnight stays were on the sex case wing and that was the reason they had kept us apart from the others. We looked over and the Geordie mug behind the server was cowering in the corner. People like him give Geordies a bad name. I didn't know this man from Adam, but he must have certainly known of the Sayers' reputation. It was good to see such a reaction; he got sacked from the server and was devastated for losing his job. I tormented him. As the screw walked away, I yelled over to him. 'Give me the nonce's letter sheet and I'll get one of my friends back home to sort it out!' For such a comedian, he didn't have much of a sense of humour.

I got my food and went back to my cell to get banged up and, when the following day arrived I finished my journey to HMP Doncaster, known locally as Donkertaz. The place is unlike any other jail I've been in as it was private and they didn't allow the Prison Officers Association to have any say in how the regime was run.

I was there to be placed on video link for the hearing, which they could have done from Durham as they had all the same facilities. I wasn't that bothered – a change is just as good as a rest.

The hearing was a trial with no jury present, and that meant that any decision would lie in the hands of just one judge. I knew that the judge had already made his decision. We won every legal point in every legal argument that was presented against us. Put it this way; if it had been a football match then it would have been 8-0 to us. It was clear that we'd won the argument but the judge decided it was in the public's interest to give us a trial with no jury and that one single judge was going to reside over our trial. It didn't look good; if we couldn't get the right decision when we'd won the eight legal points of law that had been presented against us, then how could we receive any justice whatsoever from someone so against us? To me this was like the justice the British Army gave out 200 years ago: *they shall be fairly tried and hanged with the crime of being a Sayers*.

Naturally, all of our barristers and QCs told us they'd appeal against the decision immediately and, as far as I was concerned, it was a barbaric injustice that the decision had been made in advance. Once the hearing was over I spoke to my legal team and they didn't sugar-coat it: I had to get the decision overturned at the High Court or I'd receive a life sentence and life would mean *life* for me as well as my brother. It was only the second time in history that a trial to be held with no jury was agreed in principle. The only other occasion was for terrorist activity. It was history in the making but not the kind of history you want to make. If the law is an ass, then the judge was an asshole. With a fucking wig on as well.

All was not doom and gloom though. We are Sayers which comes from the word 'soothsayer' which means a person able to predict the future and I felt it in my bones. I knew things were going to turn out OK. At times the whole situation felt surreal, as if it wasn't really happening. I couldn't believe how low Errol Hay and Northumbria Police had stooped this time. It felt like a massive conspiracy where I wanted to give everyone a shake and make them see sense.

I was taken back to the wing. I received my deposition

papers and in them it said that the degenerate Hays had arranged to do drug deals in Thailand with the full authority of the Thai and Northumbria Police. He was given apparent immunity to invite and entrap people, which he did twice. On one occasion he got a man to travel all the way from England; he received an eight-year sentence in Thailand, and the other got a six-year sentence also in a Thai prison. The conditions in a Thai prison, as you may be aware, are not for us Westerners and the poor buggers did their full sentences there. Hays received a sum of £600 and £800 respectively for getting those Englishmen locked up. When I repeatedly call this man a degenerate it is not only very accurate but also very understandable why. So I'll say it again, Errol Hay, in my opinion, is a degenerate.

My stay in HMP Doncaster lasted another three weeks before they told me I was going back to HMP Durham. To be honest, I was just glad to get back to my local jail and be among some fellow Geordies again. I contacted my solicitor when I got back and he told me it was my legal right to attend the High Court to appeal against my trial with no jury. The thought of travelling down to London and staying at four or so dirty jails on the way wasn't something I fancied, so I was quite happy letting my legal team go on my behalf. If I didn't get the decision overturned, I knew the consequences very well.

A few more weeks went by and the winter cold sneaked into my big penthouse cell. There was no heating in there; it was great in the summer but freezing in the winter. There is a privilege wing in HMP Durham; F-wing. It was previously used as a long-term wing for women; the unit McVicar was detained in and escaped from in the film made famous by my pal, Roger Daltrey. I sorted out a single cell and I got settled in nicely. I pressed the bell and when the screw came to my door I asked him if I could make a legal phone call to Richard Haswell. I didn't really call for anything in particular, just to see how the trial was going, and he give me some terrific news; my case had been up for appeal that very day at the High Court in front of the Lord Chief Justice and it seemed that wisdom and decency prevailed – he was not going to allow Northumbria Police to poison his opinion. Being a High Court judge, his opinion overruled the previous judge's decision and the decision went in my favour! The prosecution also wanted the judge who'd asked for a trial with no jury to be the judge in the forthcoming trial... fortunately this was also denied; the Higher Court judge was having none of it and he handpicked the trial judge himself. This certainly put a spanner in the works for Northumbria Police; they were probably as disappointed as I was delighted.

Richard reassured me that we stood a very good chance as the prosecution's evidence was very weak and, now we had a trial with no injustice, our hopes were high as were the hopes of our legal team. We were given a date in March and the trial was to be held at Woolwich Crown Court which was attached by an underground tunnel to HMP Belmarsh, high security prison in London.

I had two months or so to prepare for the trial so, by the time March came, I was as ready as I could be. I was sat in my cell when a screw came to my door.

288

'Stephen, you'll be moved to HMP Leeds in the morning,' he said.

The day finally arrived and I was on the move. I remember looking at Durham prison as I got into the police van. 'I will not be returning to this place, no matter what happens,' I thought. So, in my own little way, I gave a farewell and good riddance to that establishment. I can remember sitting in the back of the van and thinking that my battle for justice was just about to begin; a real *this is it* moment.

We arrived at Leeds prison; a big old-fashioned Victorian thing, for an overnight stay. I got my food and collected my bed pack, then made my way to my cell to be banged up. No sooner did I rest my head on my pillow than I fell asleep. Perfect... until I was woken up by the voice of a big Scottish screw who screamed down the landing at somebody. What a way to wake up. Every fucking prison was the same; they were all as shit as each other no matter where you were. I got washed and ready and they took me straight to reception; I was on the move again and raring to go.

I got moved further down south to HMP Bedford that was another one-night-only appearance. As soon as I was in reception I heard a Cockney shout my name and I walked over to ask him what he wanted. He asked me if I was one of the Sayers brothers from Newcastle, and told me he had a little parcel for me and discreetly passed me a quarter-ounce of cannabis. He then told me he had been in HMP Full Sutton with our John and Michael. He had some sort of privilege job as he was a red band and a trust, so he had a word with one of the screws he knew and got me a single cell for the night. 'Nice one,' I thought. Top bloke. I thanked my new Cockney rebel friend and he passed his regards on to my brothers. Now, that's how life should be. When I got to my cell I rolled and smoked a couple of spliffs and fell peacefully to sleep.

Morning came and I got shipped out to HMP Belmarsh High security prison in that there London. I sat in the back of a Category A van, handcuffed, and the sun was beaming through the tiny window. It felt nice. I felt good and I felt positive and lucky.

I arrived at Belmarsh and was taken straight to reception where I got a shower, bed pack and some food. I don't suppose there is much good in me and our John's prison time totalling 50 years between us, but one thing is for certain; when we arrived at any prison in the country our reputation always preceded us and we are always welcome with the utmost respect. Belmarsh was no different.

I was on the landing with my kit and two big bags, squeezing past people on their way for dinner. I looked up and I saw Shaka, my Yardie friend from Brixton. I have a lot of respect for Shaka. He came over to my cell and we greeted each other with big hugs. He was on a recall. He told his friends on the wing, 'The Geordie General has arrived and he shall be respected as such.'

I'd been there for a week or so and got myself to church on the Sunday morning and saw our John. We hadn't seen each other for around eight months due to all the legal shit we'd been stuck in. Like me, he was eager to get the court case going. We were on separate wings and expecting the arrival of our good friend, big Mark Rowe, who was about to surrender bail.

A year had passed since big Mark had got bail and, to be honest, I'd missed his company. He has a good sense of humour and was a terrible card player – all in all, the perfect pad mate! I was back on the wing and on bang-up when a screw came to the door and told me I was moving on to another wing. It only took me moments to pack up all my things and I was out the door. I got taken to a cell and there he was... Mark. It was a pleasure to see him – just a shame it was under those circumstances. We'd been given a three-man cell, which made it rather spacious compared to the old cells in HMP Durham. Maybe because it was a new-build, but it meant that the walls were too flimsy for us to put any picture frames or shelving up.

We went to collect our food and saw our John on the way back. We had some association for a couple of hours which was great for us as we had a lot of catching up to do. Mark told us that he'd been training and had given up smoking for a while, which was great for my ears as I still had the quarter ounce of cannabis. I knew it would get him stoned much quicker and his good sense of humour would certainly increase. He didn't take much persuading – given up smoking? My arse!

The weekend passed and they took us to court via the tunnel to the high security courts in Woolwich, just outside the gates of Belmarsh. There were lots of legal arguments for a couple of days before Hays took the stand. He claimed he'd phoned two different jury members from two different telephone boxes in Houghton-le-Spring and said that me and

Mark were present when he made these calls. Hays was adamant that he had definitely used these two telephone boxes. Then, for no reason whatsoever, he blurted out across the court that he was proud to be a police informer. 'You might be proud, but I bet your family is ashamed,' I thought. What he did has no bearing on his family whatsoever. It was proven without doubt that he was telling lies as there was only one record of a phone call to the Leeds area that night. That made it clear to everybody and the judge that the degenerate was telling lies. If he cannot be believed for one lie, how could he be believed for two?

The judge decided to adjourn the case until the following day and, when we returned, all three legal teams were rubbing their hands with joy because they knew we'd won. The judge then decided to speak for half an hour and give his decision: we were to be acquitted. It was great news for us. But, what the judge did next I found very strange. We had been found not guilty and we wanted to go home, but the judge remanded us overnight to allow the prosecution time to decide if they were going to appeal. I spoke to my QC and told him that we were innocent men and that we wanted to go home. How could he remand us into custody when we'd just been found not guilty? But we are the Sayers, remember. Three men that had been found not guilty and had no charges against them whatsoever were now being remanded overnight. We went through the same rigmarole the following day and we were taken back to court and had to sit through another full day until the judge finally dismissed us and agreed to let us go home... but not before we were taken back to prison. They kept us until half past six that night and finally released me and Mark but told us that they were not releasing our John.

They took us back through reception with our belongings. When we got outside to our surprise, there was six inches of snow on the ground. All the tubes were on strike and Kings Cross train station was ten miles away. Then they refused to give us our money or any travel expenses to get home. After a heated argument, the governor finally appeared and agreed to give us a travel warrant from Kings Cross to Newcastle but we were going to have to find our own way to Kings Cross. What a fucking farce.

We were just about to trudge our way through it when I looked up and saw my solicitor Mr Haswell in the car park and he called me and Mark over to give us a lift in his taxi over to Kings Cross. What a vision! He told us he'd spoken to the governor about our John and said, 'If you do not release this man, I will have you up in front of a High Court judge in the morning and you will have to explain why you have this man detained with no charges, fines or outstanding warrants.' The governor knew what he was doing was unlawful.

Me and Mark arrived at the train station and were having a pint in a bar across the road when his mobile phone rang. It was John! He had finally been released and headed straight to the station. The three of us were delighted to see each other... free at last!

We had our pints and our John had a glass of juice before we caught our train back home to Newcastle, arriving back at around midnight. It had been a 15-month journey and I was glad it was over. As the taxi pulled up to my flat in Byker, I was happy to see my good friends waiting for me; Fish Tams and Angie Hart. I was still stood with my bags in my hands when one of my travelling cousins from Carlisle pulled up in a van.

He jumped out and linked my arm and tried to pull me in, saying, 'Uncle Stephen, I've been fighting and I need you to come with me. I've have been fighting with a doorman in town and I need you to sort it out.'

'Are you for real, son? I'm stood here with two see through prison bags with HMP printed all over them. I've just spent the past 15 months fighting to get out. I'm not even though my garden gate!'

He left and I went downstairs to Angie's flat to have a cup of tea and catch up with her, Brooksey and Mandy Denham. I sat there for an hour and then decided to go upstairs to my flat. It felt cold and empty. The reality hit me like a tonne of bricks. I was a single man and I felt really lonely. Still though, I was free and I was home and that must have counted for something.

CHAPTER 15
SUMMING UP, M'LUD

I often look back on my life with a smile on my face. In fact, I suppose I have walked all the way through my entire life with a smile; it's just my nature. I've met some brilliant people in my line of work, some not-so-brilliant as well: the good, the bad and the ugly, you could say. There's been so much fun and mayhem over the years that the law of the land had to be changed. Twice!

I've been out on mad drinking sessions with people like Dave Courtney, when he came to visit Newcastle, and I've met just about every other dodgy character in the country. And then there's good old Charles Bronson, currently known as Charles Salvador, who has passed on his regards to me and my brothers (he's currently at HMP Wakefield... say hello from me, if you want). There's also my old mate Norman Jones, prison number A7889ac, currently serving time for a crime he didn't commit in Whitemoor.

I am a happy-go-lucky kind of man, despite the miscarriages of justice I've suffered at the hands of the police. It doesn't take a genius to work out that they've had more than their pound of flesh out of us. I only need to sneeze in the wrong direction and I'm guaranteed to get lifted for it. That's how it's been for years, even since I turned my back on crime. All that notoriety that followed us around is also something that can work against us. We've known that for years as well, but it can be a bit much. Correction; it *is* a bit much. Being accused of every major crime in the region because of your name is just a cross I've had to bear for being at the forefront of the criminal fraternity – same as my brothers, family and close friends.

When I look back over my life, I do have some regrets about it all. I've wasted a lot of years in jail because of crime, whether it was actually me or a case of the police hauling me in anyway and remanding me. Yes, that's an occupational hazard and, if you want to get on your high horse about it, of course a career criminal should expect that as part of his life. I'm no saint, I'm not whiter-than-white and I probably never will be.

If I was given the chance again, it would be nice to have had a different career, but as I said at the beginning, it was like my life was already mapped out for me. It was almost like being a Sayers was my occupation and it didn't need any more elaboration than that.

If a man goes out and shoots somebody, kills or injures them, he makes an enemy for life. If he has a straightener and sorts it out toe-to-toe, he gains respect and probably friendship. Any fool in a position of power can punish, whereupon wiser men consider compassion.

To any of the younger lads reading this who may think that crime pays... you're wrong. Yeah, a few blags here and there can set you up for a while, but in the long run, it isn't worth it. Look at the hassle me and my brothers have had over the years. If that's not a lesson, I don't know what is. Actually, I do know... our kids are now in the frame. They bare the family name and it's like a curse to them in some respects. They've been questioned over crimes and most of the time it's just the police trying to get to us by taking our kids in as suspects, no matter what damage it causes them.

If you want a man to look up to, look up to the working man; the man who gets up on a morning, earns a living and provides for his family and kids, facing his responsibilities. That's what life's about – don't waste any of that time by trying to be a criminal or a gangster because no one will thank you for having to constantly look over their shoulder, or having the front door smashed in by the police every other week. Being on remand for months is no fun; neither is being locked up for ten years. I know you've just read about me 'having fun' in those situations, but you're now reading about me wanting to escape the shadow of all that.

My story is probably full of contradictions: I say we had fun, now I say we didn't have fun, I say we had a laugh in jail, but the reality was anything but a laugh. We made the most of our time in jail, let's say. You learn from experience and I've learnt enough to be able to tell anyone reading this that the old cliché is true: crime doesn't pay.

We've gained financially through crime, but we've also lost a lot through possessions being confiscated, court costs and whatever else because of it. Seeing your family visit you in prison, to actually *see them* in a place like that, scrutinised and searched – and then have to leave you – is not good. No one deserves that. You can make up for things you did wrong, you can apologise for mistakes and try to make amends, but you can't make up for lost time.

Life is for living. Go live it.